Heart & Soul

FIVE AMERICAN COMPANIES THAT ARE MAKING THE WORLD A BETTER PLACE

ROBERT L. SHOOK

BENBELLA BOOKS, INC. • DALLAS, TEXAS

BenBella Books, Inc.
10300 N. Central Expressway, Suite 400
Dallas, TX 75231
www.benbellabooks.com
Send feedback to feedback@benbellabooks.com

Printed in the United States of America
10 9 8 7 6 5 4 3 2 1

Library of Congress Cataloging-in-Publication Data is available for this title.
ISBN 978-1935618-06-5

Copyediting by Rebecca Green
Proofreading by Erica Lovett
Cover design by Faceout
Text design and composition by John Reinhardt Book Design
Index by Robert L. Shook
Printed by Bang Printing

Distributed by Perseus Distribution
(www.perseusdistribution.com)

To place orders through Perseus Distribution:
Tel: 800-343-4499
Fax: 800-351-5073
Email: orderentry@perseusbooks.com

To Carrie, Peter, Paige, and Grace
with much love

Acknowledgments

One of the joys of writing a book is thanking all of the wonderful people who worked with me to make it happen. I greatly appreciate their support and friendship.

First and foremost, I am grateful to the men and women that I interviewed at DaVita, Mary Kay, Inc., Resource One, Starkey Labs, and World Wide Technology who took time from their busy schedules to share their views with me. They were gracious, warm, and hospitable. I feel honored and privileged to know these fine people.

As always, my wife, Elinor, is my biggest supporter. She never complains about the times when I work on weekends and into the night. I am blessed to have her as my lifetime partner.

My longtime literary agent, Al Zuckerman, founder and president of Writers House, is my close friend and best advisor. His counsel and friendship mean so much to me. I also thank his wife, Claire, who assisted me in the writing of my book proposal.

It is my good fortune that Al sold my book to BenBella Books, a boutique publishing firm in Dallas. Although a small publishing firm, BenBella is rich in talent. Publisher Glenn Yeffeth is a seasoned professional whom I rank among the best of the best publishers that I have worked with over the years (this is my 55th book). BenBella's production people who worked with me are: Debbie Harmsen, editor-in-chief of general non-fiction books; Rebecca Green, my copy editor; and Yara Abuata, production manager. Each did excellent work. Debbie, Rebecca, and Yara, you are terrific! As marketing manager at BenBella, Adrienne Lang plays an important role. Without Adrienne's insight and marketing talent, *Heart & Soul* would have no chance in today's competitive marketplace. In this capacity, her job is crucial to this book's ultimate success.

As she has done for many other Shook books, Debbie Watts transcribed all of the tape-recorded interviews I conducted doing the research process for this book. As always, Debbie did her usual excellent work, and she is a truly delightful person.

There were also some fine people I met at the five companies featured in this book who worked with me, and I appreciate their cooperation. They are: Patti Carr, Brett Cohen, Geri Colesworthy, Rachael Kuiken, JD Myers, Mark McCarthy, Yvonne Pendelton, Wanda Poling, Heather Sauber, Holly Schainker, Wendy Schutz, Areina Seay, Blaise Tracy, and Neil Waingrow.

All of the above individuals made valuable contributions to this book, and I am grateful to them all.

—RLS

Contents

Introduction

CYNICS SAY A CORPORATION can't have a heart and soul. They claim that it's hard enough to identify these qualities in an individual, let alone in a collective body of people. I disagree. I think Henry David Thoreau got it right when he said: "It is truly enough said that a corporation has no conscience; but a corporation of conscientious men is a corporation with a conscience."

Because of its elusive nature, the absence of heart and soul is more easily observed than their presence. You can't see or touch them; you can only sense them. But be assured that you will know when they aren't there. Companies that lack character are easily spotted. Their flaws are mostly apparent. And because you've been so exposed to them, you know what to look for.

The premise of this book is that a company with a heart and soul will ultimately be more successful and competitive in the marketplace. What better time than now for us to take notice of such a company? We are just recovering from a period of greed and corruption that brought on the nation's worst economic downturn since the Great Depression. Certainly, if there is a lesson to be learned from all that went wrong, it is that there must be a better way to do business.

Heart & Soul offers a better way. This book is an eclectic collection of stories about five extraordinary companies, each illustrating how caring for others is not only an acceptable way to run an organization, it is good business. Through extensive research, I have identified five companies with uncompromising values. Each has a strong corporate culture that fosters treating everyone—employees, customers, and vendors—with respect. The successes of these companies dispel the common belief that to get ahead in a dog-eat-dog business world, you must always be looking out for number one. As you will discover in this book, there is a gentler way, in which caring for people is a strength and should never be perceived as a weakness.

I acknowledge that the cynics will accuse me of looking at the world through rose-colored glasses. Unfortunately, there are many who think that accenting the good in others is Pollyannaish. I assure you that the doubting Thomases are wrong. The proof is manifest in these five stories, because this is not a book based on theory—these are five real companies, each a leader in its field. The companies I selected are diverse in industry and size and are based in different areas of the country.

Certainly I am aware that one can argue that five is too small a number to prove anything. I disagree. If five companies can succeed with high values and business plans dedicated to doing the right thing, others can follow suit. Each of these five stories provides a business model that can be emulated, and because no two are alike, this is not a one-size-fits-all message. You can pick and choose to determine which of these business models (or combination of them) works best for you.

My research to identify which companies to feature in this book included doing online searches and reviewing business magazines and journals. I also communicated with local and national associations and chambers of commerce. And I reached out to my network of personal contacts—businesspeople, writers, and so on. After giving everyone a thorough explanation about my book, I asked them to help me identify a business that met the high criteria I had set. "Can you give me a lead on a company in your city, or one that stands head and shoulders above others in your industry (association, etc.)?" It was considerably more difficult to find five companies than I had anticipated. Admittedly, I'd set a high standard. I was in search of companies with management that believes, as I do, that each of us has a fundamental duty that is first and foremost as a human being. We must treat our fellow human beings decently or otherwise be held accountable. This standard is not only applicable in our personal lives but also must be adhered to in our business lives.

I concluded that although there are American companies with a heart and soul, their numbers are few, and consequently, finding them was a difficult undertaking. All the while, I became aware that I was engaged in an important mission. I concluded that we need large numbers of companies that possess a heart and soul, which could lead the way for others to follow. I am hopeful that this book will help meet that goal by encouraging more compassionate business practices.

When you read *Heart & Soul*, you will observe that doing good is prevalent in each of these stories. It is deeply ingrained in each company's culture. To the men and women who manage these five companies, success is measured by how others benefit. They believe that *if you enrich the lives of others first, you shall reap the fruits of success*. This is not to suggest that a healthy bottom line is unimportant, because without profits, a company will surely fail, and if it does, nobody benefits. Profits and benevolence are not opposing objectives. There is ample opportunity to meet financial goals and concurrently have a positive impact on others.

In an age of information technology, looking-out-for-number-one strategies are becoming obsolete, because it is increasingly more difficult to hide bad behavior. Companies can no longer conceal their greed, irresponsibility, and unethical inadequacies. A disgruntled employee or dissatisfied customer can instantaneously spread the word globally via a spiteful blog posting or a mass email. We are at a time when a good reputation must be earned by living with integrity and by doing what is right. The good news is that those who adhere to such a strategy will discover that doing good truly is good for business.

Mary Kay Ash, founder of Mary Kay Cosmetics.

Mary Kay's Way

Mary Kay Ash, who founded the Dallas-based cosmetics company Mary Kay, Inc., in 1963, is recognized today as one of the most successful businesswomen in U.S. history. With more than two million independent representatives in thirty-seven countries, the company's wholesale revenues today are near $3 billion. At the time of her death in 2001, she was revered by millions of women around the world.

Mary Kay was a gifted speaker. In a convention hall, she could charm an audience of thousands. One on one, she conveyed enthusiasm and genuine warmth. To know her was to love her. To this day she is strongly identified with the company that bears her name. It appears on everything from product packaging to the signage on the company's regal high-rise building. Her values, principles, and beliefs are also deeply ingrained in the company's culture. She was and is the heart and soul of Mary Kay Cosmetics. Most often a company so strongly identified with a single individual finds its future in jeopardy with the passing of its founder. Remarkably, this was not the case at Mary Kay, Inc. A seamless succession was effected by a management team that clearly understood her wishes and was determined to preserve what its founder stood for; as a consequence, the spirit of this extraordinary woman lives on today. Understanding how this transition happened requires knowing about Mary Kay, the woman. This is her story and that of the company she built.

&

THE LIFE OF MARY KAY ASH is a classic rags-to-riches story—the kind that inspires books and movies. The movie *Rocky* comes to mind, in which the underdog boxer succeeds against all odds. The contrast between Rocky Balboa and Mary Kay could not be greater. Rocky Balboa is a punch-drunk heavyweight prizefighter. Mary Kay was a petite 5'2" blond, meticulous in appearance and exceedingly articulate in speech. They do, however, share one characteristic—perseverance. Like Rocky, Mary Kay came from the school of hard knocks. She, too, was a fighter who refused to quit. Of course, Rocky Balboa is a fictitious character. Mary Kay Ash was real.

As a child, Mary Kay watched her father, Edward Wagner, come home from a tuberculosis sanatorium with his disease arrested but not cured. His wife, Lula, became the family's sole supporter. She managed a restaurant in Houston, working daily from 6:00 A.M. to 9:00 P.M. Mary Kay spent much of her childhood taking care of her invalid father.

"Mother was never home," Mary Kay told me years ago. "In the morning I went to school, and when I got home, I fixed the meals and cleaned the house. At age seven, I was already taking the streetcar into downtown Houston to buy my own clothes. I really had a hard time convincing the sales clerks to sell me anything. Whenever I needed my mother, I could phone her and she would say to me, 'Honey, you can do it.' She gave me a priceless gift. She would always tell me, 'Honey, you can do anything you want if you want it badly enough and are willing to pay the price.'"[1]

In her autobiography, *Mary Kay* (Harper & Row Publishers, Inc., 1981), she wrote:

> If Daddy wanted chili or chicken or whatever for dinner, and I didn't know how to cook it, I would call my mother. Thank goodness for the telephone. That was my lifeline during those years, and my main contact with my mother. Whenever I called her, she found a way to make time for me, and to explain patiently what I had to do.
>
> She'd go through every single step, one at a time, trying to think of everything I would need to know. I hadn't been raised to be a complainer, but I'm sure she knew that this sometimes seemed overwhelming.

> Because when she was through with her instructions, she always added, "Honey, you can do it." As far as I was concerned, my mother *knew* I could do it. Her words became the theme of my childhood, and they have stayed with me all my life: "You can do it."

Mary Kay learned valuable lessons on responsibility and discipline at an early age.

At age seventeen, Mary Kay did what most young girls did in those days—she got married right out of high school. Her husband, J. Ben Rogers, was a member of a local musical group called the Hawaiian Strummers. To teenagers in Houston, he was a well-known radio star. The young couple had three children. During World War II, Ben Rogers was drafted. Upon returning from the service, he announced that he wanted a divorce.

Mary Kay recalled:

> It was the lowest point of my life. I had developed a sense of worth for my abilities as a wife and a mother, and yet on that day I felt like a complete and total failure. I didn't have time to sit around feeling sorry for myself—I had three children to look after. I needed a good-paying job with flexible hours. The flexibility was essential, because I wanted to spend time with my children when they needed me. Direct sales was a natural solution, and so I became a dealer for Stanley Home Products.[2]

Stanley Home Products dealers were originally door-to-door salespeople who sold high-quality household cleaners, brushes, and mops. The company was founded in 1931, and by the late 1930s, one of the company's dealers began giving product demonstrations to clubs and organizations to generate large orders. Other Stanley dealers also began conducting group presentations, and eventually, homemakers were encouraged to invite a few friends and neighbors to demonstrations in their homes. The "party plan" was born. At a party, a salesperson (nearly all were women) demonstrated how to use Stanley products. The hostess served light refreshments to her guests and for her participation received a gift from the company's product line—perhaps a broom or a mop.

Determined and self-disciplined, Mary Kay worked her career around her young family. Being a full-time mother and salesperson required long, tedious hours. There was little time in her day for other activities. Yet, after excelling in sales, she was soon recruiting and training other salespeople. When asked how she found time to do so much, Mary Kay liked to say, "If you want something done, give it to a busy woman." Although her performance was exceptional, she resented how the company took advantage of her because she was a woman. She was bright and innovative, yet rarely were her ideas taken seriously by management.

In 1952, Mary Kay left Stanley Home Products to work for World Gift Company, which also sold through the party plan. Once again, she moved up the ranks in sales management, but there, too, she was discouraged by being held back because she was a woman. And, typical of the times, she received far less pay than a man in the same position.

In 1963, at age forty-five and after a twenty-five-year career in direct sales, Mary Kay felt burnt out and decided to retire.

THE DREAM COMPANY THAT STARTED AS A BOOK

"Building my career and caring for my family had been everything to me," Mary Kay said in her autobiography. She went on:

> I never liked those things other people seemed to enjoy for relaxation. I never had time to learn how to play games like tennis, and I absolutely hated cocktail parties. To me, work and growth were the same, and without them I had no reason to get out of bed each morning.
>
> And so, after retirement, the only thing left for me to do was to think back over those active, productive years. During my career I had faced and solved many problems that were unique to women in business. Much of the time I was actually handicapped or held back by outdated ideas of what a woman should and should not do when working with men. "Maybe," I thought, "just maybe, I could use my experience to help other women over these same hurdles." I decided to organize my thoughts by writing down all the lessons I had learned. I was filled with

memories of opportunities denied me because I was a woman. And I hoped that making my list would clear my heart of bitterness.

Mary Kay thought about all the injustices she had encountered, and not just she. It was how all women were treated in the workforce. Yes, it was discrimination, and there are laws against it today. But in those days, it was reality.

For example, Mary Kay remembered when she was a top salesperson and had been promoted to a position as the company's national training director, making a salary of $25,000 a year. She explained:

> I was really acting as sales manager. Not infrequently I would take a man out on the road for training, and after I'd taught him the business for six months he'd end up being my superior in Dallas, at twice my salary. It always irked me when I was told that the men deserved more pay because they "had families to support." I had a family to support too! It seemed that in a male-run corporation a woman's brains were worth only fifty cents on the dollar.[3]

Mary Kay also disliked the way a lot of bosses treated subordinates. She recalled that she had once taken a ten-day round trip by bus from Dallas to the Stanley home office in Westfield, Massachusetts, a reward she shared with fifty-seven other top salespeople. The group endured several bus breakdowns but happily put up with the misery to have the honor of a personal meeting with the company president. As the highlight of the trip, on the last night before heading back to Texas, they were to be guests in his home. Mary Kay could hardly wait.

Instead of socializing with other senior managers at the president's house, however, the salespeople were taken on a tour of the plant. While Mary Kay enjoyed seeing the manufacturing facility, she recalled her main purpose:

> I was there to meet the president. When we were finally invited to his home, we were only allowed to walk through the rose garden, and never even had the opportunity to meet him. What a letdown!

> Another time, I attended an all-day sales seminar and looked forward to meeting our sales manager, who had delivered an inspiring speech. I waited in line for three hours and he never even looked at me. Instead, as we shook hands, he looked over my shoulder to see how much longer the line was. He wasn't even aware that he was shaking my hand. He treated me as if I didn't even exist. Right on the spot I decided that if I ever became someone people waited in line to shake hands with, I'd give the person in front of me my undivided attention—no matter how tired I was.[4]

There were other unpleasant memories. For instance, she thought about the home office people who begrudged commissioned salespeople their high earnings. She couldn't understand why they would resent the success of salespeople, because, after all, the company depended on them. Nor could she fathom why some company employees had no interest in taking care of customers, or gave the impression that it wasn't their job to serve customers. Mary Kay believed that serving customers was everyone's job. In her mind, without customers, a company would not be in business. And satisfied customers meant repeat orders. Unhappy customers went away and told their friends about their dissatisfaction.

Mary Kay also disapproved of managers who never made the effort to learn their subordinates' names, or showed no interest in their personal lives. She didn't like executives who felt superior to subordinates and showed it in their manner.

She wrote in her management book, *The Mary Kay Way*, which was republished seven years after her death:

> The boredom of retirement caused a deepening sense of discontent. I had achieved success, but I felt that my hard work and abilities had never been justly rewarded. I knew I had been denied opportunities to fulfill my potential simply because I was a woman, and I was certain that these feelings were not mere indulgences of self-pity, because I had personally known so many other women who suffered similar injustices.[5]

Mary Kay began to organize her thoughts. She describes it:

> I began writing my memoirs. Then I decided to write a book about selling for women. I felt that my 25 years of experience should not be wasted, that perhaps I could help other women over some hurdles I had encountered. I started to write down all the good points of the companies I had worked for. Then, after two weeks, I listed the things that I felt should have been different. Then I read all my notes and the thought struck me, "Wouldn't it be wonderful if somebody started a company like this instead of just talking about it?" I decided to put my money where my mouth was. I decided to do something about this fantastic company I had written about and give women opportunities I had been denied.[6]

For days, Mary Kay studied her lists, and the more she read, the more she was convinced she was on to something. She explained:

> As a mother strives to protect children, I wanted to help other women so they wouldn't have to suffer what I had endured. I realized that those lists were evolving into a how-to book about the right way to lead and motivate people. But who was I to write a book on leadership? I had no formal credentials in that area, or as an author. No matter how effective my ideas were, who would pay attention to them? Nevertheless, the Golden Rule—"Do unto others as you would have them do unto you"—kept racing through my mind. It seemed to me that following the Golden Rule was such an obvious way to motivate and lead.[7]

What started as a book became the beginning of Mary Kay's dream company.

FINDING A PRODUCT TO SELL

Once Mary Kay decided to start her own company, she began focusing on what product or service to sell. She describes it like this:

> I wanted a top-quality product, one that could benefit other women, and one that women would be comfortable selling. I also wanted to of-

> fer women an open-ended opportunity to do anything they were smart enough to do.
>
> After spending days and nights trying to think of such a product, it finally dawned on me one evening while I was getting ready for bed—my skin-care products. I had been introduced to them 10 years earlier by a local cosmetologist I had met during my direct-selling days. Using formulas created by her dad, she had developed creams and lotions for customers of her small, home-operated beauty shop. I, and many of my relatives and friends, had been using these wonderful products for several years, so when the cosmetologist died, I bought the original formulas from her family. From my own use and the results I had personally received, I knew that these skin-care products were tremendous; with some modifications and high-quality packaging, they would be best sellers![8]

The first products were put in a basic skin-care kit and were called Cleansing Cream, Magic Masque, Skin Freshener, Night Cream, and Day Radiance. They were packaged in small jars and bottles. On opening day, the first inventory also included rouge, lip and eye palettes, mascara, and an eyebrow pencil. The company's entire initial inventory was stored on a $9.95 steel shelving unit from Sears.

Mary Kay realized that the best way for women to get the most benefit from these products was to be taught how to apply them properly. Simply buying them over the counter and reading the instructions on the labels would result in only limited knowledge of how they worked. And a retail clerk would also know little about how to use the products. The customer would have to take the items home and figure out how to use them. And if she had any questions, there wouldn't be anyone to ask. Then there was door-to-door selling. There were many companies with armies of salespeople ringing doorbells and selling cosmetics. Here, too, customers were never taught how to use their products.

Mary Kay's intuition, based on her personal experience in buying cosmetics, told her that women were uncomfortable trying on makeup in a store. Moreover, she knew that although a cosmetics specialist could make someone look like a million dollars, most women were totally clueless about how to repeat the process.

With Mary Kay's background in direct selling, she surmised that a party-plan organization would be the best way to sell skin-care products. A salesperson would present the products to a small group of women and demonstrate how to apply them. Women could also try the lotions and creams for themselves. If anyone had questions, the informed salesperson could provide answers. Mary Kay decided to call her knowledgeable sales representatives *beauty consultants*, because unlike door-to-door salespeople and store clerks, they would be demonstrating skin-care and makeup techniques. This skin-care class would provide important personalized guidance.

The beauty consultants would be independent representatives, as Mary Kay had been throughout her sales career. In keeping with their function of personal consultation, however, they would be taught never to use high-pressure selling techniques. She knew instinctively that women felt more comfortable in a relaxed atmosphere with a group of friends.

As Mary Kay explained,

> We teach skin care. The average woman doesn't know how to take care of her skin. She has usually bought a jar of something from a department store and a jar of something from a drugstore, and she has no routine whatsoever. She mixes up different products from this company and that company without realizing the possible adverse effect of some combinations. So not only does our program give them a good skin care regimen, it also educates them on how to keep it.[9]

Another added value would be that a beauty consultant would be able to educate each woman on which lotions and creams were best suited for her. This would be part of the service, because no two women are alike, and their needs vary depending on variables from their skin type to their daily habits. For instance, some women are in the sun a lot. Some have a more active lifestyle. Each Mary Kay product or regimen could be tailored to an individual customer's needs. This would be much different from picking something up at the counter and buying a one-size-fits-all product. Mary Kay thought that this personal service would maximize the value to the customer.

Direct sales companies are no different from any business—to succeed, they must build a base of loyal customers who keep coming back. As Mary Kay, Inc.'s chief marketing officer, Rhonda Shasteen, explains, "This business depends on more than a one-time sale. Beauty consultants want their customers to come back time and time again over the years, because that's what makes it a successful business opportunity for them."[10] Mary Kay wisely chose a product that satisfied customers would reorder when their supply ran out. She determined that once a woman got in the habit of taking good care of her skin, it would be a daily ritual that could continue for a lifetime. By having many loyal customers, a beauty consultant could develop a business that gave her a steady stream of revenue—one that would continually grow as her customer base expanded.

Equally important to Mary Kay's plan was that her consultants could get as much out of the business as they were willing to put into it. Those who worked harder and smarter could earn higher incomes than those who chose to work less. Each would set her own hours and work at her own pace. It was a very democratic system. Everyone would begin the same and have an equal opportunity to succeed.

A HUMBLE BEGINNING

Mary Kay invested her life savings of $5,000 in her business venture, which she originally called "Beauty by Mary Kay." Headquarters was a 500-square-foot storefront in Exchange Park, a large bank and office-building complex in Dallas. Most of her investment went into formulations, jars, and used office equipment. She had remarried, and her plan was that her husband would manage the business end of the company while she ran the sales organization. She had recruited nine salespeople; all were her friends. One month to the day before the doors were to open, her husband died of a heart attack. Her attorney advised her to liquidate the business and recoup whatever cash she could, lest she be left without a cent. Her accountant told her that the commission schedule she had set up for her salespeople would make it impossible for the company to succeed. "It will be only a matter of time before you're bankrupt," he said.[11] Mary Kay listened carefully.

Then she did exactly what she thought was best, and the company opened for business on schedule, on September 13, 1963.

"I saw the world collapsing around me after my husband died," she said. "But when God closes a door, He always opens a window."[12] And through the window came her twenty-year-old son, Richard, who decided that he could run the financial and administrative end of the fledgling company. At the time, he was an agent for Prudential Life Insurance Company, and his salary was $480 a month. He agreed to start at Mary Kay's company with a $250 monthly salary.

Her twenty-seven-year-old son, Ben, who was married and had two children, told her, "One day I'd like to join you and Richard." Then, calmly and deliberately, he reached into his breast pocket and offered Mary Kay his savings passbook. "Mother, I think you can do anything in this world you want to," he said as he handed the passbook to her. "If it will help you in any way, I want you to have it."[13]

In her autobiography, Mary Kay wrote about the unqualified support her sons gave her on that day.

> "Mother," Richard had gently said as he put his arm around my shoulders, "Ben and I have talked about this. All our lives, we've watched you make a success out of everything you've done. If you could be successful working for someone else, we know you can do even better working for yourself."

Her sons' belief in her was the vote of confidence that Mary Kay needed. Growing up on the sidelines, observing their mother as their sole supporter when they were children, they believed she could do just about anything. They watched her succeed in her sales career before going on her own. Richard explains:

"My mother sold Stanley Home Products, and our garage was converted into a small warehouse of Stanley products. Every Saturday my older brother and sister and I packed and delivered the orders Mother had sold that week. Then we would sit around the kitchen table and count the money. If we sold more products than the week before, we would go to the movies or do something special—we were a family business."[14]

Richard also knew that when his mother was determined to do something, she became totally focused on doing it.

"When her accountants and bankers tried to persuade her to fold up and cut her losses, I can remember to this day the look in her piercing blue eyes. She had a steely resolve that blocked out their negative feedback. My mother had no fear of failure. She had a dream of creating a company that would help women and she was set on making it happen."[15]

It was important to Mary Kay that her first beauty show start off with a bang. A strong first presentation, she believed, would excite her nine saleswomen and convince them that her business plan would work. It was a dismal failure. She explained:

> I sold a grand total of $1.50. When I left, I drove around the corner, put my head on the steering wheel, and cried. "What's wrong with those people?" I asked myself. "Why didn't they buy this fantastic product?" Bursts of fear flashed through my mind. My initial reaction was to doubt the whole venture. "What did you do wrong?" I asked myself. Then it hit me—*I had never even bothered to ask anyone for an order.* I had forgotten to pass out order cards and had just expected those women to buy automatically![16]

Mary Kay learned from her failure, and so did many others who heard her tell about it.

> I want them to know that I failed at my first beauty show—but refused to give up. *I failed forward to success.* I truly believe that life is a series of many attempts and many failures, and that only occasionally do we realize success. The important thing is to keep on trying.[17]

Mary Kay had no previous experience in the cosmetics industry. Her forte was in sales, recruiting, and training. Once she had acquired the skin-care products formulas, she immediately met with cosmetics companies about manufacturing her merchandise. As she tells it,

I wanted a firm that not only made quality products, but also observed the U.S. Food and Drug Administration's regulatory requirements to the letter. With the right people in charge, we would never have to concern ourselves with that aspect of the business.[18]

After meeting with several cosmetics companies, Mary Kay chose a Dallas manufacturer who had an excellent reputation for being ethical and reliable. "I took the formulations to the president of that company," she said, "and he calmly turned the whole thing over to his son. After our tiny order, I'm sure he thought he'd never see us again. But we did come back with a second order, and a third, and so on, and so on."[19] (A few years later, Mary Kay Cosmetics invited that company president's son to join it and head its own manufacturing division.)

Mary Kay conducted skin-care parties, trained other women, conducted sales meetings, and did everything from recruiting salespeople to emptying wastebaskets. Richard ran the business end of the company. A few months after the fledging company got under way, Ben quit his $750-a-month job in Houston and moved to Dallas with his family to join his mother's venture. He took a substantial pay cut. His new salary would be the same as Richard's—$250 a month. Ben was put in charge of running the warehouse. In the early days, Mary Kay's daughter, Marylyn, was a beauty consultant in Houston. It was a real family affair.

Mary Kay, Richard, and Ben worked sixteen- to eighteen-hour days. They filled orders; they packed orders. They wrote and mimeographed newsletters. Their hard work paid off. At the end of 1963, three-and-a-half months after the company first started, their wholesale sales totaled $34,000, and they rang up a small profit. A year later, the company's wholesale revenues were $198,000. During this same year, the company moved into another building that had private offices for Mary Kay and her two sons, plus a training room and a 5,000-square-foot warehouse. By the end of the second full fiscal year, wholesale revenues totaled $800,000.

WALKING IN THE OTHER PERSON'S SHOES

We've all seen someone complain about how badly his boss treats subordinates and then treat people the same way as soon as he's promoted. It's unfortunate when people are put in a management position and lose sight of what it was like before their promotion. It's as if all their former gripes no longer have merit because now they can dish out all that they previously detested. It's as if they said, "I had to take it for all those years, and now it's my turn to make life miserable for people."

Mary Kay had the opposite reaction. What she didn't approve of as a subordinate she vowed not to do to people who reported to her. She didn't have to read a book on leadership or take a management course to learn how to treat people. She knew it from Matthew 7:12: "We should do unto others as we would have others do unto us." She knew that some people considered it naïve for a start-up company to focus on the Golden Rule, but she believed in it. Others suggested that her philosophy was too gentle, or feminine, and that to succeed, one must be strong—that if Mary Kay didn't "toughen up," she wasn't going to make it on her own. Until somebody came up with a better way to treat people, however, she was going to stick with the Golden Rule. She firmly believed that people should practice every day of the week what they learned in church on Sunday. Acts of kindness and respect for others are as appropriate in the workplace as in the home. It was a time when business schools and management conferences never mentioned the word "love." They viewed it as a four-letter word in business circles. But to Mary Kay, love was appropriate in the workplace. She respected her employees and listened to their suggestions, because what they had to say was informative and insightful. Her love was also expressed by the opportunities she provided to them to succeed.

Based on her experiences as a single working mother with three children, her priorities were always God first, family second, and career third. She said:

> I truly believe the growth of Mary Kay Cosmetics has come about because the first thing we did was to take God as our partner. If we had not done that, I don't think we would be where we are today. I believe He blessed us because our motivation was right. He knows I want women to become the beautiful creatures that He created, and to use the God-given talents that lie within each of us.
>
> I've found that when you just let go and place yourself in God's hands, everything in your life goes right. When you try to do everything alone and rely on yourself, you begin to make major errors.[20]

When Mary Kay started her sales career with Stanley Home Products, she only had time for three things: God, family, and career. There was no room for a social life. Her life revolved around her three children, work, and church. Her day started at 5:00 each morning so she could do her housework, plan her day, and give her children a good breakfast before sending them off to school. Then she conducted a party in the morning and another in the early afternoon, and made sure she was home when her children returned from school. Later, she gave them dinner, got them ready for bed, and headed out to do another party. Her babysitter put the kids to sleep before she returned. Obviously, she had a high energy level. When she could afford it, she hired a housekeeper, but she never got out of the habit of starting her day at 5:00 A.M.

Mary Kay never kept her priorities a secret. Once in business, she never deviated from telling her people that God and family should come before career. Though other managers and business owners might instruct employees to put their jobs first, she always insisted on the opposite. She would tell everyone how she managed her own career around her family. "We should never get so involved in our work," she advised, "that we lose what we cherish most: spending time with our husbands and watching our children grow up. Their early years are so important, and nobody can make the difference in their lives that you can."[21] Typically, other sales managers pushed their people for longer hours, which they figured would produce higher sales revenues. Mary Kay would tell women who neglected their families for their work that although she understood they were doing it for their families, it was self-defeating. "Perhaps spending less time on your career and more time with your dear ones will mean less financial success but more happiness overall," she'd say. Her advice came from the heart. Mary Kay wanted what was best for her sales force and employees, not her bottom line.

The fact that she was focused on the best interests of her people made Mary Kay a role model for others to emulate. Her better-to-give-than-to-receive philosophy permeated through the organization and carried over to customers as well. At the beginning of her training, a Mary Kay beauty consultant was told, "Your job is not to sell cosmetics. Your job is to go to a beauty show asking yourself, 'What can I do to send these women home feeling more beautiful on the outside, knowing full well they'll become more beautiful on the inside as a result.'"[22] The same thinking applied to each sales director. Leading by example, she focused on how to help her sales team be successful. Mary Kay understood well that if large numbers of her people were successful, her company would be successful. It was a give-and-you-will-receive philosophy. Help others to succeed, and you will succeed.

Mary Kay often told a story about how over an eight-year period, while working for a direct sales company, she had built a sales unit in Houston that generated $1,000 a month in overrides. Then her husband was transferred to St. Louis. Although she had worked hard recruiting and training her sales force, when she moved, the company stopped paying her on their future sales production. She felt this was unfair and vowed that it would never happen at Mary Kay Cosmetics. Her company wouldn't have sales territories. Every beauty consultant could sell the products anywhere, which meant that wherever she was, she could recruit others to sell for her unit. She could live in Chicago and, while visiting a relative in Los Angeles, recruit someone there to be part of her sales unit. Or a sales director could recruit while traveling on vacation. As long as she and the recruit were both active in the company, she would be entitled to receive commissions on her recruit's sales. Today, sales directors can have many beauty consultants who live outside the directors' home cities.

But what if the new consultant still required sales training? To solve this problem, Mary Kay inaugurated an adoptee program. An adoptee is a sales consultant who either was recruited by a sales director from another city or has moved to another area. Under this system, the adoptee is encouraged to attend sales meetings conducted by a sales director in her hometown. Hence, she is adopted into another sales unit, and if additional guidance or coaching is necessary, the sales director willingly provides it. Outsiders question why a Mary Kay sales director will do this without being compensated for it. They do it because it's good for the adoptee and it's good for the company. They also know that it's a two-way street. The thinking is: "Yes, I'm helping her, but somebody else is helping my recruits somewhere else."

Mary Kay people call the adoptee system the "go-give" principle. This is a philosophy based on giving, and it is applicable in every aspect of the company. Just as Mary Kay herself never had dollar signs in her eyes when she built her company, a giving and sharing attitude has been instilled throughout the organization. Of course, not everyone buys in to this philosophy. Some people are interested only in looking out for number one. Such individuals typically don't last long on the sales force or at Mary Kay's corporate office.

AN INVISIBLE SIGN

There are some experiences you never forget. One that made a lasting impression on Mary Kay, as related earlier, was standing in line for three hours to shake hands with a sales manager who never bothered to look her in the eye when she finally reached him. She talked about the incident many times throughout her career, using it as an example to teach others. She'd say,

> I have learned to imagine an invisible sign around each person's neck that says, "Make me feel important." I see this sign on everyone I meet, and I respond to it immediately. I never cease to be amazed at how positively people react when they're made to feel important.[23]

Mary Kay understood that people generally do what you expect them to do. When you anticipate that they will perform well, they do, and conversely, when you don't expect much of them, they do poorly. She wrote: "I believe that average employees who try their hardest to live up to your high expectations of them will do better than above-average people with low self-esteem. Motivate your people to draw on that untapped 90 percent of their ability, and their level of performance will soar."[24]

One way that she made people feel important was by allowing them to voice their views and listening carefully to what they said. She invited people to become involved in a new project by allowing them to participate during its initial stages. "People will support that which they help to create," she advocated.[25]

Knowing that people resist change, she sought her employees' opinions on new products and marketing innovations, which not only spawned valuable suggestions but also gave them ownership. This way, they bought in to the change, because they were a part of the process. It made them feel important, because it demonstrated that their opinions were valued. Conversely, people resist managers who announce change: "We are making these changes, and from now on, this is how it will be."

Good managers not only make their subordinates feel important by getting their support for new ideas, they seek the advice of their superiors as well. Mary Kay believed:

> Just as a manager might ask [her] staff, "What do you think?" or "What do you want?" she is wise to seek feedback from managers above her. For example, she might say to her boss, "I need your help. You've been in this business a long time, and your insight would be very valuable." It's amazing how favorable people respond when their advice is sought.

Don't think it isn't necessary to make the people above you feel important. As important as they may be, they, too, need constant reinforcement. Remember that they also have an invisible make-me-feel-important sign around their neck.

Known for her knack for making people feel important, Mary Kay showed no discrimination. She greeted everyone with a warm hello. On the company elevators and in the hallways, her friendliness to employees and visitors was legendary. "How are you today?" she'd say, and if someone replied, "I'm okay," she'd say, "You're not okay; you're great." If an employee called her, "Mrs. Ash," she would reply, "If you call me Mrs. Ash, I'll think you're either angry with me or don't know who I am. So please, call me Mary Kay." She'd tell them, "I don't want you to think of me as the chairman of the board. Think of me as your friend." She spoke with such sincerity that they knew she meant it. "If you ever need to talk to me," she'd say, "I want you to know that my door is always open." Everyone addressed her as Mary Kay, and when her son Richard became chairman of the board, employees also called him by his first name. This permeated throughout the company; everyone was on a first-name basis. It may sound like a small thing, but it made people feel important. It also made them feel good about working for a family business.

When a beauty consultant becomes an independent sales director, she is invited to the home office in Dallas to attend New Sales Director Education Week. For years, it was a tradition for Mary Kay to invite the new class of sales directors to her house. There she would chat with them individually, even when the numbers exceeded one hundred guests. Being at her home was a nice personal touch. But Mary Kay went one step further. She personally baked cookies for them. It made them feel like they were part of her family—and that's the way she felt about them. As a sales director once said, "When was the last time the CEO of your company made cookies for you?"

Having spent many years in the sales field, Mary Kay knew that the most valuable asset of the company was its sales force. She understood well that "nothing happens until somebody sells something." She continually reminded employees that if the independent sales force members were not out there selling Mary Kay products, the company would cease to exist. Consequently, nobody was more important than the women in the field. All home office employees were instructed to treat every sales consultant and sales director as a queen. When members of the sales force visit the home office, the company rolls out the red carpet. Everyone treats them royally. Throughout her career, Mary Kay never forgot where she came from. Because she spent so many years selling, she could readily identify with the women in the field. She was one of them! Her appreciation for them permeated the company, and they were always made to feel special.

"I think all company employees need to know that their jobs depend upon the independent sales force," she emphasized.

> Our manufacturing people know, "If the independent sales force doesn't sell it, we don't have anything to manufacture." We all have an obligation to back up the independent sales force, and if we fail to do so, we're not doing our jobs.
>
> Ideally, every employee in the company should be sales-oriented. It doesn't matter if that person is in research, accounting, or shipping—everyone's job supports the sales organization. Not a single major decision is made at Mary Kay, Inc., without first weighing the consequences to the independent sales force.[26]

RECOGNITION AND PRAISE

When her mother told her, "You can do it," Mary Kay rose to the occasion. As a child, she responded positively, and as a businesswoman, she always understood that most of us react the same way to praise. Throughout the years, Mary Kay Cosmetics became known for how it praised people to success. Mary Kay once said that the company's entire marketing plan is based on it. She noted:

> For most women the last bit of applause they received was when they graduated from high school or college. Sometimes it seems that the only women who are applauded are beauty queens and movie stars. A woman could work day and night caring for her home and the only time she's likely to hear a comment is if she stops doing it.[27]

What had been most upsetting to her during her sales career was being told, "Mary Kay, you're thinking like a woman." She keenly observed through her years of experience that women will often work for recognition when they wouldn't work for money.

By the same token, women customers respond well to encouragement. Every new Mary Kay beauty consultant is taught to praise her customers. They tell women in skin-care classes how wonderful they look with their makeup on. When a beauty consultant gives her first skin-care class, she may ask her sales director, "What did I do wrong?" The director is apt to reply, "Let me tell you what you did right." Only after showering her with praise will she then say, "Now let me make some suggestions on how you might improve."

Knowing how people react to recognition, Mary Kay began to reward her salespeople with gifts right from the start. When the company was in its infancy and on a tight budget, rewards were modest—colorful ribbons, pins, and costume jewelry. A gold-colored goblet was awarded to a beauty consultant with monthly wholesale sales production over $1,000, which back in the early sixties was considered a good month. When someone earned a set of twelve goblets, she received a matching tray. Mary Kay's son Richard couldn't believe it. "Do you think they'll work that much harder—for that cup?" he questioned.

"We'll make it a very exclusive club," his mother said. "Only a selected few will ever get one, let alone an entire set. They'll work hard to get it because they want the recognition that goes with it."

"I think you've lost your mind," he answered, "but if you think it will work, we'll do it."[28]

Mary Kay herself was surprised when she saw how hard the women worked to surpass their own sales records to win those gold goblets. She attributed the contest's success to people's craving for recognition, not their desire to own the gold-colored goblets.

Over the years, the company became known for the lavish gifts it awarded its top producers—everything from complete office systems to diamond rings. Top sales directors and national sales directors qualify for luxury trips to London, Athens, and Bangkok, including first-class airfare, limousine services, and five-star hotels. Not only do these prizes provide a strong incentive to qualify, but the VIP treatment makes every recipient feel very special.

It is widely known that a top Mary Kay producer can earn a pink Cadillac. In fact, the car has become a famous symbol of personal success. Every time one goes by, it's practically impossible not to think about the company. Mary Kay referred to the pink Cadillac as a trophy on wheels. Those who qualify for a pink Cadillac must meet certain sales production numbers in order to keep the car. Winners take great pride in having a pink Cadillac in the driveway, in the local shopping center parking lot, or in front of a customer's home.

The ultimate prize for achievement within the sales organization is a magnificent diamond bumblebee pin, known as the "crown jewel" in inner-company circles. The story behind it gives special meaning to this award. Years ago, aerodynamics engineers studied the bumblebee and concluded that it simply could not fly. Its wings were too weak and its body too heavy. Of course, the bumblebee doesn't know that it is impossible for it to be airborne, so it keeps right on flying. The symbol serves as a reminder to all Mary Kay people that they can achieve anything they believe they can achieve. It is also a badge of merit, and as Mary Kay often said, "Whenever you see anyone wearing one at a Mary Kay function, you know she's a distinguished person in our sales organization."[29]

There is also lots of recognition and applause at the annual Mary Kay convention known as Seminar, which is held in the Dallas Convention Center. No other company convention can hold a candle to this event. It has been described as a combination of the Academy Awards, the Miss America Pageant, and a Broadway musical. In the midst of the entertainment, glitz, and glamour, hundreds of the sales force's top performers are celebrated in the presence of their peers. Each Seminar has a theme such as "Shine On," "Dreams Come True," "The Power of Pink," and "You Can Have It All!" The company spends millions of dollars each year on this extravaganza. Each attendee pays her own expenses; yet the event is so well attended that the company holds five back-to-back three-day Seminars, with a total attendance of as high as 50,000 beauty consultants, directors, and national sales directors.

THE DREAM LIVES ON

During the spring of 1996, Mary Kay suffered a debilitating stroke. Following a period of convalescence, her visits to the office were infrequent, as were her appearances at Seminar. Ironically, one of America's most articulate businesswomen would never speak another word. She passed away on November 22, 2001.

Prior to her stroke, it was a company tradition for Mary Kay to make a grand entrance at the opening of each Seminar. But before her appearance, there was always a lot of clapping and singing. And what did they sing? Mary Kay songs, of course. Back in 1963, she had a contest that encouraged beauty consultants to create songs from a popular tune and change the lyrics. One woman wrote "I've Got That Mary Kay Enthusiasm" to the music of a much-loved hymn. The song and others like it caught on, and since then they've been sung at many Mary Kay gatherings ranging from Monday morning sales meetings to Seminar. Mary Kay thought singing was a good way to warm up a group of women. She believed that if it was good enough for schools to have a song and for congregants to sing them in churches and synagogues, singing would also have a positive effect on her sales force. She was right. And from the time the convention hall starts filling up at Seminar, there's upbeat music, and everyone starts having a grand time. It not only unites audience members, it fires them up.

Every Mary Kay entrance was spectacular. Once, a pink Cadillac convertible rose in a cloud from center stage of the convention hall. When the fog cleared, the spotlights in the dark hall were on the car, and Mary Kay stood up from the driver's seat and waved to the delighted audience. Her appearance always commanded standing ovations. At each Seminar, she crowned queens and personally congratulated and awarded all recipients for their achievements during the past year. She greeted new directors as they made their "debuts," in the presence of their peers. Seminar audiences loved her warm-hearted speeches filled with her own brand of wit and wisdom.

Until her stroke, she was active at all Seminars, starting with the first, on September 13, 1964, in the company's small warehouse decorated with crepe paper and balloons. For that one, Mary Kay herself boned chicken, cooked, and made a huge orange JELL-O salad that was served on paper plates. A director made a big cake decorated with the words "Happy First Anniversary." For entertainment, Richard hired a three-piece band. It was quite modest in comparison to today's multimillion-dollar extravaganzas.

An insightful woman, Mary Kay realized that a day would come when she was no longer active in the business. "Nobody lives forever," she'd say matter-of-factly. Over time, it became a top priority for her to assure a seamless transition in the company. A modest woman at heart, she insisted that it had been many years since the company had depended on her. She took pride in the fact that Mary Kay, Inc., had in place a strong management team and a world-class sales force of independent professionals. She was confident that they were fully capable of building an even bigger and better company even after she could no longer work side by side with them.

This could only happen if the company continued to adhere to the values and principles that Mary Kay put into place during the early years of the company. American business leaders provided precedents she could follow. IBM's dynamic founder, Thomas Watson, Sr., for example, had built one of the world's greatest companies and successfully passed the reins to his son, Thomas Watson, Jr. Other professional managers had followed the younger Watson, and IBM's principles and values had always remained intact. Likewise, Johnson & Johnson, founded in 1886 and later headed by one of the cofounder's grandsons, Robert Wood Johnson, had a strong culture that played a prominent role in its success. The company's principles and values are so deeply embedded in its daily affairs that they are spelled out in its credo today and engraved in a limestone wall at the main entrance of its world headquarters in New Brunswick, New Jersey. Johnson & Johnson's credo has never been abandoned.

Mary Kay saw her company as following in the footsteps of IBM and Johnson & Johnson, two of the world's most admired international companies, and providing opportunities to women around the globe. And always, above all else, the company would abide by the principles and values that she lived by. To assure that this would happen, Mary Kay wrote three books, including her autobiography, *Mary Kay*, whose title has been changed in the current edition to *Miracles Happen*. Each book describes what she stood for, and *Miracles Happen* is included in the starter kit that new consultants receive. "Mary Kay made a video in 1994," says Darrell Overcash, Mary Kays, Inc.'s U.S. president, "in which she asserted that the company would fare well when she was no longer here. We've shown it often at new employee orientation meetings, and it has a significant impact on everyone." Overcash pauses briefly and adds:

"When a company has a charismatic, visionary, enthusiastic founder, there is bound to be a period of adjustment when he or she is gone. We certainly had concern about how her death would affect our company. It is fortunate that she had the insight to address this issue while she was still active and vibrant. Mary Kay was known for having an effect on you, whether you spoke to her one-on-one, or you were in a crowd of 5,000 or 10,000 people. She had this ability to make you feel that she was speaking directly to you. When clips of her are shown at events, it is remarkable how viewers can feel her presence."[30]

As Rhonda Shasteen explains, "At Seminar, the most anticipated event of all was when Mary Kay made her first appearance. I don't think there is anything we can do that would create that same sense of awe and passion. However, we do show several clips of her during Seminar, and every time there are huge rounds of applause and flash bulbs start going off as if she were there in person. To this day, the sales force can't get enough of her."[31]

David Holl, the company's chief executive officer and president, explains further:

"There are so many things that Mary Kay did that were videoed and recorded as well as what she has written, and this gives us a vast selection from which to choose. So when we have a Seminar, a career conference, or a leadership conference, a message from Mary Kay is always part of the program. At Seminar, we might show a four-minute excerpt of one of her speeches. We will use it to emphasize a subject with a message that we feel it's important to communicate. Over the course of an event, several different such videos might be shown."[32]

At the 2002 Seminar, the first after Mary Kay's death, her son Richard had the audience applauding, even weeping, when he told them:

"Mother never thought about fame or wealth for herself but only about success for others. She always said, 'All that you send into the lives of others comes back into your own.' Isn't it amazing that even as we've grown to a multibillion-dollar company with a million-woman sales force, we operate today much as we did when it was just my mother and a handful of consultants and sales directors? We were like an extended family then, and we still are. It is my belief that one of the greatest measures of our success is how well we succeed in keeping our relationship-based culture at the core of all that we do."[33]

Richard ended his speech by telling them, "You are Mary Kay's greatest gift to the world, and Mary Kay's greatest gift is all of you."

With the company's emphasis on family values, it is a big crowd pleaser at Seminar today when Mary Kay's grandson Ryan Rogers takes center stage. Ryan, Richard's son and the youngest of Mary Kay's sixteen grandchildren, joined the company as a financial analyst in January 2000 after graduating summa cum laude from Southern Methodist University. Currently, he is the company vice president for strategic initiatives. An attractive young man, he is charming, like his grandmother and father, and a favorite speaker at company conferences and Seminars. Insiders say that Ryan is the heir apparent.

Ryan has spoken at Mary Kay Seminars all over the world, including in China, Ukraine, and Russia. He admires the sales forces in these countries. What particularly pleases him is how their successes with the company have changed their lives. Most impressive to him is how so many of these women, in places where entrepreneurial opportunities are rarely available, have taken advantage of a Mary Kay career. For example, he witnessed Russian women dedicated enough to travel ten hours by airplane or many days by train to attend a Seminar in Moscow. During the company's first ten years in China, the government made attempts to ban direct selling. The sales force persevered and today has become the company's largest market outside the United States.

To better understand the Mary Kay culture in other countries, in 2005 Ryan attended leadership conferences in Russia, Kazakhstan, and Ukraine. When he spoke to them in Russian, he received a standing ovation. He then journeyed to Argentina in celebration of its twenty-fifth anniversary representing Mary Kay. There, he spoke in Spanish. Later, Ryan visited China to attend a leadership conference and the opening of the company's new manufacturing plant. On both occasions, he spoke in Mandarin Chinese. His father Richard, rightfully proud of his son, said, "They tell me the applause was so intense that it shook the rafters of the new China plant."[34]

Ryan studied all three languages, and though he doesn't speak fluent Russian, Spanish, or Chinese, he spoke to the Mary Kay sales force in their language. So why and how was he able to give his speeches in these languages? He explains:

"Once when I went to Germany, I did just a few lines of my speech in German and the applause was immense. But when I went back to speaking English, the crowd was not nearly as responsive. Something definitely gets lost when you have to pause and wait for the translation. If I tell a joke, it's not funny anymore. I was also losing a huge connection with the audience. I decided that I was never going to do that again, so now, whenever I speak in a foreign country, I do it in their language. Translators help me to make sure I have the correct pronunciation. It definitely takes a lot more time and effort, but I feel it's worth it. I'd rather do a short speech in their language than a longer one in English using a translator."

He grins and adds:

"I practice these speeches to make sure I have the right dialect, and sometimes the audience thinks I speak their language. For instance, when I spoke in Mandarin, some people later approached me and started conversations in their language. Thankfully, I had a translator who explained to them that I'm not fluent in Mandarin."[35]

Mary Kay would have been so proud of her grandson, especially when he spoke at Seminars in faraway places. Richard recalls:

"Back in the fall of 2001, just before her death, Mother and I spent many afternoons looking at videos of Seminars from all around the world—from China, Russia, Mexico, Germany, and more—and of course our five Seminars here in the U.S. Each time a video would arrive, I'd take it to Mother's house, and we'd make an afternoon out of watching them together. I will never forget how her eyes intently followed the winners who crossed the stage to receive their awards. The women walked with grace and poise, and they were laughing, clapping, and hugging other winners. I looked into Mother's blue eyes and she had the same look of confidence and determination as back in 1963 when she first started this company. These images meant so much to her. And while she was unable to speak, Mother would squeeze my hand tightly and that said it all. Seeing women from so many different countries fulfilling their dreams let her know how far her own dream had traveled."[36]

MARY KAY'S PRESENCE TODAY

A salesman once walked into the lobby of Mary Kay, Inc., and seated himself in a comfortable chair. A receptionist asked, "Is there anything I can do for you, sir?" He answered, "No, I just came in to lift my spirits." The salesman explained that he loved the warm and friendly environment, and after a particularly bad day making sales calls, he needed a place to escape from the rat race. There is a good message here. When a company has a nourishing and caring culture, people sense it. They can also sense the opposite—a dog-eat-dog atmosphere releases feelings of friction and animosity. Over the years, Mary Kay's personal warmth had become deeply ingrained in the company's culture. To this day, employees emulate her friendliness and warmth.

Employees still talk about the first time they met Mary Kay in a meeting or even a brief passing in the hallway or elevator. CEO David Holl, who joined the company in 1993, recalls how he was first introduced to the company's founder:

"In 1996 I was chief financial officer, and I was walking down the hall with my boss. Mary Kay stopped to say hello and he said, 'I want you to meet a new hire of ours from Citibank, David Holl.'

"'What bank did you say that was?' she asked.

Mary Kay's original storefront (top)—where it all began; the company's world headquarters today (bottom), in Addison, Texas.

Mary Kay Ash, founder of Mary Kay Cosmetics (shown above left later in her career and above right as a young saleswoman), has been recognized as America's greatest woman entrepreneur. She poses in front of the famous pink Cadillac (below), a reward that is earned by top producers in the Mary Kay sales force.

An evening with the president—Mary Kay Ash and her husband, Mel, stand with President Ronald Reagan (above). A dynamic mother-son duo—Mary Kay dances with her son, Richard Rogers (right), executive chairman of the company.

"'Citibank—out of New York City,' I answered. She looked me squarely in the eye and replied, 'I want you to know that you are going to learn a lot more at Mary Kay than you ever could at that New York bank.'"[37]

Holl adds that Mary Kay was friendly and genuine—instantly you liked her.

'About three months later, we were talking with a big bank regarding some refinancing. I called Mary Kay's assistant and asked, 'Do you think we could get her to talk to a group of bankers at a meeting down here? I think it would be helpful in our discussions.'

"Her assistant answered, 'Mary Kay in front of a crowd? She would love to do it.' Sure enough, Mary Kay came to the meeting, and without any preparation, she talked for twenty minutes. Everyone sat there and listened. She had them mesmerized. I don't remember what she said, but it was much more effective than had I spouted off a bunch of facts and numbers. She was a superb communicator, and she had the quickest wit. I never saw anyone who could think so fast on their feet. She could handle anything that was thrown at her."[38]

During her college sophomore year in 1993, Laura Beitler worked as an intern in the company's legal department. She only met Mary Kay once—they shared an elevator—and Beitler recalls how friendly she was.

"That summer I learned about the company's values and witnessed how everyone truly cared about each other. I quickly realized what a unique and special company this was. Even though I was just an errand girl who would be working there for one short summer, the people I encountered at Mary Kay made me feel as though I was valued and appreciated. I completed my internship sincerely impressed by the incredible company Mary Kay had built."[39]

Beitler graduated college in 1995 and law school in 1998, and took a position that same year as a labor and employment staff attorney for another Dallas company. She explains:

"In retrospect, I learned so much from that summer internship about how to work with people. I suppose from that internship, I always had a passion for this company, so when I learned in 2000 there was an opening here for a labor and employment staff attorney, it turned out to be a perfect opportunity to return to Mary Kay."[40]

Once she was back at Mary Kay, Beitler was anxious to learn about the company's founder. She proactively read Mary Kay's books, listened to her speeches, and read transcripts from her speeches. Beitler says, "Listening to her words always amazes me, and I learn something new about her every day. Her views going back forty-five years are so far ahead of her time. It makes me very proud to be with this company. When I'm faced with making difficult decisions at work, I never miss an opportunity to ask people that knew her personally how Mary Kay would have handled similar situations in the past. While I know that nothing can compare with the experience of personally knowing Mary Kay, I certainly cherish hearing this information from those who knew her well. In order to be good stewards of her company, I think it's up to each of us as employees to proactively and deliberately seek out opportunities to learn more about the philosophies and values on which Mary Kay built this company. It's up to us to do our part to honor her legacy and keep this culture alive."[41]

Throughout her life, Mary Kay believed in giving to those in need. Even during her most difficult financial times when she was a young, single working mother, she made generous contributions to her church, sometimes more than her tight budget allowed. Later, as a successful businesswoman, she regularly gave large sums of money to a variety of charities and community organizations. She believed in giving back. To her it was a responsibility.

A supporter of many causes, she championed entities and projects that bettered the lives of women and their families. Anne Crews is the company's vice president of government relations and also serves as a board member of the Mary Kay Foundation. Crews explains, "It has always been her business and personal philosophy that you give back to the community that's been good to you. Initially, she gave in the Dallas area, and later, as the company expanded, she felt a corporate responsibility to give throughout America and subsequently around the world. Since the company's customer base is women, the foundation focuses on causes related to women, such as cancers affecting women and domestic violence against women and children. In addition to breast cancer, the foundation funds ovarian, uterine, and cervical cancer prevention and research. For years, we've had a Mary Kay 5K, and we've worked with the Komen Foundation since it was founded here in Dallas in the 1980s. We've also joined forces with Komen to get laws passed on the state and national levels regarding breast cancer, such as insurance coverage for mammograms, quality assurance of mammography machines, and so on."[42]

Michael Lunceford, the company's senior vice president of government relations, serves as president of the Mary Kay Foundation. As he tells it, "I think the foundation and the work it does is simply an extension of Mary Kay, who had a servant's heart. She always wanted to reach out and help people—this was the reason she started the company. The heart of this company is sharing and caring. The company was a vehicle that enabled Mary Kay to give to other people. With this in mind, the foundation was a natural extension for Mary Kay to improve the lives of women outside the company.

"Her commitment to fighting domestic violence is a good example of how she wanted to serve women. The foundation has given large grants to domestic violence national networks, but we also have a real focus on the shelters themselves because Mary Kay wanted to directly touch thousands and thousands of women in need. For this reason, she made a commitment to provide grants that went straight to specific shelters. She did it this way knowing that certain shelters with very limited resources urgently needed financial support. For example, there was one in Kentucky that had a monthly garage sale to make ends meet; they raised perhaps a few hundred dollars from a sale. You can imagine what a cash grant could mean to this shelter. Unfortunately, there are still many shelters in desperate need of financial aid. Last year, for example, we had more than 800 requests for grants, and the foundation awarded $20,000 to each of 150 shelters. We know that this money goes a long way for these grant recipients. For the past several years, the foundation has granted $3 million to domestic violence shelters. Our goal is to give these grants to at least three entities in every state of the union so we can spread our money around where the Mary Kay sales force is. During these difficult financial times, we are especially pleased to give these grants where they are needed so badly."[43]

Crews points out that the foundation is a public foundation, and it accepts contributions from the public. A major source of its funding comes from the Mary Kay independent sales force. Throughout the year, they hold fund-raising events in the United States and Canada ranging from races to fashion shows. Company employees, vendors, and Mary Kay, Inc., are also strong supporters of the foundation.

In his position as Mary Kay, Inc.'s chief counsel for intellectual property, John Wiseman is an authority on the value of a company's brand. Wiseman explains:

"Our company is in a unique position, because our brand is not a created name or coined term such as Apple or Microsoft. Our brand is also our founder. As a consequence, our brand goes beyond the expectations and other goodwill normally associated with a company's products and how it conducts business. Ours is the legacy of Mary Kay Ash based on her life and the principles and values to which she adhered. She wasn't just a talking head like many other CEOs. She connected with everyone by interacting with them here in the home office and in the field. She was constantly teaching us how to care for and respect people by her everyday behavior. Her life story is about how she overcame adversity as a young, single mother of three children and against all odds started this company with her modest life savings. Now, the company is a multibillion-dollar international corporation, and it has the same ideology that Mary Kay had when she first started it. After she passed away, Richard could have taken the company in a different direction, but he wisely realized the value of keeping the company culture."[44]

"Richard has always preferred to keep the spotlight on Mary Kay," Yvonne Pendleton, former director of corporate heritage, points out. "He always says, 'This is Mary Kay's company. She's the namesake, the star.'"[45] Not long ago, one of the networks wanted to interview him and he turned it down. Richard rarely grants media interviews.

"My father is a smart businessman," Ryan Rogers says, "and when my grandmother passed away, he was well aware of how this was not only a personal loss but it also posed a potential business risk. She was such an iconic founder. She is our brand. Her name is our brand. It would have been a terrible decision to shift gears and no longer promote her image, beliefs, and values. Well, my father realized this, and if anything, the company increased its efforts to promote the culture that she instilled. We keep doing it, and it has stayed at the forefront of what we do. We even measure it through employee surveys, and if we ever see the needle move, we become more focused on it."[46]

Richard Rogers was there from the start when the company opened its doors on September 13, 1963. Together, he and his mother built what has become one of the largest direct selling companies in the world. They were undoubtedly the best mother-son team in the history of American business. "Mary Kay was the leading lady," Richard would say, "and my job was to do everything else so she could shine in that role."[47] Mary Kay always respected Richard's judgment, even in the beginning when he was only twenty years old. She relied on him to make sure the company was managed as a business and to make sure she didn't overspend on prizes (like pink Cadillacs and diamond necklaces and bracelets) and on producing Seminars. She always ran the numbers by Richard.

In the early 1990s, an agent representing Dolly Parton came to Dallas to talk about making a movie of Mary Kay's life. Richard tells the story:

"My mother was a big fan of Dolly Parton, and she was excited about having her for the movie's leading actress. In fact, just about everyone around here thought it would be good for the company. I was absolutely against it. 'Mother, they will never give us the rights to edit the script,' I said, 'and without those rights, they'll put in some sensationalism because they'll want that sizzle to sell tickets.' I attended several meetings with advocates of the movie. I told them, 'Look, Mary Kay is bigger than life. Why do you want to expose her to anything that might hurt her image?' They agreed, and the movie was never made. I know we made the right decision."[48]

Rhonda Shasteen says of the Mary Kay brand and image:

"Our company's general counsel once asked me, 'If I could sell you all of the physical assets of the company and you start your business tomorrow, or I could sell you only the Mary Kay name and nothing else, which would you choose?'

"I answered, 'I'll take the name in a heartbeat. I can replace the building, I can hire employees, but there will never be another brand like Mary Kay.'"[49]

MARY KAY'S BELOVED SALES FORCE

Although all people were important to Mary Kay, none were more so than the national sales directors. Each of these women is an independent businesswoman who leads a large sales organization. Mary Kay could relate so well with them because what they had accomplished was what she herself had done early in her career. Like them, she spent many years in the field, selling, recruiting, and teaching women—always dedicated to helping other women succeed. Mary Kay could identify with these women, and they could identify with her because she had paid her dues, and she spoke from experience. Often she'd say to them, "If we all lifted up our skirts just above the knees, you'd see that my knees would be the bloodiest of all." How well they understood. It was like a general letting his troops know that he, too, had once been in the trenches.

Hundreds of national sales directors got to know Mary Kay personally because she spent time with them at leadership meetings and conferences. Many of these women describe their relationship with Mary Kay as like that between a mother and daughter. She liked this. She often referred to them as her daughters. "She continually told them, 'You are going to take care of things when I'm not here anymore,'" Richard Rogers says, "and they are doing that."[50]

Elizabeth Fitzpatrick is the first daughter of a national sales director to become one. In 1994, she and her mother became the company's first mother-daughter "nationals." Tells Fitzpatrick, who now lives in Denver:

"The year before that, I was eighteen weeks pregnant and I had a kidney stone. Surgery wasn't an option, so I was confined to bed rest. I was in pain and discomfort. I was miserable. One day I answered the phone weakly, and an unfamiliar voice said to me, 'Hi, this is Mary Kay.'

"I was in a bad mood and snapped, 'Mary Kay who?'

"'This is Mary Kay Ash, sweetie.'

"I was flabbergasted. I couldn't even imagine that she would call my house. 'God's delay is not God's denial,' she said to me. 'You will be a national. Just get through this time, and you'll be fine.' Her words were such a comfort, and her call came exactly when I needed it. To be able to say that the founder of the company called me when I was on bed rest is a nugget I'll keep forever. It makes me realize how important it is for us to reach out to people in need. I know the impact it had on me, so I'm going to pass it on."[51]

Fitzpatrick started her Mary Kay business in 1985. For many years, her mother, Shirley Hutton in Minneapolis, was the company's number-one national sales director and had become legendary throughout the world of Mary Kay. Hutton was a former television personality with the looks and personality of a movie star. Being her daughter had put considerable pressure on Fitzpatrick, because people expected the daughter of Shirley Hutton to also be a superstar. Fitzpatrick explains:

"I found I was always comparing myself to her, and I felt like everything I did was for my mother. She was such a leader in the sales organization that I never thought I could match up to her, so I considered quitting altogether. When I let my intentions be known, I heard from the people I had introduced to the Mary Kay opportunity. 'You can't leave,' they said.

"'I could,' I told them.

"'You're not just going to ditch us, are you?' This was a turning point for me. I realized that this is who I am, and this is my family. I don't have to be my mom. I can just be me. What matters is that I earned this position and I had to continue to lead these women. I had a brand new baby, and I decided to do it my way."[52]

When Fitzpatrick debuted as a national sales director at the 1995 Seminar, she stood there proudly with her fifteen-month-old daughter, Konnar, in her arms. Two significant others were by her side, her mother and Mary Kay. "I was onstage with four generations. These were the three most important women in my life, and they were with me to celebrate my success," says Fitzpatrick.[53] It was an emotional event, because later that year, Shirley Hutton retired.

Fitzpatrick adds that, like her mother, she had the opportunity to get to know Mary Kay.

"Every national who debuted at Seminar was individually invited to Mary Kay's suite and spent an hour with her. Then she went over what she expected of us. Mary Kay explained her philosophies and the reasons behind them. We were told that when she was gone, this is what she wanted us to do. It was very personal, because these were intimate conversations. All of the nationals spent more time with her at conferences and on the luxury trips that we were invited to take all over the world. And when we traveled, it was always first class: the finest hotels, cruise liners, limousines—always the best. She loved us and wanted to pamper us. She made each and every one of us feel as if she were a queen. It was truly amazing; she didn't sit in the background like a typical CEO. She wanted to be a part of us. Mary Kay had a vision, and she had a heart. As a woman, she could relate to our needs."[54]

Sherry Giancristoforo was a single mother and worked long hours as a nurse when she became a beauty consultant in 1976. A Minnesotan, she was recruited and taught by Shirley Hutton. Also a national sales director, Giancristoforo says, "Mary Kay always referred to the nationals as her 'Mary Kay daughters.' I liked that because after my mother, she was and is the number-one role model in my life. It is an honor and a privilege to carry on her legacy."[55]

It is said that great leaders lead by example, and innumerable stories illustrate how Mary Kay did this. Giancristoforo tells one of her favorites:

"In the winter of 1978, the company was just entering the Canadian market, and a big event was planned in Winnipeg, where Mary Kay would address an anticipated crowd of 200 to 300 women. Shirley Hutton and I drove together to Winnipeg, an eight-hour car ride from Minneapolis. When we got there, there was a terrible blizzard, and it was so bad that no one could get in or out of the hotel for two straight days. We were literally trapped in that hotel, and only fifteen people showed up for the event.

"It didn't matter how small the crowd; Mary Kay talked about the product line and the career opportunity as if there were 2,000 in the room. She had the same enthusiasm, and rather than skipping anything, she gave her complete presentation—and then some. She emphasized the great opportunities that the company offered and how Canadian women, their families, and the entire nation would benefit from everything that would happen as a result of our presence in Canada. I was so impressed, because it didn't matter to Mary Kay that the turnout was so disappointing. I remembered being told during my early training that I should never short-change a small turnout at a skin-care class: 'Always give them your very best—even if only one person shows up.' That's what Mary Kay believed—everyone deserves your best performance, like an actress on a stage, no matter if it's a full house or a sparse attendance. The show must go on. I witnessed firsthand that Mary Kay practiced what she preached. As I got to know her personally, I learned that she was always consistent. She never deviated from what she believed."[56]

Giancristoforo emphasizes that Mary Kay lived by her principles and beliefs, and today, she feels responsible to teach them to others. She says, "Once I got to know Mary Kay, I wanted to be with her and I wanted to be like her in every way. I felt she deserved to be followed. Since her passing, the company has always adhered to her personal philosophies, and in fact, management does everything possible to intertwine her beliefs, her values, and her heritage. Every company event includes video clips of Mary Kay. We feel her presence continually, and we talk about her as if she were alive. Of course, her legacy is very much alive."

Giancristoforo contributes to keeping it alive by passing it on to the 5,000+ women in her sales organization, three of whom have become national sales directors and in turn are passing it on to others.

A favorite sales force tradition is the telling of an "I" story. This is a personal story that a woman will tell about herself with an inspiring message: "If I can do it, you can, too." "I" stories are told at both small and large gatherings, including Seminars. A speaker, for example, might talk about how she was an extreme introvert before becoming a beauty consultant, "and look at me now. Here I am in front of 10,000 of you, speaking with complete self-confidence." Another might talk about how her Mary Kay career allowed her husband to leave a job he despised. This tradition started with Mary Kay when she would tell her own stories about how she was able to work her career around her three children as a single mom, how and why she started the company, and so on. Not only do these stories motivate others, they portray the values and principles that Mary Kay herself had and how she applied them.

It is the "I" stories and the messages they give that have become an oral history of the company. Today, an estimated 50 percent of the nationals have never met Mary Kay, but through the stories told by those who did, her legacy lives on. In a speech at the 2003 Seminar, Richard spoke directly to the national sales directors in the audience when he said, "You have seen to it that women who never knew her will come to respect what the name Mary Kay stands for. You have honored Mary Kay, making sure the seeds she planted forty years ago would grow. By your leadership, each of you has made a place for even more women to achieve their dreams. Our dream grows on, thanks to you."[57]

Rhonda Shasteen, who joined the company in 1984, spent many of her twenty-six years in sales and marketing in the field working with the sales force. In one of these positions, she was the manager of the product training department and in this capacity conducted workshops instructing consultants on how to sell to customers. Later she moved into sales development and worked with sales directors and national sales directors in the north central region of the United States. She then headed the sales education department that was responsible for conducting classes at Seminars, leadership conferences, and new director education classes that were held monthly in Dallas. Shasteen explains:

"Those ten years of experience with our sales force prepared me for my marketing position that began in 1999. Learning what I did in the field has made me a big believer in how much marketing people need sales experience. During those years, I learned firsthand what it's like to be in the field. I stayed in the homes of sales directors and nationals. I can't tell you how many times I was in the passenger seat of a pink Cadillac going to pick up children from school. And there were innumerable times that I went to a unit meeting with a sales director and helped her set up her meeting. I even went with them to make product deliveries to a customer.

"When you do those things, a lot of bonding happens. There's a lot of girlfriend talk, and you really get to know each other on a personal level. This is so important because this is a business built on relationships. It always has been and it always will be."[58]

As the company's U.S. president, Darrell Overcash doesn't have the background you'd expect to be responsible for a sales force of more than 600,000 women selling cosmetics. A 1983 West Point graduate, Overcash is a former helicopter pilot. A trim, 6'3" athletic man, he studied civil engineering at the U.S. Military Academy, and prior to joining Mary Kay, Inc., in 1996, he worked for seven years at Baxter Healthcare. "Most of my friends are either from the military or West Point," he says. "One of the hardest phone calls I ever made was when I called these guys to tell them I was working at a cosmetics company. After we talked a while, I'd add, 'Yeah, it's the one with the pink Cadillacs.' I took some ribbing for a while."[59]

His macho friends have since been convinced that he made the right move. "I've told them about the company's culture, and they're big Mary Kay fans now. Every single one of them," he adds with a chuckle. He goes on:

"I came to Mary Kay six weeks before Mary Kay had her stroke, so I never had an opportunity to meet her. But I do know her through all the people I've met who were close to her. I feel as though I know her well because the company has maintained her principles and values and the way she did things. Sure, there have been changes around here, but those principles and values have never changed."[60]

Today, Overcash spends a good percentage of his time in the field with members of the sales force, especially the national sales directors. He explains:

"I talk to at least one if not several a day. I'll pop in on their sales conferences, of course always invited. Every year I attend six to eight of their retreats, and pretty much anything a national asks me to do, I will try. I almost never say no. They know the sales world far better than I will ever know it. I understand the operations behind the scene. This is why I refer to our relationship with the sales organization as a partnership. We've got to stay in tune, and we've got to be doing things that support their efforts in the field. Concurrently, as the world changes, we've got to be willing to change and help them change as well.

"In the military, officers understand how you need to establish a level of morale based on trust. We must build a relationship with our unit, platoon, and company. It's the same in business. Strong relationships are also built on trust."[61]

There's a story about Overcash that has spread throughout the sales force, and it's one that would have made Mary Kay proud. After a regional conference in St. Louis, when it came time to head back home to Dallas, the weather had caused long flight delays. There were hundreds of Mary Kay salespeople who were also stranded at the airport. Overcash, who has accumulated hundreds of thousands of frequent flyer miles, could have spent the time comfortably in the club lounge. But he didn't. Instead, he mingled with the sales force in the terminal. For two straight hours, they drilled him with questions and suggestions. He took notes. "How can we do it better?" he asked them. He later commented, "It was the best two-hour flight delay I ever had." One sales director later said, "It reminded me of what Mary Kay would have done."[62]

Each April, an Inner Circle meeting is held in Dallas. The top nationals are invited. In 2009, to be included in this elite group, a national had to earn $325,000 during the twelve-month period ending December 31, 2008. At this meeting, these women meet with the top executives of the company. Prior to the meeting, the nationals are urged to submit any ideas and suggestions they want to discuss. They let management know what they are thinking, and it's a two-way street. Management lets them know what it is thinking as well.

Sherry Giancristoforo explains:

"We have a national sales director feedback system that encourages us to email the company's top executives anytime about anything. And they read every email we send in. In addition, any national can pick up the phone anytime, and chances are she'll get through to any executive, or at the very least, her call will be returned. But the Inner Circle meeting is a particularly good place to discuss something new—a product, a program, a new idea. Management knows that it must get the support of the Inner Circle nationals so that in turn, we will take it to the field."[63]

Barbara Sunden, of Old Tappan, New Jersey, started her Mary Kay business in 1972. Today, she is the number-one national sales director and has been a member of Mary Kay's exclusive Inner Circle a record twenty times and a top-ten national nationwide sixteen times. She has developed and promoted eight other national sales directors. Sunden estimates that she has more than 15,000 people selling Mary Kay products in seven countries (the United States, Canada, Mexico, the United Kingdom, the Philippines, Brazil, and South Korea). She holds many sales records that include having commissions in excess of $140,000 in a single month and annual commissions in excess of $1,047,000. Her career commissions are in excess of $11 million.

Sunden explains:

"When I started my business, it was just for fun. I loved the product and enjoyed conducting skin-care classes, but I quit three months later when my son was born. At the time, I looked at it as a job selling skin-care products. I didn't really know much about the company mission. My experience reminds me of a story about two railroad workers who were having lunch on a bench. The company president walked by and greeted one of the men, and after a brief chat, he left. Afterward, the other worker asked his friend, 'How is it that you and the president are such good buddies?'

"The man answered, 'We both came to work for the railroad at the same time and worked side by side doing manual labor.'

"'But he's the president and you're still a laborer.'

"'Yes, I know,' the man answered. 'You see, I came to work to earn $1.40 an hour, and he came to work to build a railroad.'

"I first came to Mary Kay to sell cosmetics, and only later did I learn about the opportunities that the company offered women. Then I learned about Mary Kay's principles and values, and that's when I realized what was available to me. Once I knew there was so much more to this business than conducting skin-care classes, I became focused on the big picture."[64]

Richard Rogers couldn't agree more with Sunden. As he puts it, "When we first started this business, we didn't have a mission statement. We had goals. But now our mission statement says that we provide opportunity for women around the world. Back then we said that Mary Kay's mission was to enrich women's lives, but as you can see, it's the same thing. For years I've been saying that we happen to be in the cosmetics business. That's the product. But that's not the business we're in. Our business is to provide opportunity to women throughout the world. I think everyone in this company knows this. It's part of the culture."[65]

A FAMILY BUSINESS

In October 2001, Richard Rogers promoted the company's chief financial officer and treasurer, David Holl, to president and chief operating officer. A few days later, Richard told Holl, "Mother is not doing well, and it's likely that she won't make it through the end of the year." Weeks later, on November 22, Mary Kay passed away. Richard kept the titles of CEO and chairman of the board, but on a day-to-day basis, it was up to Holl and the management team. Of course, as the largest shareholder of the company, Richard stayed involved in all major decisions. In late 2005, Richard told Holl, "I am going to take another step back. You need to be the CEO." The following April, Holl became the company's chief executive officer.

"By then, I knew the sales force well," Holl explains.

"I had attended many career conferences and leadership conferences, had conversations with nearly all of the nationals, and worked with them at Seminar. Of course, at Seminar, all of the management team gets involved. No matter who you are, you're in the backstage area helping out. When there is something going on, whoever is closest to it is the person who handles it. A perk is when one of our top sales force comes onstage and, as one of the men on the team, you get to escort her onto the stage and down the steps. It's also another way of getting better acquainted with our top field people. And although I'm certainly not Mary Kay or Richard, I make a lot of speeches at Seminar and other conferences. After I was named CEO,

Richard made certain to appear onstage with me, and sometimes Ryan was there, too, with me in the middle. This sent a message to the field: 'Okay, this guy is the CEO, but we are still a family business.' Sandwiched between the two Rogerses, I wasn't shy about telling the audience, 'The company is going in this direction, and we'll get there with Richard's help.' I'd sometimes add, 'Someday it's going to be Ryan up here, not necessarily me.'"[66]

Holl often points out that because the company is family owned, its management thinks long term. He points out:

"We don't have to meet quarterly forecasts to satisfy Wall Street. Instead of thinking just three months or a year out, we think of where we'd like to be five and ten years from now. I remember someone asking Richard after his mother passed away if he planned to sell the company. He said, 'No, and it wouldn't matter what anybody would offer me; the company is not for sale. This is a family company.'"[67]

In his role as executive chairman, Richard doesn't come to the office on a daily basis. He says, "I might not be there every day, but I never take my eye off the company. I read all the financial statements, including the monthly and quarterly reviews. I love reading the minutes of every quarterly review when management from across the world come in to make their reports. I enjoy hearing what they have to say. While I rarely attend Seminar, you will find me at annual budget meetings."[68]

The only family member active in the company today is Ryan, who has made a big hit with both corporate employees and the sales force. Ryan has fond memories of his grandmother, as the following story illustrates:

"When I was a small boy, every time I'd see my grandmother, she'd ask me, 'How are you?' and like all her grandchildren I was expected to respond, 'Great!' When all my cousins, my brother and sister, and I would visit her, before we could play, it was a ritual for us to stand in line and be greeted by Grandmother, one at a time. As the youngest, I was usually the last in line, and it seemed like forever before it was my turn. She'd ask each of us personal questions about school, soccer, whatever we were into. She knew what was going on in our lives, and she spent so much time being attentive to each and every one of us.

"Finally, when it was my turn, she'd start the conversation by asking, 'How are you, Ryan?' I'd answer, 'Fine.' And she would correct me by saying, 'No you're not. You are great. And don't you forget it, Ryan.' Having gone through this routine so many times, we all knew to say, 'Great,' but I didn't like to play by the rules. When I was older, I wised up, and when she'd ask how I was, I'd say, 'Oh, I am wonderful, thank you.' Or, 'I'm terrific,' or 'I'm doing splendid.' But I wouldn't say great. Grandmother would give me a look as if I had done something wrong, but she couldn't help giving me a little smile and then a wink to let me know she was on to me It was kind of a game we played, and I could tell she enjoyed it."[69]

In 1984, when Ryan was seven years old, Mary Kay's second book, *Mary Kay on People Management*, was published. Mary Kay gave him a copy with the inscription: "To Ryan: Learn all of this to use when you are President of Mary Kay Cosmetics!! Love, Grandmother." Ryan says that the book is his prized possession and that he keeps it in a safe. For the 2008 rerelease of this book, now titled *The Mary Kay Way*, Ryan wrote the foreword, and he discusses how Mary Kay's business philosophies continue to guide the company.

Barbara Sunden agrees that the company still operates on Mary Kay's principles; in fact, she's had firsthand experience with that for thirty-two years. She explains:

"Shortly after I became a national, my mother was diagnosed with breast cancer. Our doctors in New Jersey were not optimistic. When I told Mary Kay about my mother's diagnosis, she insisted that I bring her to Dallas to be treated by her personal physician. My mother and I flew to Dallas, and after examining her, the doctor had her admitted to his cancer clinic. As a result of this treatment, I am convinced my mother lived an extra three years. I couldn't get over how Mary Kay took such a personal interest in my mother. On several occasions she visited my mother, and I find this mind-boggling. It would have been one thing had I been the one in the hospital, but this was my mother, who was one person removed from Mary Kay. Now, have you ever heard of the CEO of a company going over to the hospital to check on someone's mother? Later on, Mary Kay's assistant picked my mother up in Mary Kay's personal pink Cadillac and took her to the office building for a tour. Afterward my mother visited with Mary Kay in her office. I couldn't believe how my mother's spirits were lifted from all the VIP treatment. It was better than any medicine! When you talk about a family business, I think this epitomizes what Mary Kay created. Her actions went far beyond business. She instilled these values in all of the nationals, and today we treat our people the same way. We learned from her that everyone is important and deserving."[70]

Sunden explains that what Mary Kay taught the nationals is now being passed along to others.

"Mary Kay was so good about calling people on both happy and sad occasions, whether it was to express her condolences when a loved one passed away, to wish a speedy recovery to a sick person, or to congratulate someone for anything from a big anniversary to a wedding. We all got enough of those calls and knew how meaningful they were that we became conditioned to do the same with our extended family. Today the company sends out a monthly update to all the nationals to let us know who needs a word of encouragement for whatever reason. And, just like Mary Kay did, we send out a note."

Executives at the company do likewise.

THE COMPANY CULTURE

In addition to the company's rich oral history, volumes of books, and audio and video recordings, there is the Mary Kay Museum that opened in 1993. Housed today at the company's 600,000-square-foot world headquarters building, the museum is located inside a soaring glass lobby, occupying more than 3,500 square feet. It displays a collection of artifacts that document the life and times of Mary Kay Ash and the company she and her son Richard founded. You can't help but feel good when you visit it; you come away a believer that dreams do come true.

Richard always joked that his mother saved everything, refusing to discard old possessions. "Someday, we'll have a use for all these," she'd tell him. Perhaps she was thinking ahead, because today, many of those very items are on display in the museum, including the original skin-care products. Also on display are some of the prizes and awards from the past and present, including the first diamond ring presented at Seminar awards night in 1968 and twelve diamond bumblebee pins like those awarded to top sales force achievers and patterned after the original bumblebee that Mary Kay personally wore. The museum also exhibits gowns worn by Mary Kay at Seminars. And it has a collection of the suits that directors wore over the years. Because a new director suit was designed each year, viewers are enthralled to see the fashion changes over the decades.

Jennifer Cook, who formerly was Mary Kay's personal assistant, is now the Mary Kay Museum curator. During a tour of the museum, she says with a smile, "Look at that pink hard hat. The construction workers wore them when the building was under construction." She points to a photograph and adds, "That's a bulldozer that was painted pink when the Atlanta distribution center was being built."

The museum is open to the public, and during Seminar, when up to 50,000 members of the sales force come to Dallas, it is perhaps the most visited place in the entire state of Texas. Just walking through the lobby is a treat. There is a dining room with thick, three-story-high columns designed to replicate giant lipstick tubes. Photographs and paintings of Mary Kay adorn the walls in the hallways. There is a photo of Mary Kay with Ronald Reagan and another with her longtime friend, Norman Vincent Peale. You'll even see the sheet music for Paul Anka's "My Way," which became Frank Sinatra's signature song. The words "my way" in the song have been changed to "Mary Kay's way."

On exhibit in the Keepers of the Dream Gallery is a large crystal sculpture that resembles a pink eternal flame. It rests on a polished faceted full–lead crystal base. The sculpture was inspired by Mary Kay's priorities of God first, family second, and career third. The base is permanently attached to the flame, creating a single sculpture. The eternal flame serves as a reminder of how Mary Kay often talked about the women she groomed to be role models for her dream company and how the torch would be passed on to them. She said that they were destined to be keepers of the flame.

Nearby, another wing off the lobby houses a hall of honor with portraits of the national sales directors from throughout the world. In the same area is the milestone wall, which displays interesting photos of the sales force's "firsts" including Helen McVoy and Dalene White, the first two national sales directors, who both debuted in 1971; Ruell Cone, who debuted in 1976 as the first African American national sales director; Shirley Hutton, who became the first member of the Million Dollar Circle of Achievement in 1980; Maria Alvarez, who became the first Hispanic national sales director in 1991; Shirley Hutton and Elizabeth Fitzpatrick, who became the first mother-daughter national sales directors; Dacia Wiegandt, who in 2005, at age twenty-six, became the youngest national sales director; and Anne Newbury, who in 2006 became the first national sales director to earn $1 million in commissions in one year.

In another area of the museum, there is a theater where visitors can select and view continually playing videos that reveal the life and times of Mary Kay. The museum is filled with honors accorded Mary Kay during her lifetime, including the Horatio Alger Distinguished American Citizen Award. Even after her death, Mary Kay was named the Greatest Female Entrepreneur in American History by a Baylor University academic study published in 2003, and in 2004, the Wharton School and PBS named Mary Kay to its list of the twenty-five most influential business leaders of modern times.

"The sales force loves walking through the museum," says David Holl. "It is a little piece of their home. It's our history."

Certainly, the museum, books, and video tapes are valuable tools that contribute to reinforcing the company culture. But the scores of endearing stories that are told and retold also reveal the character and personality of Mary Kay. Oftentimes, the stories are about little things this remarkable woman did—incidents that perhaps evoked a slight smile or a chuckle, acts and gestures that nobody thought would ever be remembered, let alone repeated years later. These are being passed down as an oral history that today defines Mary Kay, the woman. For instance, they still tell the story about how Mary Kay once walked into the office of Michael Lunceford, senior vice president of government relations. It was during the noon hour, and Lunceford was having a quick lunch at his desk. He was enjoying a hamburger from Whataburger, a local favorite fast-food restaurant in Dallas. Although there was no conversation about the meal, many times afterward, Mary Kay would cut out a Whataburger coupon from the newspaper and drop it off at Lunceford's office. Another time, she noticed an employee who had brown-bagged his lunch but had fast-food ketchup packets on his desk. "It's my favorite ketchup," he explained somewhat sheepishly, "and I can't get it anywhere else." Evidently, Mary Kay enjoyed a good hamburger, too, because afterward, she would periodically stop by his office to drop off more packets of that same ketchup.

Rhonda Shasteen has her own favorite personal story. She was the emcee at a career conference in Orlando with 4,000 people in attendance. She explains:

"Every year, there would be a contest to determine which conference Mary Kay would attend, and it wasn't until the last minute that I found out it would be this one. Now, I had done these conferences for ten years, so it wasn't any big deal for me to do one. But now, all of a sudden knowing Mary Kay would be there, it became a big deal. I felt a bit nervous. The convention center had filled up, the music was playing, and the consultants are standing and starting to wave their pompoms. My adrenaline was starting to pump because I was getting ready to go to the podium to kick off the meeting. At this point, nobody else knew Mary Kay would be there, and I was getting ready to introduce her. Mary Kay was behind the curtain in a portable office that had been prepared for her.

"I started to visualize in my mind how it was going to go—greeting everybody and then surprising them by welcoming Mary Kay. I was really starting to get butterflies, and I started to think, 'What if I trip on my way up the stairs? What if I mess up the introduction?' I wanted it to be perfect. I started to pace back and forth, and I got a tap on my shoulder. It was Nancy Thomason, a bodyguard who traveled with Mary Kay. Nancy said to me, 'Rhonda, Mary Kay wants to see you, right now.'

"'What have I done wrong?' I thought to myself. 'I hope I didn't say anything to someone in the sales force that upset her and she told Mary Kay. If so, I'm in trouble.'

"I followed Nancy to where Mary Kay was. She was dressed beautifully in a business suit and sitting on a small loveseat. She had her shoes kicked off, but this wasn't unusual. In her office, she nearly always kicked off her shoes under her desk. I nervously approached her and timidly asked, 'Yes, Mary Kay, can I help you?' My voice cracked, and she could see that I was shaking. She looked up at me with a big grin on her face.

"'Rhonda, hon, my right eyelash has come unglued. Do you think you could glue it back on for me?' She took out her makeup bag and handed me a little tube of eyelash glue. She gave me a wig pin that she used to put the glue on the strip of the eyelash.

"I was very much relieved that's all she wanted to see me for. In retrospect, I knew that Mary Kay put her eyelashes on every day. She would have had no problem gluing that eyelash on herself. But because she knew I was a little uptight, by letting me know that she needed me, she totally diffused all of my nervousness. That's how well she understood people."[71]

Although the customs, politics, and lifestyles vary in the thirty-seven markets where Mary Kay products are sold, the one thing that remains constant is the company culture. It has universal appeal to women around the world. The Mary Kay culture transcends borders and is accepted everywhere because it is so basic. Women in faraway places, from Brazil to Kazakhstan and China to Russia, are inspired by Mary Kay's words: "God didn't have time to make a nobody, just a somebody." Referring to his mother at the 2002 Seminar, Richard Rogers said, "Mary Kay's true greatness was her ability to inspire, the wisdom to praise people to success, and to literally bring out greatness in everyone."

Ryan Rogers talks about a sales director he met in Russia.

"She told her 'I' story, and it's one I'll never forget. She said that her husband had left her, and as a single mother with a small son, being on her own was much more difficult than she had imagined. 'I thought about suicide,' she said, 'thinking my son would be adopted by a family or taken care of by the state, and he'd have better opportunities than what I could give him in this country.' A day after contemplating suicide, she was introduced to Mary Kay and became a beauty consultant. 'Mary Kay didn't just change my life,' she said, 'it saved my life.' Today, she is a top sales director. I asked her how her son was doing, and she told me, 'Oh, he's in college in New York City.'"[72]

"A magazine had a feature article on lipstick in Siberia," Yvonne Pendleton tells. "It reported how women in some of its harshest climates love Mary Kay lipstick and our moisturizers because they work so well. Our chief scientific officer commented, 'You know your product is good when women in Siberia can't live without it.'" Pendleton points out that Mary Kay's regional teams select what best suits their market from the brand's global palette.

It is said that the big reason why Mary Kay is so well received globally is in part because the company has good products. The rest of the credit goes to the company culture. Ryan Rogers sums it up perfectly when he says, "Women have an emotional connection with Mary Kay's story. They strongly resonate with these values. The Golden Rule is something easy for them to understand and to relate to from a business perspective. Women appreciate the whole idea of a balanced life. Here, it's God first, family second, career third. To an Asian woman, we say faith or spirituality first, family second, and career third. When a company lives this, it's the company you want to do business with."

Bill Austin, on a mission in Victoria, Mexico, goes face to face with a small child who just received hearing aids provided by Starkey Laboratories.

So the World May Hear

Starting in his basement in 1967, William"Bill" Austin opened a small hearing aid clinic and repair shop that later became Starkey Laboratories. Starkey is America's largest hearing aid company and is the world's leading manufacturer of custom hearing instruments. Starkey, a privately owned company, is headquartered in Eden Prairie, Minnesota, and Austin serves as its chief executive officer. The company employs 3,700 people in twenty-six facilities around the globe. Starkey has annual revenues in excess of $700 million and conducts business in more than one hundred markets worldwide.

An industry innovator and leader, Bill Austin is hailed as the most admired American in the hearing aid field. His proudest accomplishment is the Starkey Hearing Foundation, a nonprofit organization he founded in 1984 that is dedicated to providing the gift of hearing to those who can least afford a hearing aid. Starkey missions are conducted each year that provide more than 100,000 hearing aids to needy people, mainly children. Accompanied by a team of Starkey employees and often his wife, Tani, Bill personally spends more than four months each year on missions visiting the underprivileged in countries such as India, Vietnam, the Dominican Republic, and South Africa. During these missions, Bill works side by side with his fellow missionaries fitting people with hearing aids. In addition to the costs for administrative, travel, and payroll expenses, the Starkey Foundation gives away more than $50 million (retail value) of hearing aids annually.

&

> Oh you men who think or say that I am malevolent, stubborn, or misanthropic, how greatly do you wrong me. You do not know the secret cause which makes me seem that way to you. For six years now I have been hopelessly affected by the said experience of my bad hearing. Ah, how could I possibly admit an infirmity in the one sense which ought to be more perfect in me than others, a sense which I once possessed in the highest perfection, a perfection such as few in my profession enjoy or ever have enjoyed. Oh I cannot do it; therefore forgive me when you see me draw back when I would have gladly mingled with you. My misfortune is doubly painful to me because I am bound to the misunderstood; for me there can be no relaxation with my fellow men, no refined conversations, no mutual exchange of ideas. I must live almost alone, like one who has been banished; I can mix with society only as much as true necessity demands. If I approach near to people a hot terror seizes me, and I fear being exposed to the danger that my condition might be noticed.
>
> —LUDWIG VAN BEETHOVEN, *October 6, 1802*

HUMBLE BEGINNINGS

Born in Nixa, Missouri, on February 25, 1942, Bill was the only child of J. E. "Dutch" and Zola Austin. His paternal grandfather was a sharecropper in Alabama and raised thirteen children. Dutch quit school after the third grade to help his father plow cotton. He migrated north to Missouri during the Depression. Dutch found work on a small farm, and he married Zola, the farmer's daughter. Dutch was classified 4-F by the military because of his poor vision and flat feet and was unable to enlist during World War II. To help with the war effort, he worked in a munitions plant. Zola worked at the same plant, loading shells.

Bill talks about his early years:

"For the first five years of my life, I was mainly raised by my grandparents. My grandmother was a wonderful woman who had a strong influence on my life. She talked to me as if I were an adult. A religious woman, she took me to church with her on Sundays. She always had a wise saying to apply to what she wanted to teach me, and hearing them when I was so young left a strong impression on me. One in particular that she drummed into it me was that the idle mind is the devil's playground.

"Products of the Depression, my parents and grandparents constantly worried about money. It was something that stayed with them all their lives."[73]

Zola had a brother, Paul, in Oregon who claimed there were lots of jobs to be had out West. When Bill Austin was five years old, his family moved to Oregon. He says, "My father got a job as a lumber grader with Georgia-Pacific. Later he started his own bartering business collecting and reselling. To make ends meet, my mother and I picked up beer and soda bottles on the roadside. We'd pick them up, put them in our gunny sacks, and when they were filled, we'd get a couple of pennies per bottle for our labor. In the summer, we picked wild blackberries in the fields. I remember how my arms and legs would get scratched up. It was no big deal. It was just part of the job. In the winter, we cut bark from Chittum trees in the forest that we would peal and dry. Then we sold the bark, which was used to make medicinal products. When I was seven, I was old enough to get a paper route.

"I saved my money in a big piggy bank that my uncle gave me. One day I came home from school and discovered that my father had raided it. All my money was gone. He used the money to make a down payment on a house in Bay City, Oregon. I never saw that money again, and he made no attempt to pay it back to me. I know my father never thought that he had done anything wrong. Even as a young child, I understood his motive, and I didn't dwell on it. Money was not important to me back then, nor has it ever been. Knowing how it meant a lot to my father, there were times when I went to school without money for lunch, and when my father would ask, 'Do you need lunch money?' I'd tell him, 'No. I'm okay.'"[74]

Dutch's frugalness was ingrained in him during the Great Depression. For most of his life, Dutch had been dirt poor. He knew the value of a dollar and wanted to make sure his son did, too.

Dutch worked hard in his trading business and built a good reputation for being an honest man. He repeatedly told his young son: "Your word is your bond. If you say something, that's it! That's the way it has to be. If you make a mistake, it doesn't matter if you lose money. That's irrelevant. You must always keep your word."[75] This advice made a lasting impression on the young lad. Above all else, everyone who knows him will say that Bill Austin always honors his word.

Over time, his father made enough money to buy a fifty-two-acre farm near Salem, Oregon. With no freeways back then, it took several hours to get there from the Austin house. It was a small farm with a few pigs, a cow, and some chickens, and it required someone to do the daily chores. Apparently, his parents had a lot of confidence in their nine-year-old son, because in the summer of 1951, they dropped off young Bill at the farm, where he lived by himself for one month. He explains:

"I was responsible for feeding and caring for the animals. My parents told me that if I had any problems, I should walk over to the neighbor's house, which was about a half-mile down the road. And in the event of a dire emergency, I could use the phone on the wall. It was one of those old ones you had to crank, and I never once used it."[76]

Bill was a nature lover and, as a young boy, wanted to someday be a forest ranger. But after reading a book about the life of Dr. Albert Schweitzer, he changed his mind. "I was enamored with his life's work in Africa."

Bill took Schweitzer's words to heart: "I don't know what your destiny will be, but one thing I do know: the only ones among you who will be really happy are those who have sought and found how to serve."[77] By the time Bill had finished the book, he had determined what he would do with his life. "I decided to be a missionary doctor. I wanted to contribute to humanity. I knew that someday I would."[78]

By his teenage years, Bill had developed a strong work ethic, and observing his father's bartering and scrap-collecting endeavors, he decided to make extra money by doing the same thing. The industrious teenager would find abandoned cars and trucks and remove the metal parts, which he would then sell to salvage yards. He did well enough to pay for his own clothing and pay cash for his first car by the time he was fifteen. Bill graduated high school early and took a night job at Georgia-Pacific, earning enough money to pay for his education at the University of Oregon, where he studied for two years.

As a member of the cleanup crew at a Georgia-Pacific sawmill, he performed what was undoubtedly the lumber company's least desired job. He explains:

"Those who had this job were paid for pushing a broom around, and they didn't take pride in their work. This was evident from the sawdust and debris that had collected over the years in corners that were not cleaned. When the job was assigned to me, I took it upon myself to clean the place so it would look like a showroom. My thinking was that whatever your job is, you should do your very best at it. You must take pride in your work to avoid getting trapped into thinking, 'I have a miserable job, and I'll do as little as possible but enough to stay on the payroll.' I believe you should find meaning in whatever you do."[79]

Bill's sentiments are reminiscent of the famous Martin Luther King, Jr., quote:

"If a man is called to be a street sweeper, he should sweep streets even as Michelangelo painted, or Beethoven composed music, or Shakespeare wrote poetry. He should sweep the streets so well that all the hosts in heaven and earth will pause to say, here lived a great street sweeper who did his job well."

Between his sawmill job and operating his scrap business, the assiduous young man was able to pay his tuition and purchase a small rental house as an investment. The real estate transaction was relatively easy—so much so that he briefly considered buying many more properties, thinking that over time it would be a sure way to become rich. "It was something I believed I could do with ease," he reflects, "but the notion of accumulating wealth was not my first priority."[80]

To make extra money while in college, Bill also worked as a deliveryman for a furniture store. Noticing his young employee's limited wardrobe, the owner gave him his old dress shirts. Bill recalls:

"They were good shirts, but the elbows of the sleeves had holes in them. I had accumulated three sweaters that were given to me as gifts during the past two years, and by buying two more, I was able to wear a different outfit for a full week. Being a good dresser for the first time in my life was good for my self-confidence. Then one day I noticed that people didn't really care about how I was dressed. They were more interested in themselves. From that day on, I decided that I would only dress simply, so the focus would be on the other person. Every day I wear the same black outfits so that my attire will not become a subject of discussion, allowing the focus to move to the other person and their interests."[81]

On the advice of Uncle Fred, his mother's brother who lived in Minnesota, Bill transferred to the University of Minnesota. Bill points out, "This is where Earl Bakken, who developed the first wearable cardiac pacemaker, and Dr. C. Walton Lillehei, who is referred to as the 'father of open-heart surgery,' were making incredible medical advances in the 1950s. Lillehei performed the first successful open-heart surgery, and he developed new procedures for medical devices such as pacemakers and heart valves. I was interested in doing life-saving work, and knowing that researchers like Bakken and Lillehei were there, I thought it was the place to be."[82]

BILL'S EPIPHANY

In 1961, to pay for his education while attending the University of Minnesota, Bill worked for his Uncle Fred's company, Minnesota Hearing Aid Center, in a small shop that made earpieces for hearing aids. In the beginning, it was just a job. He had no interest in hearing aids. His intention was to work there solely to pay for his education. He explains his thoughts:

"My first impression was that the hearing aids business was rather mundane. Medicine had far more appeal. I'd be saving lives and be surrounded by young, attractive nurses.

"In those days, hearing aids were primitive compared with today's. Control of feedback was a challenge. The molds had to fit tightly, and if not, the aids would whistle. My job was making the earpiece, putting it on the patient, and testing it to make sure its seal was tight. One day I fit this elderly man, and the way he reacted afterward had a profound influence on my life. His entire face glowed with absolute joy. As long as I live, I will never forget his expression. When I observed that he could hear, it dawned on me for the first time what hearing truly meant. That night I said to myself, 'Bill, the reason you want to be a doctor is so that you can help people. If you do this work, you will be able to help them and you won't kill anyone.'

"I knew that over a lifetime, a doctor was certain to lose patients. I accepted this as part of practicing medicine. You can't prolong life forever. As a young man, I knew that when I was a doctor, I could only do so much with my time and my two hands. However, with hearing aids, I could foresee when working with teams of people and the combined hands of many, I could contribute to improving significantly more lives.

"I used to have these conversations with myself. I'd say, 'Bill, it is unlikely that you'll ever be a Jonas Salk. You don't enjoy chemistry, nor do you have the patience for research.' I wanted the immediate satisfaction of treating a patient."[83]

One night, the nineteen-year-old student had a dream, one that changed his life forever. He recalls:

"In my dream, I was talking to Bill Austin. 'Bill, you're a clinical guy. You are going to treat one patient at a time. Perhaps you will see fifteen or twenty a day.' Then my dream fast-forwarded. I had a vision of myself as an old man in a casket that was being lowered into the grave. People were standing around the burial plot. The mourners were saying, 'He was a nice old doctor, and he helped our community.'

"My immediate inspiration was that in the hearing aid business, I could contribute much more to the world. I could be a citizen of the world. I said to myself, 'You have one life to live and one life to give. You must make it count for as much as you can. I can give the gift of hearing, the vehicle that creates love and caring between people. And it allows them to learn so they can live more productive lives.' This thought changed the course of my life. When I awoke in the morning, I knew exactly what I wanted to do. It was my destiny to serve people with hearing impairment."[84]

Bill recalls his thoughts at the time and his attitude about the hearing aid industry.

"It was my opinion that it was on the slow track. That was okay with me. If you want to win, you should be on a slow track. I say this in candor, knowing that some people in this field might take this as an insult. However, I could see so many things that were being done inefficiently. I recognized that there was so much room for improvement. And I could see that during the course of making those improvements, I could attract a team of people, and with that core group, we could add teams of people. Then by multiplying this process, I could attain the leverage that was required to make a significant contribution to life."[85]

That morning Bill rode a bus to work. On a panel on the ceiling, he read an anonymous quotation: "The true way to be humble is not to stoop till thou art smaller than thyself, but to stand at thy real height against some higher nature that will show thee what the real smallness of thy greatness is." He recalls his reaction:

"I reread those words and repeated them until I knew them by memory. It was exactly how I felt. I wanted to challenge life. I wanted to be the best in what I did and still see the smallness of my greatest greatness. I was overcome with inspiration, but I had no leverage. I knew what I had to do. I had to build leverage, and I realized that it would take time, because I was starting out with absolutely nothing."[86]

SCHOOL OF HARD KNOCKS

In 1961, Bill dropped out of school and went to work full time in his Uncle Fred's hearing aid store in Sioux Falls, South Dakota. It was a replica of his uncle's clinic in Minnesota. Only the name was different. In Sioux Falls, it was called South Dakota Hearing Aid Center. And like its sister clinic, Minnesota Hearing Aid Center, its name projected an image of a large company. Bill's uncle owned several other stores like it throughout Minnesota and the Dakotas. All of them were small hearing aid clinics, each having a staff of one to three employees.

The store was managed by an ex–school teacher. Bill recalls:

"There was so little traffic that one day the manager announced, 'I can't take it anymore. I quit. I'm going back to schoolteaching.' I told my uncle that I can run this business, and just like that, I was his new manager. There were days when not a single person came in. We had a sales area and three examination rooms. A young woman in a white nurse's uniform was always present in the front. I watched people that walked by take a peak at the window display, glance at the receptionist at her desk, and continue on walking down the street.

"Since they weren't coming in the door, I decided to take a more aggressive approach. I went outside, and I waited for those window shoppers to come by. As they stopped to look at our window display, I approached them as if I were just or returning from a coffee break or lunch. I'd casually say, 'Why don't you come inside? We'll check your hearing, and it will only take a minute. There's probably nothing wrong and nothing needs to be done. But you might as well find out how your hearing is. It's a free service we provide.' It worked, and our sales shot up."[87]

A natural-born salesman, Bill Austin is likeable, compassionate, and trustworthy. He has always had a strong work ethnic, and most importantly for a salesperson to succeed, he never took it personally when a customer said no. For this reason, he never became discouraged or lost confidence in his ability to sell. Above all else, he possessed a strong conviction in his product and services. This conviction was so evident that people sensed it, and they knew that what he did for them was in their best interests. All of these attributes are what it takes to succeed in the sales profession, no matter what the product or service is.

Bill didn't rely only on window shoppers as prospective hearing aid patients. He would venture out away from the shop to solicit business. He explains:

"I would visit small towns in the area and go door to door down the street. 'I am doing a survey. Is there anyone who lives here that has a hearing impairment?' If there wasn't, I'd ask, 'Do you know anyone who has a hearing loss or wears a hearing aid?' In a small town, everybody knows everybody, so it didn't take long for me to come up with a list of people with hearing impairments. Sure, not everyone was friendly, but enough were that I was able to get my foot in the door to serve people who needed hearing aids."[88]

Once, he had called on an elderly couple in Woonsocket, South Dakota. He tells the story:

"I introduced myself at the door and said, 'I understand you have a problem with your hearing. I test hearing.'

"'My husband has a loss,' the woman said.

"'If you want to test our hearing, that's okay,' she said, 'but I'll tell you up front that we aren't going to buy anything. It's up to you, but you'll be wasting your time.'

"'Fair enough,' I replied.

"As it turned out, they both needed hearing aids. They were very friendly and commented on how professional and courteous I was.

"'Our son is Dr. Frank Lassman who heads the audiology department at the University of Minnesota. Do you know him?' the husband asked.

"'I don't know him personally, but I do know of him,' I answered. (Several years later, I did meet Dr. Lassman, and we became good friends.)

"'Our son warned us that we should be aware of the Austin gang because they're crooks,' he said.

"'Do you know who I am?'

"'Well, no,' they both nodded.

"'I'm Bill Austin.'

"They both laughed, and when they saw I was serious, she said, 'You can't be. You're much too nice to be Bill Austin.'

"They both bought hearing aids that night. I had a habit of selling just about everyone I talked to. That's because I didn't like to waste my time, and besides, I considered it a mental challenge to overcome their resistance. I felt that I was on a mission to help anyone who had a hearing loss. For this reason, I didn't accept it when someone said,

'No, I don't want a test,' or, 'I'll wait until later.' It was just a game to see if I could be 100 percent effective.[89]

Bill acknowledges he didn't bat quite 100 percent. "Nobody does," he says.

"I did get chased off someone's property. Actually it happened twice. Both times it was by husbands who didn't want their wives to have hearing aids. These men simply didn't want to spend the money on their wives. One husband said, 'Every autumn I go hunting in the Black Hills, and if I bought my wife hearing aids, it would mean I couldn't hunt this season.'

"'You can't be serious,' I said. 'Your wife has been your helpmate all these years and you would deprive her of her hearing so you can go hunting.'

"'That's right, young man. Do you have a problem with that?' the man replied.

"I took great pleasure in telling him what I thought before I left."[90]

Bill says that he recalls his failures as well as the names of all his early patients. He possessed a near photographic memory, and after every sales call, he would review what transpired. He explains:

"Every time I sold a hearing aid, it would be like coming back from the moon. As soon as I hit the seat of my car, I debriefed myself and I remembered every word of an entire conversation. I realized it's about timing, the psychological impact. It's not what you say but how you say it and when you say it. It's creating the emotional why. I would go through this exercise and analyze what transpired, and I'd analyze what I did wrong—even when I made the sale. After every call, I'd ask myself, 'How could I have been even better?' I went through this exercise religiously."[91]

The same analytical approach he applied to selling was his *modus operandi* in all facets of his career. He demanded constant improvement. Bill Austin was, and to this day is, a man obsessed with it. As he tells it, "I was constantly analyzing how to interface the device to the ear. I wanted to prove to myself that I was better today than last month. I drove myself to develop skills so that I could apply a hearing aid to deformed ears, surgical ears, and soft cartilage. I was determined to help those with the most difficult hearing losses. As time went on, I realized that like people's fingerprints, no two ears are the same.

"In a matter of time, I got to the point where I could sell and fit hearing aids no matter how tired I was, no matter how sick I was. At the risk of sounding boastful, I knew exactly what to do. That's because I was so analytical about every phrase of this business. You meet all kinds of analytical people in other fields but not in this one. For instance, there are golfers who have an obsession for the game. They can have scratch handicaps, yet they are continually refining their swing. This is why I don't play golf. This is what convinced me to say to myself, 'Bill, there are too many golfers out there that keep taking lessons and keep learning.' Well, I knew I'd never be an Arnold Palmer. In this business, however, I was seeing people who had learned the basics and then were doing it by rote, never analyzing what they are doing, and for this reason, they were remaining static. They reached a point where they never improved. I knew I could be better today than yesterday and better tomorrow than today. Consequently, I found it easy to leave the competition in the dust.

"My work is my hobby. It is my life. It is what I derive the most enjoyment from. There is no meal that could be prepared with the finest quality of foods and wines that would be as satisfying to me as the joy I receive from fitting patients. There is no entertainment—no Super Bowl or concert performance—that could match the enjoyment I receive from what I am able to do for my patients. Sometimes I think I am selfish because I am doing exactly what I want to do.

"People were trusting, and they trusted me. I expected them to trust me because I was going to do my best for them—and I did. I know making cold calls is a tough way to build a clientele, but that's what I had to do. If this is what it took to help people, I was happy to do it. Sure, not everyone welcomed me with open arms. One time I called on a man who had been cheated by a hearing aid salesman. Somebody had taken his money and never delivered the hearing aids to him. When I knocked on his door and introduced myself, he shouted, 'You people are crooks!'

"He was an old man, but his age didn't stop him from picking up a chair and chasing me around his dining room table. I kept a few steps in front of him, and while I was being chased, I kept saying, 'Hey, I've never been here before. I came to be of help. I'll try to help you.' Finally, he calmed down enough to hear me out. I was able to help him, and when he received his hearing aids, his hearing was restored. He was very grateful and referred several other hearing-impaired people to me."[92]

With Bill running the store, business was brisk at South Dakota Hearing Aid Center in Sioux Falls. Bill was winning prizes for his sales production. Once, he won a suit, and another time, it was an all-expenses-paid trip to a hearing aid conference in Chicago. To his dismay, his uncle reneged on both the suit and the trip. Bill recalls:

"I sold more hearing aids than anyone else, and I was disappointed that Uncle Fred didn't keep his word. However, I refused to let it get to me.

"Meanwhile, I had a lot of accumulated commissions that was being held in a reserve. Knowing these back commissions were due me, I put down a deposit on a cottage in South Dakota. My plan was to collect the money from my reserve so I could close the deal on the house. I asked Uncle Fred to mail it to me, but a check never arrived. If the check didn't come soon, my deposit would be forfeited. I drove from Sioux Falls to my uncle's office in Minnesota. When I got there, his assistant said that he was too busy to see me.

"'I need my money so I can close on a house,' I told her.

"'I'm not authorized to pay you,' she said, 'so you'll have to talk to your uncle.'

"I waited all day but kept on being told: 'He can't see you now; he's with someone,' or, 'He stepped out for lunch,' and, 'He's in a meeting and unavailable.' At the end of the day, I drove back to Sioux Falls without being paid. As a consequence, I lost my deposit on the house. 'I'll never work for him again,' I vowed, and I quit. I worked like a dog for my uncle. He never had a more loyal employee. Had he paid what was due me, I would have never left him."[93]

A few days later, Bill was on an airplane to Oregon to sell the rental property he had purchased a few years earlier.

With the money from the sale, he went back to Sioux Falls and opened a small retail hearing aid storefront. Applying the same sales techniques as before, he slowly built his business.

Bill enjoyed modest success in Sioux Falls. Envisioning greener pastures in a larger metropolitan market, in 1967 he migrated to Hopkins, Minnesota, a suburban community of 15,000 just west of Minneapolis. Here he opened Professional Hearing Aid Service, a combination clinic and repair shop. Not only did he work with patients and repair hearing aids, he did repairs for other dispensers. He began fixing their equipment, and what they found most appealing was that he did it at a fixed rate.

In time, all brands came to Bill's shop. He systematically broke them down and studied how they were built. He listened to how they sounded. He methodically analyzed them. Then he kept an inventory, sorting the various parts in bins and drawers. An intense improviser, Bill was usually able to make necessary modifications, and the unfixable became fixable. He developed a keen expertise on how hearing aids worked mechanically, and working with products made by a variety of manufacturers, he was privy to what each company did best.

Meanwhile, Bill continued to serve patients who came into his store. He reveled in the joy of restoring a person's hearing. No matter how many repair jobs were in the back room, being one-on-one with a patient was what he most enjoyed. Everyone received his full, undivided attention. A perfectionist, he made sure each received the best hearing aid for his or her condition. Every mold had to be properly fit, and every fit must be made so it could be comfortably worn. A fitting that was off by the thickness of a coat of paint was enough to cause a hissing sound; a fitting that was too tight caused discomfort or even pain to the wearer. When it came to taking care of a patient, it didn't matter how much time it took to make sure he or she received maximum results. Bill was not a clock watcher. There was never a meter running that kept track of his time with a patient. Yes, those in the reception area might have to wait for their turn, but few objected, because they knew that when it was their turn, they would be treated by a man who truly cared about their hearing.

As the owner of his company, Bill wore many hats. He put in a full day's work with his patients, and nightly he could be found taking apart and reconstructing broken hearing aids. He also found time to make calls on other dispensers, buying their broken hearing aids and used parts they hadn't bothered to discard. He was able to convince them that since they had never before used the relics collected in cabinets, they should sell them to him. Typically, a dispenser had twenty, fifty, or even hundreds that were just sitting there, and Bill Austin would relieve the vendors of what they viewed as nothing more than junk. Their junk was his treasure.

Professional Hearing Aid Service was building a good reputation for repairing hearing aids. However, its real growth came when the twenty-something-year-old entrepreneur decided to expand the company by providing equipment repair services at a set rate to dispensers. This opened doors to the hearing aid community across the country. It also required him to spend a lot of time on the road. Once in a dispenser's office, he was able to buy their discarded parts, which he added to his growing inventory. Having accumulated a large stock of hearing aid parts, he solicited these same dispensers for their repair business. Within three years, his start-up company had more than thirty employees.

"My Uncle Fred passed away, and I got a call from his widow, Thelma," Bill tells. "She said to me, 'You owe it to me to buy our company.' I wasn't sure why I owed it to her; however, I bought the business because I knew she needed the money."

STARTING STARKEY

Technically, Bill Austin didn't start Starkey Labs. It was a company he bought in 1970. The company made earpieces for hearing aids and, in particular, ear molds. It was housed in a log cabin in Maple Plain, twenty miles west of Minneapolis. Paul Jensen had purchased the company from Harold Starkey, who had moved to Black Duck, Minnesota, to spend his remaining years. Bill paid $13,000 for the company with assurances from Jensen that he would stay on and continue to make molds.

"In his early thirties, Jensen had come to America. He was sponsored by his cousin, Harold Starkey's wife. Jensen started working for his cousin-in-law in 1964, and five years later, he became the company's new owner. Bill had molds made at Starkey, and one day he made Jensen an offer to buy him out. Bill explains:Jensen's mother lived in Denmark, and he never had the time to visit her. He couldn't get sick. If he had a cold and didn't work, no molds got made that day. It was a one-man band. 'If you sell me your company, you'll get to see your mother,' I told him. 'And you'll see the business grow.' Jensen's eyes lighted up when I said that. 'When it grows, think of how we will be contributing to the employees. They will have more meaningful lives because their good work will enable people to hear.' When I said this to Jensen, I could see in his expression that we were on the same page. I bought the company *for* Paul. Jensen was the best person I knew at cutting molds. I wanted his skills."[94]

Under Jensen, Starkey had remained a small, three-person shop. In addition to Jensen, it employed a secretary and a man who was mentally challenged.

Jensen, who speaks with a heavy Danish accent, says, "Everything Bill told me came true. I did visit my mother in Denmark many times, and the business really grew. Two years later, Bill bought another company I owned, Jensen Supplies, that had an inventory of parts we used to build hearing aids. I received $30,000 for it. He was very fair with me, and I stayed with him until I retired at age eighty-one in 2008. The best thing I ever did was sell the company to Bill Austin."

Following his $13,000 purchase, Bill moved the acquired company out of the log cabin and into his St. Louis Park site, where Jensen would continue making molds. He decided that it was also time for a name change.

"I'm going to change the name of Professional Hearing Aid Service to Starkey Laboratories," Austin explained to Jensen.

"Why would you do that?" Jensen questioned. Why not name it Austin Labs?"

"I want this company to be bigger than I am. I don't want it to be always associated with me. I want Starkey people to accept certain philosophical principles as their own. They should live by them, and when I am no longer here, these principles will live on. The most difficult job I will encounter—and it will be my last job—is to have built this company so that it can go forward and its people will *not* do everything that I did. Instead, they will adapt to the times, and at the same time, they adhere to our core values. For this to happen, they must take ownership in these principles."[95]

Bill insists that he never had ambitions concerning money.

"I never said I hope that someday we'll be a $10 million, $100 million, or $1 billion company. How big we are never mattered to me. Size isn't what's important. It's the character you bring to work. From the day I decided to devote my life to the hearing aid field, I was determined to help people with their hearing impairments. I wanted to do it by being the best I possibly could be, and I wanted to constantly keep improving and growing. To accomplish this, I know I'd have to apply leverage so that a maximum of people could benefit. These are the bedrock principles I based my future on, and I want these principles to live on through the people that succeed me."[96]

But why name it *Starkey*? Bill explains:

"Back in those days, there were so many hearing aid companies with 'tone' in them. There was Beltone, Goldentone, Audiotone, Microtone, Sonatone, and I wasn't going to be another tone. Let's do it our own way. We don't have to copy what the competition is doing. It might take people time to get used to it, but we're going to be the trendsetters in this industry."

"Besides," Bill adds with a smile, "I thought the name Starkey was a name that people could relate to. I liked the combination, 'star' and 'key.' We want to help people reach the stars and we want them to find their key to success."[97]

When the deal for the company was finalized, Bill handed a check in the amount of $13,000 to Paul Jensen. "That was the last day I have ever written a check," Bill states. "Since then, other people have handled money matters for me."[98]

BILL AUSTIN'S EARLY INNOVATIONS

In the 1970s, Starkey Labs had steady growth spurts. During this period Bill came up with several innovations that forever changed the hearing aid industry. For the most part, the cynics resisted the changes he introduced.

When he was a student and made ear molds for his uncle, Bill was appalled by the lack of service in the industry. He couldn't believe that no company offered a trial period allowing a customer to bring back a defective device for service. The industry edict was: "If you bought it, you own it." There was no such thing as a return policy.

Once Bill operated his own shop, he instituted a very informal return policy. Customers didn't have to pay anything unless they decided to keep the products. On occasion, there were individuals who returned hearing aids because they couldn't afford to pay for them. Bill explains:

"If I knew a patient was truly so poor that he couldn't afford to pay me, I'd say, 'Keep them and you can pay whatever you feel comfortable paying, but I don't want you be without them. I will trust you.' We didn't have a credit department. We had an honor system. It was the same way when we repaired aids for dispensers. Again, there was no credit department, and here, too, I said, 'It's an honor system, and I trust you. I will give you an open account. If you don't pay me, your account will be closed.' We rarely had someone welch, and by eliminating the costs of running a credit department, we were ahead of the game."[99]

For practical reasons, patients could not keep their hearing aids indefinitely and then receive a full refund. They were given ninety days to make their decision. Today, the Food and Drug Administration requires a money-back guarantee, but Starkey was the first to offer it at a time when it wasn't mandatory by law. Some competitors cried foul play. Others claimed, "Bill Austin is crazy, and it's just a matter of time before his company goes belly-up." When the company started to pick up market share, the competition declared that he would ruin the industry. There was one attempt to have Starkey blacklisted and a letter mailed to dispensers that called for a boycott. When it became evident that customer satisfaction was high and the ninety-day return policy resulted in few returns, the boycott was totally ineffective. Within a few years, all of the competition came out with return policies.

Although Starkey Labs had matured into the industry's leading repair company and continued making hearing aid molds, Bill never stopped fitting patients. Above all else, this was his first love. He enjoyed the excitement people had when their hearing was restored. Over time, he worked with thousands and thousands of patients. His vast experience combined with his quest for continual improvement proved to be a formula for success. He acquired superior skills and insight that even his competitors could not deny. Energized by his passion for his work, he worked long hours, always honing his craft. Driven to serve hearing-impaired people, he strived to find ways to make new products. He thought about his work every waking hour. Long before the phrase became popular by a best-selling inspirational book, Bill Austin lived a purpose-driven life. It was an obsession.

In the trade, the biggest objection to wearing hearing aids was a result of the stigma they carried. People are vain. They didn't want to be perceived as impaired or elderly. Knowing his patients, Bill understood that people's vanity played a significant role in their buying decision. The small laboratory had successfully cast inner ear molds. Bill wanted to make in-the-ear devices that were barely detectable. Up until this time, the behind-the-ear models were most commonly worn. Bill was sensitive to his patients' needs. "We could do better," he'd repeat. "There has to be a way where we can overcome this stigma *and* give them even better hearing." Observing how patients unconsciously pointed to their ear when he tested their hearing, what should have long been so obvious became evident to him. "They point to the entrance of the ear," he reasoned. "Of course they do. That's because they don't hear from behind the ear but from the ear's canal. I am going to make devices that are placed in the ear."[100]

In 1973, three years after the acquisition, Starkey introduced its first custom in-the-ear hearing aid. "It has to be this way," Bill claimed, "because no two ears are the same." Within the industry, the reaction was, "Customize each hearing aid for each patient? It can't be done. It will cost too much. This time Austin has lost touch with reality. It's only a matter of time before Starkey is out of business." The public didn't see it this way. To them, customized in-the-ear hearing aids made a lot of sense.[101]

Because of the heavy demand, Bill went on a hiring spree and brought in experienced hearing aid technicians. It didn't take the company long to establish itself as the leading producer of this revolutionary product. In 1975, Starkey moved into its current headquarters in Eden Prairie, a suburb of Minneapolis.

Randy Schoenborn is the president and owner of NewSound Hearing Aid Centers located in the South Texas area. NewSound has more than thirty stores and sells more Starkey products than any other hearing aid brand. Having known Bill Austin for over twenty-five years, Schoenborn says, "There is no other CEO of a major hearing aid company that has spent even a fraction of the time with patients as has Bill Austin. Based on many years of personal experiences, Bill recognized that people wanted small, unnoticeable hearing aids. Understanding the psychology of the patient, he emerged as the leader in promoting smaller and even smaller hearing aid devices. For instance, in 1973 Starkey introduced its first CE model custom-fit in-the-ear amplification device. Today Bill Austin is frequently referred to as the 'father of the in-the-ear hearing aid.' It was also Austin's no-questions-asked return policy that led the way where other companies followed suit."[102]

The custom in-the-ear hearing aid was a suitable antidote for people stigmatized by how they thought other people viewed them. Interestingly, having impaired hearing is comparable to having poor vision, but wearing eyeglasses doesn't have the same stigma as wearing a hearing aid. This is true in part because hearing loss is more often associated with aging, and America is a youth-centered nation. Stigma aside, Bill plainly states, "If you need glasses, you get a pair. If you need hearing aids, you take care of it. It's no big deal."[103] In addition to easing people's self-consciousness about wearing hearing aids, the in-the-ear device helped improve their hearing. This improvement was possible because of the physiology of the ear: the closer to the inside of the ear the device is placed, the more efficient the amplifying process.

There was no marketing and advertising blitz to launch the CE hearing aid with in-the-ear technology. In fact, it couldn't have been more low-key. Bill recalls:

"On January 1, 1973, I sent a two-sentence introduction out in a letter to our dispensers. It read: 'We do something besides repair hearing aids and make ear molds. We also offer an in-the-ear hearing aid worthy of your consideration.' That was it. Brief and right to the point! From that moment forward, my problem wasn't selling hearing aids. It was keeping up with the production and maintaining quality control."[104]

To make hearing aids affordable to the needy, Bill started the Starkey Fund in 1973. In the beginning, dispensers recycled their used batteries through Starkey, and in turn they received credit that was donated to those who needed financial assistance in purchasing a hearing aid. Several years later this fund evolved into the Starkey Foundation, a vehicle of Bill Austin's that fulfills his biggest dream—it provides hearing to the most needy people around the world.

By the late 1970s, Starkey was making diagnostic equipment and key research tools, including the CHAT hearing aid tester, the Tinnitus Research Audiometer, the HAL Hearing Aid Lab, the ST-1 Power Stethoscope, the BC-1 bone conduction aid, and the RE Series Probe Microphone Systems. These and other inventions were more sophisticated and patient-specific than what was previously available, and they led to future specialized development of hearing aid models.

In 1980, Starkey introduced the world's first in–ear canal hearing aid. The INTRA was the latest of a series of hearing instruments made by Starkey. Each was a technological advancement that was smaller and less conspicuous to the wearer. It was an immediate hit, and phone calls came in from across the country from patients, dispensers, and audiologists.

FIT FOR A PRESIDENT

One call was from Byron Burton, a dispenser from Santa Anna, California, who was a Starkey customer and Bill's good friend. From previous conversations, Burton recalled being told that ever since Bill was a small boy, he had been a big Gene Autry fan. Bill tells the story:

"Byron remembered a story I told him about when I was four years old and my Uncle George Austin from Oregon came to visit us in Missouri. I hid in my uncle's car trunk because I knew he was heading back to Oregon. I wanted to go out West and see my hero, Gene Autry. Luckily, my hiding place was discovered before the car pulled out of the driveway. With my boyhood story of mind, Byron called me.

"'Shooting blank pistols in all those cowboy movies caused Autry to have some hearing loss. He wants to be fitted for new hearing aids. Why don't you come with me and you can fit Gene?'

"I went to Palm Springs where Autry lived and fit him. It was the start of a long friendship, and he was one of the reasons why I later bought a house in Palm Springs. I liked hanging out with Gene Autry. He was a good friend of Ronald Reagan from back in the days when Reagan was in the movies. Autry was quite satisfied with my work, and during a visit in 1983 at the White House, he told the president about his hearing loss and how well he was hearing since I treated him. Reagan also suffered significant hearing loss when a blank gun cartridge had been shot off close to his ear on movie sets. Autry told me how impressed the president was with the hearing aid I fitted him with and remarked that he couldn't even tell Autry was wearing one."[105]

Shortly afterward, Bill received a call requesting that he come to fit the president. Because of his loss of hearing, Reagan had been experiencing difficulties in his interactions with dignitaries and the press. Wearing imperceptible devices appealed to him. He was the oldest president in the nation's history and conscious of his image. He didn't want to appear as an elderly person.

To be sure, President Reagan had a lot of important matters on his plate. Shortly after the president received his new Starkey canal aid, a Russian military plane shot down a Korean Air Lines Boeing 747 (Flight 007), killing all 267 passengers aboard, including a U.S. congressman and sixty other Americans. At first the Soviets denied any knowledge of the shootdown. Later, Premier Yuri Andropov admitted that Russian fighters downed the jumbo jet, justifying the shooting by saying it was on a spy mission for the United States that was flying through Soviet airspace. Of course, there was no basis for Andropov's claim that the Korean jetliner was an American reconnaissance aircraft. This happened at a time when the Soviets and the United States were discussing nuclear arms reduction.

The Flight 007 incident dominated the news for weeks, and polls showed it was hurting President Reagan's popularity. The White House needed a positive story to offset the negative news coverage. Meanwhile, his wife, Nancy, and staff members were commenting to him about how his hearing had vastly improved. The office of the White House press secretary picked up on this and announced the wonderful news about the president's new hearing aids. The announcement was a boon to Starkey, generating enormous media exposure, particularly at a news conference when Reagan acknowledged Starkey by name and commented on his new state-of-the-art hearing aids. Millions of Americans and viewers worldwide could see that the president didn't even look like he was wearing any! It was also newsworthy for the president to admit he had a disability and be so open about it. His openness had a positive effect on alleviating the stigma of hearing aids. If arguably the most important man in the world wore them, there was no shame in wearing hearing aids. It was a publicity coup for Starkey. Immediately, the phone was ringing off the hook. Bill explains:

"We received so many orders that our people were working overtime, including Saturdays and Sundays trying to keep up. However, the company experienced tremendous growth that came at a steep price. Quality control declined significantly. Getting parts was another problem. Repairs that took a week were taking a month or more. The back orders were piling up, and the company started to unravel.

"Someone once said to me, 'Having such a jump on the competition with the INTRA canal aid, you must have made a lot of money.' I replied, 'No, it cost me millions of dollars because we had prosperity disease. We lost some good, longtime customers, and we experienced high service costs. We lived through it, although it took over a year.'"[106]

Ronald Reagan wasn't the first VIP to wear Starkey hearing aids, but the pursuing news coverage on the president certainly caused more publicity than the company had ever experienced. "There were others prior to President Reagan," Bill points out, "such as Buckminster Fuller, the famed American futurist and author of *[Operating Manual for] Spaceship Earth*; Japan's emperor, Hirohito; and a few sundry kings and other celebrities."[107]

Other U.S. presidents that Bill has treated include Gerald Ford, George H. Bush, and Richard Nixon. He has treated Jimmy Carter's wife, Rosalynn, as well. Worldwide personalities include Mother Teresa, Nelson Mandela, Imelda Marcos, and Pope John Paul II. Other celebrities are Walter Cronkite, Billy Graham, Scott Carpenter, Carol Channing, Frank Sinatra, Paul Newman, Steve Martin, Arnold Palmer, and billionaire Warren Buffett. Bill thinks that the more open high-profile people are about wearing hearing aids, the less is the stigma to wear them. "Remember now," he says, "these are not anything like your grandfather's hearing aids."[108]

In recalling the VIPs who have benefited by wearing Starkey hearing aids, a wide grin appears on Bill's face.

"The word just spread around the world, and I often wondered, how do you know when you've really become a significant force in the industry? Well, I was looking at some orders that came in, and I happened to come across two orders. One was from a Russian commissar, and the other was from a prostitute from Thermopolis, Wyoming. She was embarrassed because her behind-the-ear hearing aid kept falling from her ear while she was engaged in various activities with her customers. It made me think, a commissar from Russia and a hooker from Wyoming. We have arrived! Now we are a real company! We were serving society at all levels and all places."[109]

A FAMILY BUSINESS

In his early twenties, Bill had a brief marriage that ended in divorce. He has two children from this marriage, an adopted son, Greg, who works side by side with him fitting patients, and a daughter, Alex, who works in the company's Government Services program. Brandon Sawalich, a son of his current wife, Tani, is the company's vice president of sales and marketing. Tani's other son, Steven Sawalich, is a film director who produces videos for the company. Tani is very involved in the Starkey Foundation, so it's a family affair. She describes her husband as having a purpose-driven life: "He's on the job 24-7. But I don't consider him a workaholic. It's just who he is. He loves it."[110] To Bill's good fortune, his wife and children are active in the business.

Tani Austin grew up in the hearing aid industry. Her mother, Pat Manhart, who was divorced when Tani was a small child, has been a dispenser for fifty years. For twenty-five years, Pat operated her own hearing aid company in southern Illinois and then in California, where she currently has her own practice. "It has always been a part of my life," Tani says. She continues:

"Patients were our gardeners and our babysitters. My siblings and I always made extra money working for my mother.

"When I was old enough, I had a franchise with Miracle Ear. I served on their franchise advisory counsel, and I was vocal about saying what was on my mind. My mother always cared about her patients, and I grew up sharing her sentiments. At Miracle Ear, the emphasis was on the dollar, not the patient.

"In 1990, after attending a counsel meeting in Minneapolis, I was at the airport waiting to board my flight to the West Coast, and I saw this tall, distinguished man with a head full of white hair. 'Who is that guy? I know him,' I thought to myself. It was Bill Austin, who had received an Entrepreneur of the Year award that I read about in a trade magazine. I knew of his reputation about how he cared for patients, so within a few minutes, I built up enough courage to walk over and introduce myself to him.

"Very quickly into our conversation, he started talking about product quality and caring about patients. He spoke with such conviction that I knew he was sincere. Still I couldn't help thinking, 'Is this guy for real?' What he said was the opposite of what I had been trained in."[111]

About six months later, Tani was still thinking about her chance encounter with Bill Austin. She had become disillusioned with her practice and decided it was time to either change or shut the doors. She explains:

"I called Bill and asked him for his opinion. He told me that Starkey was having a class that weekend for a group of its dispensers and invited me to attend. Our conversation was on a Tuesday, and that Thursday, I was on an airplane to Minneapolis.

"I attended the weekend session, and it was like having worked in black-and-white and going into living color. I immediately knew that this is what I wanted to do. This is what this business is about. When I got home, I changed to Starkey. I had a million-dollar business, but I was just selling hearing aids, and I didn't like it. I closed four of my offices and let six people go. In no time, I was doing a better job, and I was having fun again. When patients came back after a week of wearing Starkey hearing aids, they'd say, 'I love these hearing aids and have been wearing them all week.' At Miracle Ear, we'd tell them to wear them just one or two hours a day and 'you'll soon get used to it.' I realized that Starkey's technology was far superior to the competition. This is what made my work fun again.

"I was so enthusiastic about the product and applying the Starkey program, I had immediate success. I kept sending my results to the marketing department, and one day Bill called me. 'I wish my salespeople would listen to me as well as you do,' he said. 'I think you are the only person in the country that listened to what I said that day.'

"'I remember saying to my father that night, 'I think Bill Austin offered me a job, and I would like to take it.' I called Bill back and asked, 'Did you just offer me a job?'

"'Well, maybe,' he said.

'I would really like to do it. I will show other dispensers how I do it with my practice so that they will do a better job with their patients.'"[112]

Tani started working for Starkey in Minneapolis in January 1992. And as Tani says, "The rest is history. Bill and I dated. That May, we moved to Dallas, where Starkey had a distribution facility, and lived together for eight years. We were married in 2000."[113]

Greg Austin studied the acoustics of sound at Camden County Community College and then spent the next few years learning how to train racehorses. Afterward, he went back to college to study the physiology of hearing. When he came aboard full time, he worked in several different departments ranging from manufacturing to the business side of the company. Today, approaching age fifty, he works side by side with his father, fitting people for hearing aids. "To me," he says, "the most rewarding job here is working with the patients. What makes this so special is that every day I get to see how my work impacts people's lives."[114]

A chip off the old block, Greg adds, "My father has a lot of compassion for people and, in particular, for those with hearing problems. He has a successful company today, and he could be busy running it all day, or if he wanted to, be on the golf course or on a yacht enjoying the good life. But this is what he enjoys more than anything else. My father put together a team of top managers, and he lets them run the company. He trusts them explicitly, and this frees him to do what he literally lives for. It's a calling he has. Like I said, I could be working in other areas of the company, but I followed in his footsteps because I share his passion for working with patients."[115]

Greg believes that when employees see his father working with patients every day, it sends a message that the patient comes first. "It doesn't matter if you're in accounting, engineering, or sales," he states. "The patient is our top priority. When Starkey people see that the company founder and CEO is totally focused on the patient, it lets them know what the number-one priority is around here."[116]

Everyone who knows Bill Austin, with his years of experience and dedication to constant improvement, shares the opinion that he is the world's best at fitting patients for hearing aids. Bill doesn't dispute the fact. He is certain that this is true. It is not his ego saying this—it's a fact. Like a great heart surgeon who makes split-second life-and-death decisions, Bill has confidence in his abilities in what he does. He says, "If I can find someone better than I to do a job, I stop doing it and let that person take over so I can conserve my energies to be used for needed tasks and thereby better use my time. Well, I used to think I was the best wax guy in this field—I could clean ears better than anyone else, better than any doctor. Then one day I watched my son. Now, I have steady hands, but Greg's hands are even steadier. His hands are perfect. He could have been a fine surgeon. I watched him working and I said, 'I quit.' Greg does it now because he's the best at it."[117]

There are many companies that employ relatives of the boss but are never described as a "family business." But the description fits Starkey. That's because employees feel like they work in a family atmosphere where people care about each other. It starts at the top with Bill Austin.

Ray Woodsworth has good reason to feel this way about the company. Ray was a hearing aid dispenser in North Carolina when he met his wife, Laura, a Starkey employee, in 2001. He and other dispensers had been invited by the company on a Caribbean cruise. Ray and Laura fell in love, and to be near her, Ray took a job at Starkey's Center for Excellence in Eden Prairie, where he currently works closely with Bill fitting patients. When the couple got married, the wedding ceremony and reception were at the Austin house.

As mentioned previously, today, Randy Schoenborn owns NewSound Hearing Aid Centers in Texas. In 1983, Schoenborn's father-in-law, Dr. Harlan Conkey, who has a doctorate of education in audiology, recruited him to the company. Dr. Conkey had been a general manager at different Starkey manufacturing facilities in Canada, Oregon, and Texas. Working initially under his father-in-law's guidance, Schoenborn was eventually promoted to the position of general manager of a Starkey facility in Austin, Texas.

In 2001, Starkey acquired a three-store company from an Austin dispenser. Its original owner operated the three stores for the next twelve months and then left the field altogether. Being based in

Austin, Schoenborn was asked to manage the three stores until other arrangements were made to sell them. He says, "I kept my general manager's job. I took over the books and managed the people at the stores. Although time consuming, I enjoyed it.

"Bill and I would talk from time to time, and in reference to the stores, he'd ask, 'How's everything with your retail business, Randy?'

"'I'm really having fun with it.'

"'That's interesting,' he'd say.

"These conversations went on for a while, and one day he asked me, 'How much time are you spending at the plant?'

"'Not a whole lot,' I answered. 'Bill, I really like the retail side of the business and think I want to go in that direction.'

"He said that would be fine and never pressed the issue. He let me decide what I wanted to do. A couple months went by before we met in person, and we made a deal whereby I would leave the company and buy the three stores. It was a very easy transition. I followed the principles that I learned from Bill over the years—caring about people, building relationships, and knowing that I was put on this earth to serve people. These principles were a very good formula to succeed in any business."[118]

Schoenborn is grateful to Bill for providing him with the opportunity to buy the small retail chain from the company. He is also appreciative for what happened just prior to his departure. He explains:

"Ten years earlier, my sixteen-year-old son, Jake, had brain surgery to prevent seizures. In 2002, he required additional surgery at St. Paul's Children's Hospital. Bill delayed taking me off the payroll so my son would be included in the company's health plan. Jake's medical expenses over the years have exceeded $1 million, and as a privately owned company, a lot of that comes out of Bill's pocket. All I can say is that Bill is a very generous man."[119]

Bill's generosity extends to family, friends, and strangers. A few years ago, a farmer from Arkansas came to see Bill to be fitted for hearing aids. When Bill put a video otoscope in the man's ear, he discovered a tumor. He explained the problem to the man and was told, "I'm fine. I'll take care of that later."

"You've got to get this looked at now," Bill said.

"Later, but right now I can't afford it."

"I'm sending you to Michael Paparella, a friend of mine who is an excellent ear, nose, and throat specialist," Bill insisted.

Reluctantly, the farmer consented, and a Starkey employee drove him to Dr. Paparella's office. Following an examination, the man was admitted to a local hospital for surgery. The surgery was successful, and the farmer fully recovered. Bill paid the entire cost, which exceeded $20,000.

Asked why he paid the farmer's medical expenses, Bill modestly replies, "When you extend a helping hand, it enriches the other person's life as well as your own."[120]

YOU WIN WITH PEOPLE

Back in the days when Bill had an epiphany to make a positive difference in other people's lives, he was certain that by applying leverage, he could multiply his efforts by delegating the operations side of the company to others. By doing so, he would be free to personally work with individual patients. For years now, this is exactly what has occurred. Today, he spends most of his time with patients, and the managing of his $700 million company is delegated to others. More than 400 audiologists work at Starkey Labs now. Today, the company employs more audiologists than any enterprise other than the government. Eight audiologists work alongside Bill fitting patients all day. Patients referred by dispensers and audiologists daily trek to the fifteen-acre campus of the Starkey Center for Excellence to see Bill Austin. Many of them are the most difficult cases. For this reason, they come from afar to be treated by the man who invented the custom in-the-ear hearing aid—a man reputed as the best in the world at his craft, a man who has fitted far more patients than any other person on the planet.

Of the big six hearing aids manufacturers, Starkey is the only one that is headquartered in the United States. The other five are Oticon, ReSound, and Widex, all three based in Denmark; Phonak in Switzerland; and Siemens in Germany. Of these companies, Starkey

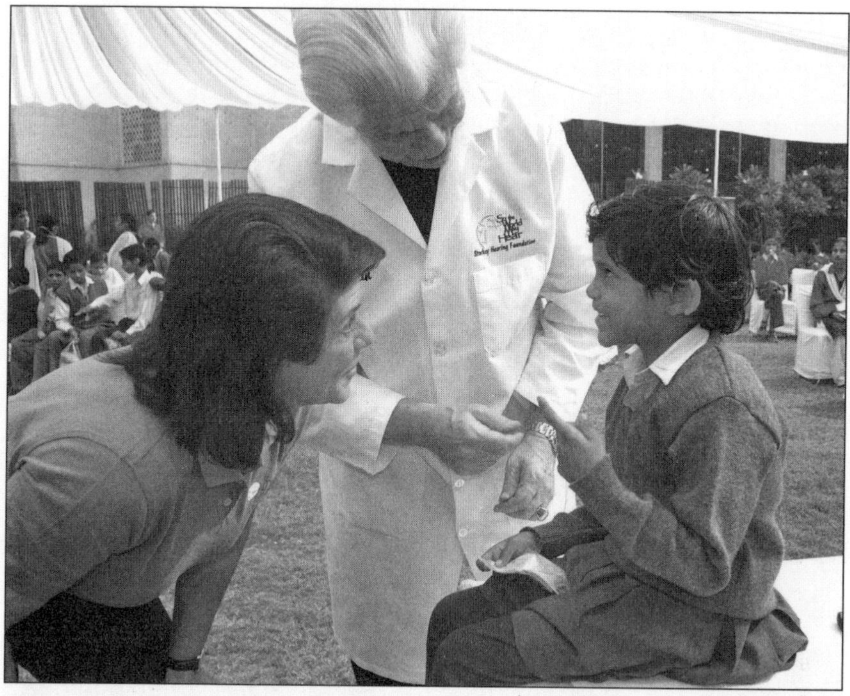

Tani and Bill Austin speak to a little boy on mission in Delhi, India, in 2008.

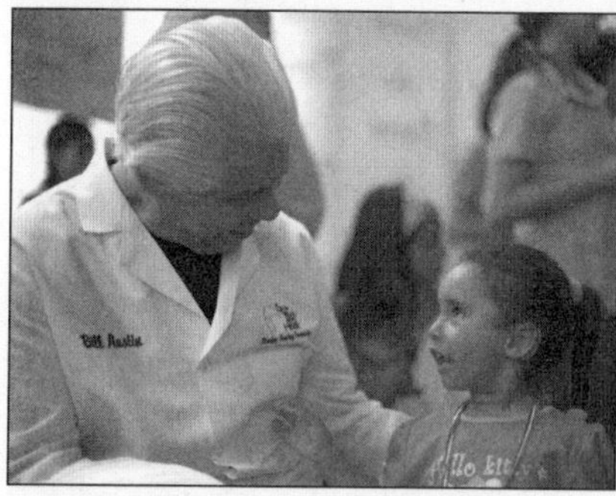

Bill Austin listens to a little girl in Lima, Peru (above), and shakes hands with a young boy in Panama who presents him with a statue (right).

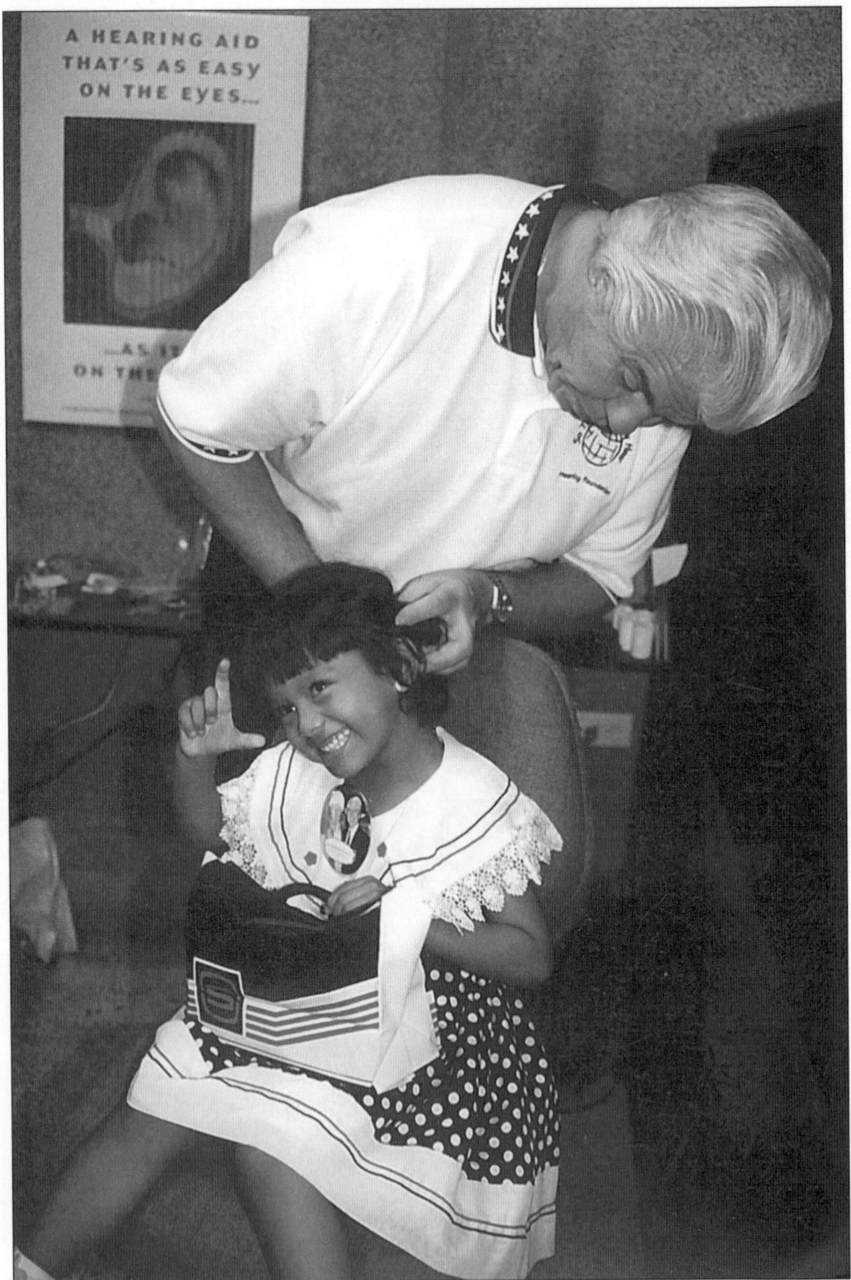

"A little more volume, please." A young girl in El Salvador smiles about the new hearing aids she's receiving.

Fellow humanitarians Bill Austin and former South African president Nelson Mandela meet in Mandela's office on October 29, 2008 (top). Passing on the torch: Bill Austin with Jerry Ruzicka, Starkey's newly named president, on January 1998 (bottom).

is the only company still owned by the founder. Be assured that Bill Austin is the only CEO of these companies who treats patients daily; although, in fairness to the others, he may be a one-of-a-kind in *any* industry. It is doubtful that there is another CEO of a sizeable company who is as hands-on as Bill Austin. CEOs that head pharmaceutical companies don't prescribe medicine. CEOs of automobile manufacturers don't assemble cars. Perhaps CEOs and senior managers at other companies should find ways to spend at least a minimum of time with their customers. By staying close to customers, Starkey has managed to stay ahead of the competition. There is nothing quite like a CEO being on the firing line and getting firsthand information straight from the customer.

But then somebody has to mind the store. Without a strong management team in place, Bill could not spend long hours seeing patients. A CEO must have absolute trust in his management team's capabilities to run the company and, equally important, *stay out of their way*. A common tendency of entrepreneurs is to think that no one else can run the business as well as they can. Without delegation, such enterprises have limited capacity to expand. To Bill's good fortune, he is surrounded by top-notch people who he trusts explicitly.

One such person who has earned Bill's confidence is Jerry Ruzicka. Ruzicka joined the company in 1977 at age twenty-one, just after receiving a computer technology degree. For a short while, he had worked at Telex in its hearing aid division. Using his technology background, Ruzicka started out at Starkey as a repairs technician. Starkey quickly realized his supervisory potential and within two months promoted him to the position of line leader. In this capacity, he managed a small group of assembly-line workers. Before the end of his first year, he was promoted to department manager. His real talent surfaced when he found ways to shorten the time between when a repair order came in to when the hearing aids were fixed and shipped back to the customer. Ruzicka explains:

"Getting repairs out the door quickly is crucial in this business. It should only be here a couple of days. If your television set doesn't work, you can survive without it, but when you can't hear, you're unable to participate in life. Bill has always been totally focused on a fast turnaround, and frankly, I was good at helping him improve the service and turnaround time. I continued to grow with the company, and by the time I was twenty-nine years old, Bill promoted me to vice president of manufacturing. In 1998, I became the company's president.

"Bill kept giving me more responsibility because he believed I could handle it. Every time I took on a new job, I continued to maintain my old job, too, so my responsibility kept expanding. As vice president of manufacturing, I kept looking at what had to be done next, and shortly after taking on this position, I started developing the company's engineering group."[121]

Ruzicka learned a lot from his boss and mentor. In particular, he adapted well to Bill's philosophy of caring for people. Ruzicka says, "Most unusual is how Bill lets people grow. I quickly learned that he never sets specific goals, and in fact, he's never told me what to do. But he always asks me, 'What are we doing, and how are we going to do it better?' This is very powerful. For instance, somebody can say, 'Well, you are going to run a three-minute mile.' But if you are running a six-minute mile, and you're told that you're going to run it in three minutes, your reaction will be, 'No way. I can't do that.'

"However, if someone says, 'You are running a six-minute mile, and we want you to improve on that,' you accept the challenge. You ask yourself, 'What do I have to do to get better?' It might be losing weight. It might be more training. So it causes you to think about various things. This is more effective than saying, 'I want you to grow the company by 30 percent.' Asking the question, 'What are we doing to get better?' made a huge difference on how I view what we can do as a company. This supports Bill's philosophy, which is based on service."[122]

Since the time when Ruzicka joined Starkey, annual revenues have grown from $8 million to $700 million. Ruzicka emphasizes, "As a big company, we keep trying to be a small company. We value the relationships that we make with our customers—dispensers and audiologists—and our job is to build strong relationships with them.

To do this, we have to help them do a better job, because what it all boils down to is doing what's best for the patient."[123]

Ruzicka points out that all people in leadership positions at Starkey know a lot about the company's products.

"When working with patients, Bill is always searching for ways to make our products better. Like Bill in his early days, I was a repair technician, and I also built new hearing aids. Many of the other companies in this industry have marketing and research organizations that are telling them how their products are working and what the customers are saying. In this respect, we are an anomaly. We don't hire any outside sources to take surveys. We don't because we are so hands-on, and that evolves from Bill. It is in our DNA, and it is who we are. When we are developing a new product, Bill doesn't participate in the strategy of what that product should be. But when we have the first one ready, he's the first to get it, and he's going to use it on patients. Rest assured, he is going to be our most critical customer. He will be our toughest customer. We want to give him a product that will make him proud and he'll tell us how great it is. When this happens, it's an improvement, and we'll go forward. When we know that we've helped him to do a better job with his patients, we know that we succeeded."

The company president pauses briefly and adds, "I can't imagine any CEO being more hands-on than Bill Austin. He's constantly dealing with the end user, and because he is, the rest of us are drawn to that. Another thing about this company is that there isn't a lot of bureaucracy in this organization. Bill can walk into anyone's office, pull up a chair, and talk. So can I and anyone else here. By removing layers of bureaucracy, your message doesn't get watered down. It's a family atmosphere where people aren't afraid to talk to one another."[124]

In 1994, Brandon Sawalich started his career at Starkey at age nineteen. Like his stepfather, he began in the repair lab, buffing and polishing and sorting old hearing aids that were sent in for repairs. He worked with all makes and models, learning the nuts and bolts of the business. Brandon says,

"When you're nineteen, you think, 'My mother is engaged to the boss; boy, I've got it made.' In reality, it was the exact opposite. I was under a microscope where everybody was watching what I did to see if I was getting special treatment. Bill wanted to make sure that I learned the business by starting with the basics. This way, I'd have a future in the business. He made sure I learned the blocking and tackling. Had he started me out in a cushy job, I would have been set up for failure. Although I didn't appreciate what he was doing for me at the time, I do today."[125]

Brandon worked his way up the corporate ladder starting on the ground floor, and in his mid-thirties, Brandon is vice president of sales and marketing. Nobody who has followed his career ever claimed that Brandon got to where he is today because he's related to the head honcho. All agree that he has earned his stripes. A personable and energetic man, Brandon is well respected by his coworkers and peers throughout the industry. And much like his stepfather and mentor, Brandon has a deep passion for the business. It would be hard for him not to. He has been exposed to the hearing aid industry since he was a small child. His mother and his maternal grandmother were hearing aid dispensers. "I didn't want to be in this business as a young boy," he confesses. "Like other kids, I wanted to be an astronaut or something more fun."[126]

As vice president of sales and marketing, Brandon heads a sales force of more than 200 people. In this position, he contributes to developing the marketing strategy. He sums up his job by plainly saying, "I'm responsible for getting orders in the door. Keeping the place open."[127] As it is said in sales parlance, "Nothing happens until something is sold."

When asked to describe the company's sales and marketing strategy, Brandon explains, "It's basically about making sure that we are serving our customers better than anyone else—that we are engaging with our customers better than our competition." [128]

When Brandon talks about the company's customers, he's referring to the 5,000 or so dispensers and audiologists that sell Starkey devices to end users. He explains:

"This is our customer base. When we advertise, it's generally in trade magazines. We don't advertise directly to the public. We don't attempt to build the brand, because this is a people business. It's like when you get a hip replacement. You don't ask who makes the artificial hip. You don't care. You want the best doctor and the one who will give you the best care. It's not about building the Starkey name; it's about providing the best product and service to over 5,000 customers that, in turn, serve their patients."[129]

In addition to the daily calls made by the sales force to provide everything from technical information to fitting information, there is one other significant service that the company provides to its dispensers and audiologists. What puts Starkey in a league of its own is the way it educates and trains its customers. Throughout the year, Starkey conducts about forty invitation-only seminars that include two days of intensive classes at Starkey's headquarters. Approximately 200 customers at a time migrate to Eden Prairie, where they take crash courses on how to better serve their patients. The company picks up the tab for their airfare, lodging, food, and beverages from the time the customers arrive at Minneapolis-St. Paul Airport on a Thursday to when they head home that Sunday. Which customers, prospects, and new accounts are invited to these sessions is determined by the sales staff.

The classes are professionally conducted and provide the best continuing education in the hearing aid industry. During these four-day visits, customers are able to exchange ideas with their peers. Tours of the company's manufacturing and repair facilities are conducted, and visitors are able to meet the men and women who make and service Starkey products. They see Bill Austin working with patients, many of whom are the most severely hearing impaired. Sometimes, they may catch a glance of a celebrity who is there for a fitting.

Many of the hallways and walls of the Center for Excellence are adorned with large photographs of the rich and the famous who use Starkey products. These photographs serve a dual purpose. First, they let visitors know that VIPs who are hearing impaired are not slowed down; this message helps to remove the stigma associated with using hearing aids. Second, when customers discover that past presidents, heads of states, show business people, and other well-known people use the company's products—individuals who can afford the very best—it sends a message that the most discriminating people in the world wear Starkey devices. It is likely that many dispensers and audiologists make this point to their patients. In reference to the VIP photos, Brandon comments: "We don't make a big deal about it. We let the photos of these high-profile people speak for themselves. They serve as testimonials."[130]

Brandon refers to the customers' visits to the home office as "the Starkey Experience." He comments:

"When they take their time away from their personal and professional lives, we want to make it worth their while. From our viewpoint, we think of them as the most important people in the world, and we make sure to go that extra mile to make them feel special.

"Our competition is trying to figure out how to beat us. They keep asking themselves, 'Why Starkey?' Well, it's pretty simple. It's about the people. It's not about some brochure, and it's not just about a product. Starkey is a community. Everybody who works here does it for more than a paycheck. They truly have heart and passion. This is what separates Starkey from the competition. When our customers come here, this is what they take away when they go home."[131]

THE MISSIONS

The World Health Organization reports that there are 280 million people around the world who suffer from moderate to severe hearing loss. The report estimates that two-thirds of them live in developing countries, and most of them would benefit from hearing aids. In the United States, it is projected that there will be a population of 33 million hearing-impaired individuals in 2010.[132]

In 1973, Bill agreed to donate free hearing aids to dispensers who in turn gave them to their patients who couldn't afford them. The program was called the Starkey Fund. These donations were on the condition that the dispensers would provide free fitting services to the recipients.

Bill got his first opportunity to give away free hearing aids outside the United States in 1974, when a hearing aid dispenser from California called him for a donation. The caller was with a group that called themselves the Flying Samaritans. These people flew to Mexico on private planes to help poor people in remote rural villages. "A friend of mine is a doctor in Mexico," the dispenser told Bill, "and he knows some children that badly need hearing aids. Can you help us out, Bill?" Bill tells the story:

"I never say no to someone that asks for hearing aid help. 'Of course, we will do that,' I replied. After we discussed it, I agreed to supply hearing aids for eighty children that he said would be more than enough. I also told him that I'll send Paul Jensen to Mexico to help fit the ear molds. 'Paul is a world-class ear mold expert,' I said. 'He's a good man to have with you in Mexico.'"[133]

"We were there for four days, and we treated twenty-five to thirty kids a day," Jensen recalls, "but we only took along eighty hearing aids. It was our first venture outside the U.S., and we didn't know what to expect."[134]

Shortly after the mission to Mexico, a deaf school in Nepal requested hearing aids. Here, too, Bill consented to help. He explains:

"Nepal seemed like an interesting place to go, but it could have been a call from anywhere in the world, and I would have been compelled to comply, because my purpose is to help people with their hearing. This time we took a large enough supply to fit several hundred. Soon afterward, we went to places like Israel and Turkey. And later, we were traveling around the world to Africa, Asia, Central and South America—we went to all corners of the planet. As we did more missions, we found ways to be more efficient. Early on, we thought that if we could fit 200 people a day, that would be terrific. Now remember, that's 400 hearing aids. Later we started sending an advance team to a country to do the fittings prior to our arrival, and by doing this prefitting, we could see 250 and 300 people a day. Then, working in teams, we figured out how to serve 500 people a day. We kept getting better and better at it, and the more people we'd see, the more good we could do. Our current record is 635 patients in one day; we did that in Kenya. Also, seeing more people meant being more cost-efficient, because there were a lot of fixed costs incurred for moving a team of our people to faraway places. In addition to the transportation costs, there were lodging, food, and local transportation expenses, and so on."[135]

It was just a matter of time before requests for free Starkey hearing aids came pouring in from around the world. Although Bill was eager to help, his policy was that there had to be an identifiable person with a hearing loss for each pair of hearing aids. "I wanted to be certain that there was a designated individual so our hearing aids wouldn't be put in an inventory for future use," Bill says. "If that were the case, there was the risk of having our products getting stored away in a warehouse and never be[ing] used."[136]

As he conducted missions around the world, Bill realized the scope of the need for providing hearing aids in impoverished countries. "After seeing the sheer size of the problem, I knew that I could never be able to solve it alone," he says.[137]This thinking prompted him to establish the nonprofit Starkey Hearing Foundation in 1983, an independent entity separate from Starkey Laboratories. Unlike the Starkey Fund, it is a 501(3)(c) public tax-exempt charitable organization, which means the IRS permits it to receive tax-deductible contributions from donors. "We can now encourage others to participate, and through leverage, we can expand our efforts to serve many more people. I also wanted to set up a foundation so it would continue after my death," Bill points out.[138]

Tani Austin works full time at the foundation as secretary-treasurer. To keep expenses low, she works with a bare-minimum administrative staff of a handful of people. But many other Starkey employees help the foundation by donating tens of thousands of hours. The Starkey Foundation is committed to providing more than 100,000 hearing instruments each year to those in need. Bill spends about five months of the year on missions. Most of the time, Tani accompanies him. Neither are remunerated for their work. With less than 2 percent of its money going to administrative and fund-raising costs, the foundation ranks among the top American charitable organizations with the highest percentage of its donations going directly to its recipients.

The foundation has thousands of volunteers and donors around the world. Many of the missions today are sponsored by Starkey suppliers and vendors. For example, Knowles Electronics, an international company that makes a wide range of components for hearing aids, sponsored a 2009 mission to the Dominion Republic. Rayovac sponsored a mission to Guatemala. Rayovac also donates hearing aid batteries that Starkey gives to the needy around the world. Glen Taylor, a successful businessman and owner of the Minnesota Timberwolves, is a major contributor. A personal friend of Bill's, Taylor has also gone on several missions. Don Kendall, the founder and former chairman of PepsiCo, has sponsored missions, and Pepsi has donated products that are served to thousands of children and their family members during Starkey missions. In 2009, a group of Canadian Starkey dispensers contributed $500,000 to the foundation. Randy Schoenborn, the former Starkey employee and owner of NewSound, has sponsored missions to Mexico. Seventy-five percent of Starkey's employees make personal contributions to the foundation. The list of supporters goes on and on. As the foundation's motto states: "Alone we can't do much. Together, we can change the world."

Today, as a result of a lot of trial and error, the missions run with few hitches. But the foundation must always be ready for the unexpected when traveling to third-world countries. Tani explains:

"Once we were in Malawi. There were forty of us, and we had brought all the equipment, hearing aids, and batteries with us. We were all set to go, but the kids didn't show up. They didn't have enough money for gas for the buses to transport the children to us. There we were. We had flown from the Midwest in the U.S. to this remote place in the middle of Africa, and there were no children. They embarrassingly explained the situation to us. Bill said, 'We'll buy the gas,' which we did, and the next day we had to work double time to catch up for the lost day. I've heard my husband say many times, 'It's not about us. We're not important. The children give us our importance.' I used to say, 'Yeah. Yeah, right.' But when the kids didn't show up that day, it dawned on me that was what he was talking about.

"Today we prescreen them. In some countries, we send in our own people, some of whom are Starkey employees and dispensers that sell our products. Other times, it might be a government entity, like it is in Mexico. In some countries, it might be one of our local customers, such as when we go to Peru. National and international civic organizations such as the Lions or Rotary Clubs work closely with us to identify the needy in many countries we visit. These groups help with the advance work before the mission by arranging transportation, securing a location such as a local hospital or school for us to set up shop. They also help coordinate the mission with the local government.

"In Peru, for instance, a Starkey dispenser is close to a priest who identified a lot of hearing-impaired children, many that are orphans. In Mexico, the Department of Infants and Families that takes care of poor people determines who is poor and deaf. It also makes sure to get these people to us when we're there. In Turkey, the schools identify the children that can't hear, and they bus them to us. In India, we took hearing aids to the people in a compound where Mother Teresa did her wonderful work. While we were there, we fitted Mother Teresa with hearing aids, which she wore the last two-and-a-half years of her life."[139]

Two key people who travel around the world to do the legwork prior to the missions are Rene Perez-Bode and Fredreic Rondeau. Rene, who was born in Cuba, migrated to the Dominic Republican, where he attended medical school. He currently lives in Minneapolis, where he is employed by Starkey. He speaks fluent English, Spanish, and Portuguese. Fredreic is the international director for the foundation. A native Canadian and former professional soccer player, Fredreic was educated in the United States and today resides in El Salvador with his wife, Carla, and three children. He speaks fluent English, French, Spanish, and Portuguese. Both Rene and Fredreic travel extensively, visiting the countries where Starkey has missions each year. Over the years, missions have been conducted in nearly every Latin American country. Many have been made to the Caribbean basin—that is, the bigger islands—and one-day missions have been made to many of the small islands via a cruise ship that stops for day visits. Starkey employees see about 300 hearing-impaired patients per port. Because of Rene's and Fredreic's particular background and language skills, both men have expertise on the cultures of this part of the world.

The advance work is crucial to a mission's success. Fredreic explains:

"There are many issues to consider. First, we want to know if there's an infrastructure that we can work with. For instance, are there professionals available, or do we have to develop talent? Do we have to provide equipment in order to do the event? Is there an infrastructure in place that will identify qualified individuals? Are there schools for the children and young adults to attend after they've been fitted with hearing aids? Then we look at such things as customs regulations, safety issues, lodging, travel logistics, et cetera, et cetera. In some countries, there are obstacles such as paying tariffs and even high taxes to bring hearing aids in. Since we don't have unlimited funding, these are matters we must deal with. Of prime concern is whether we will be able to build alliances with local entities, and in particular, there is the immediate task of our having permission to reach out to the patients and later being allowed to provide them with solutions. From the time we start our discussions, it can take anywhere from six months to a year to do a mission in a country."[140]

Missions are regularly made in many countries throughout Africa, the eastern bloc of the European countries, and Asia. "We've covered the globe," Fredreic says. "About the only countries we purposely stay away from are such places as western Europe and places like Canada and Australia, where they provide subsidized hearing aids through their social and health programs.[141]

While attending the University of Virginia, Fredreic met Carla, who was studying audiology at Radford University, also in Virginia. Then Carla enrolled in graduate school at Gallaudet University in Washington, D.C., the world's only university specifically designed to accommodate deaf and hard-of-hearing students. Following her schooling, the Rondeaus moved to her native country, El Salvador, where she opened a hearing clinic. To her dismay, only about one out of every fifteen of her patients was able to afford hearing aids. Consequently, she started doing nonprofit work testing people for hearing loss and began searching for ways to accommodate her poor countrymen with hearing loss. Over a period of two years, Carla screened an estimated 3,000 poor people and identified 1,200 patients who needed hearing aids. Meanwhile, Fredreic was working full time as a consultant, advising international companies on how to do business in Latin America. Joining forces with his wife's fund-raising efforts, they raised $10,000, a small amount of the funds needed to help the underprivileged with hearing loss in El Salvador.

In July, 1996, Carla and Fredreic made a pilgrimage to Miami, where they attended the annual American Academy of Audiology convention. In addition to attending the usual meetings, they planned to solicit suppliers for support of their nonprofit project back home. As is typical at professional and trade conventions, all the major companies in the hearing aid industry had set up booths to sell their wares. Carla's and Fredreic's game plan was to make the rounds, booth by booth, looking for a backer to subsidize their efforts to help the needy in their Latin American homeland. Fredreic explains:

"There was no interest, with the exception of one or two suppliers that offered a little support but with strings attached. 'If you sign a contract to buy all your hearing aids exclusively from us, perhaps in a few years from now, we'll donate some freebies,' one said. Another told us, 'If you bought 200 pairs a year, we will give you 10 free pairs.' There was no sincere desire to help us.

"On the last day, with just two hours to go before the convention was over, we stopped at the Starkey booth. We had already spoken to a company sales manager, but philanthropy wasn't his area so we got nowhere with him. We were down in the dumps, and a man who was an assistant of Bill Austin said to us, 'What's up? You're usually upbeat. What's going on?' We quickly told him our story, and he said, 'Have you talked to Bill Austin about it?'

"'We're young pups, and he's a mogul in this industry,' I said. 'How would we ever be able to talk to an icon like Mr. Austin?'

"'Stay around,' he told us. 'I think Bill will want to hear about what you're doing in El Salvador.'

"I told him that we had to leave because they were closing down the convention and we didn't have any credentials to stay. He told us to sit down and be patient. He sent a Starkey employee to the hotel where Bill was attending some meetings to bring him back to the booth to meet with us. The thought of meeting with Bill Austin put us on edge. We managed to boot up our laptop and have the file ready to give our presentation when and if he would actually show up. Sure enough, he came to the booth. Not only is he a huge VIP in this industry, he's 6'2", and in person, he seemed bigger than life. And we were feeling quite small, unqualified, and insignificant.

"'Okay, I understand you need my help,' he said in a booming voice. He seemed very interested, and he listened to us for a few minutes and then interrupted: 'I can see that you are in your early twenties and just starting in this business. You've done all this work, and you have this strong commitment to your people, but you had no guarantee of finding help?'

"'We just think this is the right thing to do,' Carla said. 'We have nothing else to provide but labor and ability.'

"'I find this amazing," he said. 'Everybody comes to me and usually pitches a dream about what they plan to do, but in reality they haven't done any work. Tell me, how do you plan on funding all of this now that you've done this work?'

"'We've raised ten thousand, but that's it,' I said. Then I went on telling him about how we went to different companies to fund-raise. I suppose I talked too much about it because he said, 'If you bring up money again, that's the end of this conversation.' Then he started asking us questions about how we were going to do the molds.

"'We make them in our small lab, one at a time,' Carla said. 'As we find the funds, we'll do them one at a time.'

"'Do you have any molds you made here?' he asked.

"'Yes, we have some in our hotel room.'

"'You brought them here?' he said. 'I really like you guys. But I am going to do them for you in Minnesota. What are you going to do about batteries?'

"'We will give them a pack when we fit them,' Carla said, 'and hopefully they will be able to fund their purchase of batteries.'

"'I will give you the batteries. Forget about doing the batteries. What about the hearing aids?'

"'We've got 1,200 patients, and about $10,000,' I said, 'so if somebody helps us at about $100 a hearing aid, we can can fit 100 patients a year, and we'll keep doing this every year.'

"With that, he threw his arms up in the air and said in a booming voice, 'What? You've created all this and you're building people's hope and you're only going to fit 100 a year? That's disgraceful! How dare you do that!'

"He was really getting upset, and I said, 'Look, Mr. Austin, we're just trying to do the right thing. But we only got ten grand.'

"'I don't care how much money you have. Do you have it here?' I did, and I reached into my pocket and showed him a check. He grabbed it from me and put it in his pocket. 'Now I've got it. Now don't even bring it up again.'

"At the end of the conversation, he said, 'We are going to help everybody.'

"'Mr. Austin, if you are going to do this for the people of El Salvador,' Carla said, 'I can't accept only the hearing aids. You must come with us to participate in this event.'

"'I can't believe you guys,' he said. 'Everyone else comes to me for $20,000, $50,000, or $100,000 and asks for help, but you guys actually want me around and you want to share the dream with me.' His face lit up, and he was thrilled.

"Bill took out a little black book and looked at his calendar. 'I have a gap here. In four weeks from now, we will come to El Salvador to take care your people. Can you be ready?'

"We had no clue if we could be ready, but I said, 'Of course.' Then, he got on the phone and made some calls. We heard him say, 'We're going to El Salvador in four weeks. Get ready.'

"We had the patients lined up, so it was just a matter of contacting them to tell them to come. In a month, Bill and his Starkey team were in El Salvador. It was a big event for our country. The press gave it a lot of coverage. Bill was given the keys to the city. At a reception, he met the president. The secretary of defense had a daughter with a hearing loss, and he personally brought her to meet Bill. Back then, like our neighbors, El Salvador was not a safe place for visitors, so Starkey hired security people, and the secretary of defense had to disarm at the main entrance. I've heard Bill tell his story about this mission, and he likes to tell people, 'Even secretaries of defense are disarmed when they meet me.'

"Carla and I drove to the airport with Bill, and he invited us to work with him and the foundation in fulfilling his dream to give hearing aids to poor people around the world. I've been working with him ever since."[142]

El Salvador is about the size of Rhode Island and has a population of about six million people. Today, Carla owns and operates the biggest hearing aid clinic in the country and one of the largest in Latin America. Her clinic employs twenty-two people, repairs hearing aids, operates a mold laboratory, and conducts speech therapy and sign language classes. It exclusively sells Starkey hearing aids. Fredreic spends seven to eight months each year traveling around the world on Starkey missions.

Tani Austin recalls a mission in El Salvador: "We were fitting a small child, and when we fit him for hearing aids, he heard for the first time. It was like turning on a light switch. He came alive. This little boy had been thrown in a trash can. A woman found him there. Every child has a story."[143]

"They are not children of a lesser God," Bill states. "They are children of a God who cares. He sends me to help them."[144]

Antonio Esteban represented the Dominican Republic as participant in the windsurfing competition at the Olympics in Los Angeles in 1984. In 1990, he won a world championship and was the Dominican Republic national champion for ten years. Esteban was employed by multinational companies, such as Citibank and 3M, as well as a Dominican Republic telephone company. His life changed when his wife gave birth to healthy baby boy who was profoundly deaf. At age two, his son had a cochlear implant, and he had a second at age nine. He is now living a normal life, doing well in school and in sports. His son's loss of hearing inspired Esteban to become a hearing aid dispenser.

To learn the business, he worked for a Spanish clinic that opened Santo Domingo, volunteering to work without a salary. Esteban recalls:

"I read books about hearing, observed doctors and nurses, and I asked many questions, and I learned how to do fittings. When I heard Starkey would be doing a mission in our country, I volunteered to help fit patients. In a four-day period, I worked side by side with Bill Austin, treating 1,300 children. On the last day, Bill asked me, 'You did a good job. Where do you work?' I told him about my son and how I volunteered to work at the clinic without pay. He suggested that I start my own business.

"'I have no money, and I've never been self-employed,' I said.

"'I want you to come to Minnesota, and we will teach you.'

"I said I'd have to talk to my wife first. A week later, I had borrowed money for the plane ticket, and I showed up in Eden Prairie. Bill put me in the classes, and I went through an extensive training program. He paid all my expenses for lodging, food, and the cost of the training. When the training was over, I was all set to open up my own clinic, but I didn't have any money to get started. I needed thousands of dollars worth of equipment to test patients, and of course, I needed an inventory of hearing aids. Bill sent me to the accounting department to establish my credit so I could charge whatever gear I needed to get started. 'Give him everything he needs,' Bill told them. 'He'll pay me back.'

"I never met anyone as generous as Bill Austin. He changed my life. He believed so strongly in me that I had to succeed so I wouldn't let him down. Today, I only sell Starkey hearing aids at my clinic, AudioNet. Of course, it helps that the company has the best product and best warranty, and they always want to help their dispensers."[145]

Bill recalls:

"I remember a woman in Guatemala who brought her four children to see us. She had three sons and one daughter, all in their teens. They all had very bad hearing, obviously genetic. I was able to fit them with our tandem superpower behind-the-ear aids. After they left, someone told me that the mother had to sell the family's only cow so she could pay for transportation to bring them in. I handed a $100 bill to one of our people and said, 'Give this to that woman so she can buy another cow.' Unfortunately, the family was already gone, and we couldn't find them."[146]

Tani remembers:

"They were so happy to be able to hear that they were all crying with joy. Fortunately, our photographer took pictures of them. Bill had also given his business card to her, and five years later, she sent a letter to us asking for more hearing aids for her children. I showed the letter to Bill and the photo of her family. 'This is the cow lady,' he said. We were able to contact her and refit all of her children."[147]

Mark McCarthy, the Starkey photographer who often photographs and films missions, recalls one in India. "These hearing-impaired children were wearing T-shirts that read, 'Institute for the Handicap and Backward People.' This was a school that was chartered in 2000, not some old institution that was established fifty or a hundred years ago. When we saw these children's faces, we certainly did not think that they were backward or handicapped."[148]

In November 2008, a twelve-day Starkey mission to India made stops in Delhi, Agra, Guwahati, and Kolkata and then went to Kathmandu, Nepal. A total of 7,000 hearing instruments were given away. On Thanksgiving Day, the foundation set an all-time record when the Starkey team fitted 565 children with more than 1,100 hearing instruments—the most in a single day! "There is no better way to give thanks than to demonstrate our respect to the world through our care for others," Tani said.[149] That record was eclipsed during the 2009 mission to Kenya.

Bill talks about a young woman in her early thirties who was a doctor in El Salvador.

"She had kidney failure, and dialysis or a transplant was not available to her. As her condition progressed, she lost her hearing and her eyesight. It was only a matter of a short time before she would die. She had heard about our mission and wanted to be fit for hearing aids before she passed away. The woman was brought to me in a wheelchair, and I had the privilege to help her hear. She was so grateful. It meant so much to her to be able to thank the people who had cared for her. To be able to help someone like her was a priceless experience for our team."[150]

Another time, a grandmother came with her young grandson to a local hospital in Juarez, Mexico, where a Starkey mission was being conducted. Bill recalls:

"The old woman watched intently as we fit her grandson, and when she saw that he could hear, she cried uncontrollably with happiness. I was touched by her behavior and wanted to know more about her. I found out that she had come a far distance and had waited three months with the child for our arrival. 'Why didn't you wait at home?' I asked. The woman said that she was afraid she might miss us. She said that she was terminally ill and didn't have long to live. The woman explained that her grandson had no one else to look after him, and he would be unable to take care of himself if he couldn't hear. Through a translator, she said, 'I now know my grandson will have a chance in life, and I can now die in peace.'"[151]

Bill talks about a mother of a small child who lived in a remote village in the Amazon region bordering Venezuela. The woman's three-year-old daughter was deaf, and the community raised money to buy hearing aids for her. After wearing them for the first time, the child went out to play, and the mother put the hearing aids in her purse. Then somebody stole her purse. She was devastated. The mother knew that without hearing aids, her daughter would be unable to develop speech. She felt that she couldn't go back to the community for another pair. Bill explains:

"When she heard on the radio that we were doing a mission in southern Brazil, she made a decision to come to us. The mother and daughter traveled by bus for five days and five nights to get to see us. They arrived just before we started packing up to leave, and we were able to fit her daughter with hearing aids."[152]

The Starkey Foundation has been providing hearing aids to children in Vietnam since 1994 via Americans Helping Asian Children (AHAC), an organization that does wonderful charitable work for children at orphanages and deaf schools. AHAC was founded by

Dr. Bruce Johnson, a San Diego gastroenterologist. "A few years ago, Bruce called us to say they were having a fund-raising event in October and wanted to honor Bill," Tani says.

"I said that it would be our honor and privilege to attend, but then Bill said to me, 'I've been on the road so much this year, so I'd like to pass on this one.' I told him that I already consented and I wanted to go. Reluctantly he okayed it.

"We flew to San Diego, rented a car, and when we arrived, they gave us the red carpet treatment. There were media people everywhere, waiting for Bill. TV crews and anchormen were lined up to interview him. The AHAC had flown in an eighteen-year-old young man from Vietnam who had been in school, known there as a school for deaf, dumb, and defective children. The young man stood at the podium and talked about receiving hearing aids from Starkey. He said that by being able to hear, he was able to attend a normal school and go on to graduate valedictorian of his class. With watery eyes, the young man looked at Bill and said, 'Because of you, I now have a chance in life.' Tears rolled down my cheeks, and I thought to myself, 'What if we hadn't been there for that young man? We must always say yes we can when someone asks for our help.'"[153]

Bill adds, "Imagine having a person with a fine mind like that young Vietnamese man being trapped in that school for defective children. An interesting thing is how we have been going back to the same countries for years now, and we see how many of the recipients of our hearing aids have since grown up. And because they can hear, they are productive and responsible citizens today. This is what lets me know that what we do is good work. Being able to hear makes a person feel like he or she is part of life itself. We feel connected to life through our hearing. Hearing enables us to communicate with our family and friends.

"Helen Keller and others like her who lost both sight and hearing early in life have expressed that if they could only choose one, they would rather hear than see. I suppose that people get used to bumping into things, but they don't get used to not being able to communicate with another person, not being able to say, 'I love you,' or, 'I care about you.' People want to express their feelings. They want to share their feelings."

Bill pauses and adds, "It's important to help the children, because they are the future of the world. If we neglect the children, we won't have a good future. We live on into the future through our gifts back to the community and to humanity."[154]

A while ago, a man came into the Starkey office with a smashed hearing aid in his hand. He showed it to Greg Austin and said, "This belongs to my mother, and I need you to fix it right now."

Greg saw that it was a powerful one, which meant his mother would be unable to hear anything without it. "I'm afraid it's broken too badly and can't be fixed," he said, "and there are some parts missing."

The man was frantic. "You must do something. My mother is dying, and we can't talk to her." He explained that she was on her deathbed and in a coma. "We keep talking to her, but she doesn't even open her eyes. We think that maybe she would respond if she could hear us."

"Let me see what I can do," Greg answered. He took the hearing aid, and using spare parts for the missing pieces, he reconstructed a workable device.

The son thanked him, rushed out the door, and went to his mother's bedside. He then put the hearing aid back in his mother's ear, turned up the volume, and spoke to her.

Her eyes opened. She looked at her son and daughter and said, "What's for lunch?"

They were hoping she'd have something more meaningful to say on her deathbed, but they were delighted to converse with her. They read the lunch menu to her. "What sounds good, mother?"

"Everything," she insisted.

"You couldn't possibly eat all that food," the son said. "But I'll order it, and I'll help you eat it.

When the food came, she started to eat. He started to take some, and she said, "That's my food. If you want some, get your own."

The son and daughter ordered lunch, and the three ate together. During their meal, the mother told them stories about their family history that they had never heard. “We sat there and listened,” the son says.

“We were enthralled and enjoyed every moment. It was a wonderful afternoon. Then my mother asked that we move her wheelchair to the window. She looked outside and said, ‘It is a beautiful day.’

“‘Yes mother, it is a beautiful day,’ I answered.

“Then she said, ‘It *really* is a beautiful day,’ and with that, her head went back, her eyes closed, and she was gone.”

The next day, the man came back to the Starkey office. He handed the hearing aid to Bill Austin and said, “My mother died, and I am returning her hearing aids.”

“What are you doing here?” Bill replied. “We don’t need this hearing aid. Go be with your family. Do the things you must do.”

“No, I must be here. I came here to tell you the story so that you might share it with others so they can know the meaning of hearing.”

Bill explains:

“I thought about what he said, and it made me realize that to be able to hear for one afternoon is priceless. I thought about how it would be to be terminal and dying and having my family coming to see me. What it would be like to see their lips moving and not knowing what they were saying. Not being able to hear, ‘We love you, Dad.’ Hearing those words, even for one moment, makes hearing priceless.”[155]

On a six-country mission in Africa in 2008, the Starkey Foundation gave thousands of children and adults hearing aids. The final stop was fitting children from a local school for the deaf in Johannesburg. While there, Tani and Bill met with Nelson Mandela and his wife, Graca Machel. She gave her support and became the Starkey Hearing Foundation’s official Patron for Early Detection of Hearing Loss in Infants and Children. First Lady Graca asked Bill what she could do to help his work with children. She was impressed when he answered, “We just need more children to help.”[156]

Jerry Ruzicka says:

“Companies that are publicly owned have a responsibility to serve their shareholders. Shareholders want to earn a return. But when you have a spirit like Bill has, he does not demand that the company have a certain level of profitability. But we plan for a certain level of profits because that helps us grow. It helps us do the next good thing. I talk to industry analysts because we compete with publicly held companies, and they try to quiz me about our profitability. 'Wait a minute,' I say. 'That's not a fair comparison to make because they don't have the same investment strategy that we do. Part of our investment strategy might be to help support the work that Bill wants to do.'

Still, our business philosophy is to keep the company healthy so it makes money, because this allows the owner to have the freedom to really do what he wants to do. I think this is what he has me here for—and I hope I do it well for him. He doesn't worry about money. My wife doesn't either. But I do."[157]

Like other Starkey Lab employees, Ruzicka has gone on several missions. When asked why, he says, "I'm primarily here to take care of the business, which is a big job. However, I don't want to get disconnected with Bill's passion, and for this reason, I participate in missions."

Ruzicka adds that with all his mission work, Bill has fit by far more people for hearing aids than anyone else in the world.

"That's what he loves to do, and he does it day in and day out. It may be that he's fitted one hundredfold more hearing aids than any other person ever has. Combine this with his dedication and intellect, and this is why he's the world's best person at it. I've been with him for more than thirty years, and he still asks me the same question from when I first started at Starkey. 'Jerry, what are you doing better?' I absolutely live to make this a better place for him. That's what I'm here for.

"I don't think you're going to find another Bill Austin in this world. The thing about Bill is that there isn't a difference between a good day and a bad day. Every day is the same for him. When Bill sees patients, he treats them all the same. It doesn't matter if they have no money and are the poorest people in Calcutta or a Warren Buffett. Whoever he's treating at the time is the most important person in the world to him, and they all get the same level of care and consideration."[158]

THE STARKEY FOUNDATION'S U.S. PRESENCE

The Starkey Foundation's Hear Now Program assists U.S. hearing-impaired citizens with limited financial resources. Bill has vowed that no one will be turned down because he or she is unable to pay. Tani says, "Bill understands business, but at heart he is a true missionary."[159]

The biggest fund-raiser for the foundation is an annual gala held in Minneapolis and is undoubtedly the most spectacular fund-raising event of the year in the state of Minnesota. Tani, the mastermind behind the event, spends much of her time working on the galas. "I've watched celebrities tell Bill that they would like to help," she says, "but Bill kept saying, 'It's all right. Don't worry about it.' I said, 'Why can't we have a fund-raiser? Everyone else has a fund-raiser, and they are offering to help.'"[160]

In 2001, Tani wrote eight letters to honorees, and seven of them accepted. Among those who came to the foundation's first gala were Carol Channing, Walter Cronkite, and Scott Carpenter. Eight hundred people attended, and $500,000 was raised. In 2007, Jay Leno, Glenn Frey, Arnold Palmer, Jim Belushi, Kenny Loggins, Goldie Hawn, and Jane Seymour came. "Most of our honorees are usually people who wear hearing aids," Tani says, "and have benefited from what we do."[161]

In 2008, 1,500 guests were present at the gala, and $5 million was raised. Celebrity guests included Garth Brooks, Norm Crosby, Marlee Matlin, Jon McLaughlin, and Billie Jean King. Garth Brooks, one of the evening's performers, thanked Bill and Tani for helping to restore the hearing of his twelve-year-old daughter, Colleen, who has been fitted with Starkey hearing aids. Billy Crystal served as the master of ceremonies at the 2009 gala. Other performers were Tony Bennett, Gladys Knight, and Sir Elton John. In spite of the weak economy, more than $5 million was raised, edging out the previous year's record.

PREVENTING HEARING LOSS

A small percentage of people are born deaf, and there are unavoidable causes of hearing loss, including genetics, high fevers, infections, and head injuries. As we get older, we also have hearing loss largely because of exposure to noise over time. There are, however, ways to prevent hearing loss.

Susan Dalebout, an audiologist with thirty years of experience in the field and a former associate professor for the Communication Disorders Program at the University of Virginia, is the author of *The Praeger Guide to Hearing and Hearing Loss*.[162] A leading authority on hearing loss, Dalebout writes in her book:

> [O]ur world is getting louder and louder. Hazardous noise occurs in our workplaces, our homes, and our communities. People of all ages are affected. Because the hazard is odorless, tasteless, invisible, and (usually) painless, people don't understand—or choose to ignore—the danger until it's too late. Perhaps it's unfortunate that dangerous noise doesn't make our ears bleed; if it did, people might pay more attention.

Dalebout states that people differ in their susceptibility to damage from noise. The harm caused from exposure to the same noise for the same length of time varies from person to person. Someone may suffer severe damage; another will not. The level of noise that is considered hazardous also fluctuates. Generally, it occurs with prolonged or repeated exposure to sound levels of at least 85 decibels, or roughly the level of a gas-powered lawn mower. As a rule of thumb, noise is potentially dangerous when you have to shout to be heard by someone who is an arm's length away, if your ears hurt or ring during or after exposure, or if sounds seem muffled or speech is hard to understand during or after exposure. Just as constant exposure to loud sounds can cause hearing loss, so can a single, intense sound such as an extremely loud impulse noise that occurs close to the ear (for example, a gunshot or an explosion).

Working in tandem with the GRAMMY Foundation and Best Buy, the Starkey Hearing Foundation launched a hearing conservation program, Sound Matters, to educate the public about responsible hearing. Educating the public is crucial, because people today are losing their hearing at a rate two-and-a-half times faster than their parents and grandparents. Bill explains:

"To be sure, during World War II, the booming noises caused by the close proximity to gunfire and shelling from heavy artillery were sources of considerable hearing loss. Awhile ago, we used to say that the rock bands were too loud, but they performed in big rooms. Then there were the boom boxes that young people carried around, placed on the floor, and they danced. Yes, they were bad, but the worst thing to come down the pike was when the young generation started putting devices right in the ear and played loud music. This is the most damaging due to the small space and the accompanying noise that is being driven right into the ear. This is particularly destructive due to the proximity, because sound diminishes according to the square of the distance. This means that if you are four times as far away, the sound is sixteen times as weak. Conversely, when the tip of that device is in your ear and eardrum, the noise level is literally deafening."[163]

You might be suspect of a person who manufactures hearing aids expressing concern about preventing hearing loss. Is it not the same as biting the hand that feeds you? This is certainly not applicable to Bill Austin, a man who has dedicated his life's work to helping people with hearing loss. Bill's interest is to help people. Pure and simple. Money has never been his objective. This is a man who has never measured success in terms of monetary gain. His success is measured by how well he serves others.

To create awareness among the general public and specifically young people, Sound Matters has recruited people in the entertainment industry to help deliver its message. Well-known performers include Michael Bolton, Sara Bareilles, Taylor Swift, Trisha Yearwood, Steve Martin, Dan Akroyd, Marlee Matlin, Lou Ferrigno, Jim Belushi, and Jane Seymour.

Songwriter and country singer Taylor Swift, 20 years old, says that she feels an obligation to her young fans to tell them to listen responsibly to music to avoid hearing impairment.[164]

"Hearing this message from performers that they admire," Bill says, "is an effective way to reach young people."[165]

Three-time Grammy winner Trisha Yearwood became involved with Sound Matters after meeting Bill Austin at a Teammates for Kids event. After Bill showed her a video of one of the foundation's missions, Yearwood burst into tears and said, "I have to go." She has since traveled on missions to different countries and has worked side by side with the Starkey team fitting children for hearing aids. "It's amazing to see their faces when they hear for the first time," she says. "Some cry because they don't know what it is; others get wide-eyed and laugh and smile. I can't imagine not being able to hear, to hear music. I feel like this is the cause I'm supposed to give my time to, not just my name to."[166]

To get the word out to young people, the foundation promoted the slogan "Don't Say What." It is a simple message that reminds people that they are often in places where the noise is too loud, and if you have to say, "What?" to hear a person in a noisy room, then it's likely that the noise is too loud. Bill advises parents that if their child is listening to music in the house, they should apply the "Don't Say What" rule and when applicable, turn down the music. "Parents have to be proactive," Bill says, "to protect their children. And if your child is wearing headphones and you can hear the sound from three feet away, it's too loud and potentially unsafe."[167]

In addition to the photographs of the rich and the famous on the walls of the Center for Excellence, there are photographs of children from around the world showing expressions of joy as they hear sound—a singing bird, a dog's bark, their mother's voice—for the first time in their lives. These photographs tell the Starkey story better than any words this author can write. There are also handwritten letters from some of these children.

Bill received one letter from a young boy who wrote: "I think you are really a doctor, a doctor of the soul. Thank you for helping me and my father hear better."

Another letter from a young girl reads: "Thank you for my new hearing aids. They made me very happy. You are very kind and generous. Everyone at Starkey has been so nice to my family. You really made me feel like a star. Love, Samantha."

Employees at InRETURN transform waste material into something recyclable, helping other companies meet EPA regulations in the process as well as giving meaningful work to those who've suffered from brain damage.

Brotherly Love

In the 1938 movie Boys Town, *a small boy is carried piggyback by a slightly older boy, who says to Father Flanagan, "He ain't heavy, Father. He's my brother." Today, this memorable line is the motto of the world-famous Boys Town orphanage in Omaha. This story about Rob Groeschen and his brother, Tom, also depicts how brotherly love inspired someone to achieve the extraordinary. Tom was in a near-fatal accident, and years later, its consequences prompted Rob to start a company, Resource One, and subsequently, InRETURN, a nonprofit company that offers employment opportunities to individuals with brain injuries and related disabilities.*

ROB AND TOM, two years older, are the two youngest of LaVern and Jack Groeschen's brood of six children. Growing up in Fort Thomas, Kentucky, as they did, during the late 1960s and 1970s was like living in a Norman Rockwell small-town setting. The picturesque hilly community sits on the banks of the Ohio River, which divides the two states. On many of the town's hilltops facing west, you can clearly see the high-rise buildings in downtown Cincinnati. If it were not for this visibility, it would seem as though Fort Thomas were far removed from big-city life.

The brothers thought of it as a wonderful place to grow up. Parents felt safe letting their small children walk to and from school. Families and friends gathered to sit on their front porches, and people were greeted everywhere by their first name—at the neighborhood grocery store, at McDonald's, and walking down Fort Thomas Avenue, the town's main street.

In the springtime, the landscape is plush with green grass, budding daffodils, and pink and white magnolias. The summers are hot and humid but mild in comparison to the weather farther south. During football season, the autumn leaves are richly colored in a variety of brilliant reds, oranges, yellows, and browns. Come wintertime, the weather seldom gets bitterly cold, unlike the weather one hundred miles north in Columbus or Indianapolis. Only occasionally does a snowstorm leave enough snow to accumulate on the ground. So although there are plenty of hills for good sled riding, there are some winters when children's sleds get little or no action.

Growing up, the two Groeschen brothers were partial to the warm weather. Avid fishermen, they loved fishing at nearby Wilbur's Lake and in the Ohio River and its tributary streams. There were always enough neighborhood kids to round up for a pickup baseball game. Tom, one of the best ballplayers in the neighborhood, was usually a team captain, and when he was, Rob was always one of his first picks, because he knew that his little brother would otherwise be picked last. Tom knew that this would have been hurtful to his kid brother. And whatever hurt Rob also hurt Tom.

The two brothers were inseparable. It was a sure bet that whenever you saw Tom, you would see his kid brother, Rob, not far behind. Yet, they were very different. Tom was big for his age, gregarious, and strong. Rob was small for his age, shy, and scrawny.

Many youngsters look up to their older siblings. Rob Groeschen really looked up to Tom; he idolized him. And with good reason. First and foremost, his big brother always looked after him. However, Rob was not the only kid who looked up to Tom. Others did, too. Tom was a good-looking natural leader and a gifted athlete.

Jack Groeschen worked hard to support his family of eight. Early in his marriage, he was employed as a carpenter by his father's small construction company. When his dad retired, Jack took a job as bartender at the local VFW hall and also managed the lodge's banquet hall. LaVern Groeschen recalls:

"Jack went to work around suppertime just before I put food on the table for the children, and he'd come home at one or two in the morning. He was rarely around to put the younger ones to bed or help them with their homework. In the morning, he'd be sleeping while I was getting them ready for school. He disliked this being away from the family, so he studied to get a real estate license. Once licensed, he got up the courage to quit his VFW job and work on straight commission selling homes. This work required him to show homes at night and on weekends, so again, he was often away from the children.

"Jack talked me into getting a real estate license. 'If anything ever happens to me, LaVern,' he'd say, 'you can always sell homes for a living.' I got my license, and for a year I worked with him in the same office. It turned out that he'd given me good advice. At fifty-two, he had a sudden and fatal heart attack. With no savings to speak of, the family had to live from week to week. With six kids ranging in ages between eleven and nineteen, I assumed the role as the family breadwinner."[168]

Selling real estate provided LaVern with the flexibility to schedule her business appointments around the time she had to be with her six children. And as her husband had, she showed homes in the evenings and on weekends. Working on a straight commission, she had no choice but to succeed in real estate. LaVern was outgoing, smart, and energetic—all the qualities needed for selling real estate. She explains, "Back in those days and being a woman, my broker treated me more like a secretary than an agent, and I felt this held me back. That prompted me to get my broker's license and open up my own office. I bought a small building at a foreclosure, and with my five sons, we paneled the basement so it could be used as a conference room for sales meetings. Our offices were on the first floor. I built a thriving firm, having at its peak as many as ten licensed agents."[169]

Rob was eleven and Tom thirteen when their father died. The loss brought the two boys even closer together. Tom perhaps instinctively felt that he should protect his younger brother, because that's exactly what he did. While Tom was in the spotlight, he never neglected to find time to be with his younger sibling.

"In retrospect, being the youngest child of a large family without a father as a role model, it was obvious that I lacked motivation," Rob says.

"Consequently, I did just enough in school to make passing grades, and that was pretty much how I was in all facets of my life. At best I was mediocre in sports, although people expected me to shine like Tom. The truth is I was content having Tom in the limelight, and as long as he was the star, I was a happy camper. I was so proud to be his brother. He was very popular in school, and in fact, anywhere in town we'd go, everyone recognized him because his picture and his feats on the football field were always featured in the local newspapers. That's the way it is in most small towns across America, and with my brother's good looks and charisma, he played the part of football hero quite well. In fact, central casting couldn't have picked anyone better for the role."[170]

By the time Tom turned seventeen, he stood just shy of six feet and weighed 180 pounds. His body was solid as a rock. He was the star running back at Highlands High, a powerhouse that was perennially ranked as one of the state's top teams. In 1982, his senior year, Tom was named to the Kentucky's All-State first team. That same year, the blond-haired, amiable athlete was voted the school's homecoming king and prom king.

The media tagged him "Mr. Everything." That's because Tom could do it all on the gridiron. He was a hard-hitting running back who also played linebacker on the defensive squad. The moniker applied even when Tom wasn't playing football. He excelled at nearly everything. His mother often said, "If any of my kids end up in politics, it will be Tom. He has one of those winning personalities. Everyone loves him."[171]

For two straight years, the Groeschen family trekked to Louisville to see Tom play in the state championship game. LaVern's brothers attended, and so did her sister and her family who came from Memphis. Highlands won back-to-back state championships in 1982 and 1983. Tom was the team's star player. LaVern remembers:

"All of my children and our relatives were so proud of Tom and none more so than Rob. He lived vicariously through his brother's stardom. Every time Tom made a big play, he'd cheer his head off and made sure to let everyone seated nearby know, 'That's my brother!' Rob was not what you'd call an animated boy, and I cannot recall him being as excited about anything as when Tom made a big play.

"Seeing how excited Rob was at Tom's games, I said, 'Rob, why don't you play football?' 'What do you want me to do, Mom? Get killed?' In high school he was slight built for his age, but now he's 5'11"and has filled out.[172]

"At a banquet honoring the Kentucky All-State team, Tom insisted that his little brother sit beside him. Photos of the two sitting side by side show Rob with a beaming smile on his face. Tom looks stoic, humbly accepting the accolades. 'Seeing my brother being honored was one of the happiest times of my youth,' Rob recalls. After a brief pause, he looks at an old photo and adds, 'Notice how much bigger Tom was than I. I looked like a runt compared to him.'[173]

"In the autumn of 1982, Tom headed off to Eastern Kentucky University in Richmond, about one hundred miles south of Fort Thomas. Carl, the fourth of the Groeschen siblings, was in his third year at 'Eastern,' as the school is known to state residents. With more than 13,000 students, the university dominates Richmond (population 27,000). Having played every season since the peewee football days, Tom decided to take a year off as a college freshman and didn't try out. During his first semester, he had a 2.1 grade point average. Disappointed, he decided to buckle down and earned a 3.5 in his second semester. 'That was typical of Tom,' Rob says. 'He was one of those guys who can say, "Hey, wait a minute. I can fix this, and away he goes. Once he became determined to do something, he would focus on it and get the job done. Now how cool is that?'"[174]

Meanwhile, Rob finished his senior year in high school. It was an uneventful year, but he did make several weekend trips to Eastern to see Tom. Upon his graduation, Rob, too, enrolled at Eastern and eagerly looked forward to coming there as a freshman. That summer, Tom took an outside job working for a local landscaper, and Rob worked indoors at a local hardware store.

A LIFE-CHANGING ACCIDENT

It was nearly one o'clock in the morning on August 11, 1983, when there was a loud and abrupt knock on the Groeschen's front door. It awakened LaVern from a sound sleep. She put on her bathrobe and went downstairs. She recognized the two policemen on the front porch and invited them in.

"Two of your sons have been in a car accident," she was told.

"Anyone injured?" she asked, feeling terrified.

"We are certain it was Tom, and we think your son Carl was also in the car."

"No, Carl went out around here with his friends, not Tom."

Just then, Rob walked in.

"It's a serious accident," the cop said. "You should get to the hospital."

St. Luke Hospital is just a mile down the road from their house. All six of the Groeschen children were born there. Rob volunteered to accompany his mother, and they parked in the hospital's empty lot, headed to the emergency room, and asked to see Tom.

The woman at the desk looked through the nightly admittance sheet and said, "We don't have a Tom Groeschen here."

"That's strange," LaVern said.

Another woman at the front desk spoke out. "Oh, that's the one they took straight to University Hospital."

A chill ran down Rob's back. "Why would they do that?"

LaVern felt weak-kneed. She knew that there was a trauma center near downtown Cincinnati, and she feared that her son might be seriously injured. Perhaps he broke an arm or a leg. Or maybe cracked some ribs. Or it might be that University is closer to where the accident occurred and she was overreacting. "Come on, Rob, let's go."

Once on the road, she asked Rob, "Where did Tom go tonight?"

"There was a party on a friend's houseboat on the Ohio River. And afterward, the guys like to meet at Dixie Chili for a late snack. But to answer your question, Mom, I'm not really sure where he went."

On their way, they drove down Interstate 471, and Rob saw Tom's green Dodge Charger being hauled out of a ditch. It had smacked into the guardrail and looked like it had rolled over. "Seeing how badly damaged the car was, I knew then that Tom might have been badly hurt," Rob says, "and it scared the hell out of me."[175]

What they didn't know then was that earlier, the police had found the wrecked car, and Tom's friend was lying outside the car with a broken nose and multiple cuts. Nor did they know that it was unclear who had been driving, because Tom was found unconscious in the rear of the car. As it turned out, the police records never determined who was driving, and neither boy remembered. Tom had suffered severe head trauma and a collapsed lung, and his heart had stopped for a few moments.

Once inside the emergency room area, they were instructed to fill out the usual admittance papers. Soon after, a young woman said to LaVern, "Would you please come with me? Your son can finish the paperwork." She led LaVern to a small room.

"It dawned on me when I heard the tone of her voice," LaVern says, "that this was really serious. I said to her, 'Tom has a sister and three other brothers. My sister, Mary Bertha, is a nun. She's very close to our family, and my children are comfortable with her. Should I be telling them to be here?'" The woman nodded her head. LaVern felt devastated. She recalls:

"I dialed Mary Bertha's number. 'I am sorry to be calling you at this hour,' I apologized. 'Tom has been in a very bad accident. Rob and I are at University Hospital. I'd like so very much please for you to go to my house, pick up the rest of my family, and bring them to the hospital.' She said she'd go at once. I wasn't sure she'd be able to wake them up, so I called the Fort Thomas police to also go to our house. They banged on the door until everyone was up. My oldest son was working the night shift, but the others quickly dressed and, with my sister, came to the hospital."[176]

In a close-knit community like Fort Thomas, word of the town's star athlete being in a terrible accident spread quickly. It was believed to have originated with one of the ambulance crew, who had said that it looked as though Tom's pulse had stopped and he was dead on arrival. Thankfully, an alert doctor at the hospital detected a faint pulse and went right to work on Tom. By the next morning, though, most of the young people in the community had heard that Tom Groeschen had not survived a terrible automobile accident.

While the family was huddled together at the hospital, Tom was unconscious. "He will be lucky if he makes it through the night," one doctor said, preparing them for the worst.

There was nothing any of them could do except wait—and pray—which they did. Rob says, "Sitting there in a small reception area and waiting to hear about my brother's condition was like living a horrific nightmare. I was exhausted and kept dozing off and waking up every few minutes, thinking I had had a bad dream. Then I'd look around the room, pinch myself, and realize it was not a dream. It was around 8 o'clock in the morning before we were allowed to see Tom. I took one look at him and couldn't believe what I was seeing. 'That can't be,' I thought to myself. His head was so swollen it was as if someone had inflated it like the Pillsbury Doughboy. I felt faint, but I knew I had to be strong in front of my mother."

Rob's eyes water, and he continues, "The side of his face and head were raw flesh. His whole body showed gashes, and he was covered with blood. The hospital staff had never taken the time to wash him. They were too focused on saving his life. I thought it would be impossible for him to ever look human again. When they cleaned him up, he was still hardly recognizable. I was scared out of my mind seeing him just laying there so still, not being able to function. Before, he was always so full of life. 'How could this be my brother?' I kept asking myself."[177]

Three days had passed before the family knew that Tom would live. Then, a social worker informed LaVern, "You will have to bury the person you knew and accept the person you have now."[178]

Because of a bad infection and high temperature, Tom fell into a coma, and he lingered in this state for more than three months. For the rest of the summer, Rob visited his brother every day. He recalls:

"Tom would lay there, unable to make a motion. He was unable to do anything—he couldn't communicate, feed himself—he couldn't do anything. Still, we were told that nobody knows what's going on inside a coma patient's mind. I always felt some hope he might be capable of comprehending what we said to him. So I'd sit there for hours having one-way conversations with him, trying to be positive, but without having any idea if anything was getting through to him. We'd all take turns talking to him but never a response. We'd rotate turns massaging his feet and ankles. I remember one time when my sister Ann became frustrated and whistled so loud it could be heard on the other end of the hall. Then, as loud as she could, she shouted, 'Tom, wake up!' It made her feel good to let off some steam, but still no response.

"Friends would ask about Tom, but none of us could relate what was going on or what I was going through. One time, when Tom moved his hand a few inches, our family got all excited. That's all it took to give us some hope. Just the least little thing. Later on, I'd tell my friends, 'My mom and I were there and saw his left thumb move.' They gave me blank looks, but we viewed it as a blessing.

"When the doctors told us, 'Tom is going to have permanent brain damage, and he may not remember anything,' I'd think, 'They don't really know.' Or when they'd say, 'If he does survive, he might only live two to five years,' again, I'd think, 'How can they be so sure?' Meanwhile, we kept right on giving my brother a lot of caring and loving, always thinking outside the box, never giving up hope."[179]

LIFE GOES ON

When it came time to matriculate at Eastern, Rob said he was staying in Fort Thomas to be near Tom. He explains:

"My reason for choosing Eastern was to be with him. Without Tom there, I had lost interest in going to college. Tom had always looked after me, and I was so comfortable with that. I expressed my views to my mother, and she replied, 'Tom would want you to go to college. He would be upset to know that you didn't go because of what happened.' I knew she was right, and I was aware that his future life would be challenged. So I needed to get a good education and to excel so I wouldn't also be a burden to my family."[180]

In September, Rob and Carl drove down to Richmond, and they came home every few weeks to visit their brother. "I had always envisioned having a great time with Tom at Eastern," Rob says.

"Being there without him was hard to accept. I tried to enjoy college life, and I focused on my studies. To everyone's surprise, I became a decent student. I liked my classes and, in particular, the open structure that allowed me to make my own decisions on what courses to take and what classes to attend. Meeting new friends and working my way through college helped me take my focus off the accident. I matured quickly and became aware of how precious life is. Having a front-row seat witnessing what happened to Tom, I realized that someone could have everything and suddenly lose it all. It made me appreciate what's important in life and what's not."[181]

In bed motionless for three months, Tom withered down to 135 pounds. "One day I picked up his leg and was sickened to see how spindly it was," Rob says.[182]

"By November, Tom emerged from his coma. He couldn't talk, sit up in a chair by himself, or even smile. But his eyes were open, and he could move his left arm. Tom could recognize family members and friends, and although he couldn't speak, he kept trying, and this was encouraging to the family. 'He was able to respond when I'd talk to him,' Rob recalls, 'which was a good sign. I remember picking him up to move him to a chair and saying, "Could you believe it, big brother, that I weigh more than you now?" [Though he was] unable to smile, I nonetheless could see a slight twinkle in his eye that let me know he thought that was funny.'"[183]

Later in November, Tom was released from the intensive care unit. A social worker at University Hospital advised LaVern, "Find a nursing home, or he will be a vegetable for the rest of his life."[184]

After doing her homework on this, LaVern made arrangements for Tom to be admitted to Cardinal Hill Rehabilitation in Lexington. Rob and Carl drove home from college to pick him up. The next morning, they fastened Tom into the front seat of LaVern's car, and with Rob in the backseat, they headed for Lexington, ninety miles south of Fort Thomas. Tom looked out the window throughout the trip but, according to Rob, had no clue what was going on.

Once at Cardinal Hill, therapists started to work with Tom on everything from speaking to holding a fork. Initially, their goal was to get him to where he could feed himself. Cardinal Hill was only a thirty-minute car trip from Eastern, and Rob and Carl visited several times a week. "In the beginning, it was difficult to see Tom in this environment," Rob says.

"There were a lot of old people who sat in chairs, looking at a blank wall, appearing not to move for hours at a time. Once I came to visit Tom and found him on his bed in a fetal position. I had no idea if he had been like that for two hours or two days. Slowly, Tom started to show small signs of improvement. Although the doctors kept telling us that he'd never be the 'old Tom,' I started to think that it would take a long time, but someday he'd be himself again. We believed those guys at Cardinal Hill were professionals and they would get him to where he needs to be. And sure enough, by February 1984, Tom was able to feed himself and even stand up, and holding on to his wheelchair by pushing it from the back, he could walk. We were thrilled with what they had done for him at Cardinal Hill. It was time now for him to come home and live with Mom. At this point, we had become convinced that in time Tom would be able to live a normal life again. 'Let's take him to the next step,' my mom said. And by this, she meant getting him back in school and getting his life restarted."[185]

The Groeschen family's dining room was used only on special occasions such as Thanksgiving and birthdays. For children, the room was otherwise off-limits—no one even dared to walk in there. When Tom came home, the entire family celebrated his homecoming in the dining room. It was a great occasion. Tom was thrilled to be home with his loved ones. Although a smile could appear on only half of his face, he was clearly enjoying himself. And he was laughing. It wasn't a robust laugh like the old Tom's, but it was a laugh.

Tom still needed help getting dressed and using the bathroom. But his brothers and his mother were there for him. Eventually, he could manage these functions on his own. Standing up and then pushing behind his wheelchair gave him mobility. Only rarely did he actually sit in it. His oldest brother, Steve, took Tom to the YMCA, where he enjoyed water exercises that developed his sense of balance and helped to restore his ability to walk. Over time, Tom gained back much of the weight he had lost, and he was able to have limited conversations. He still had plenty of scars, and when people outside the family saw him, they could see something was not quite right.

LaVern's point of view was: "Let's get Tom back in school. Rob and Carl can look out for him at Eastern." Her mind-set was, "Hey, you don't know unless you try it," so Tom was signed up for a couple of courses at nearby Northern Kentucky University (NKU) in the autumn. But his short-term memory was weak, and he couldn't retain what was being taught. One month later, he dropped out. Plan B was less ambitious. The family decided that Tom would learn a trade or perhaps receive on-the-job training working at a local company. He enrolled in a vocational school but was still unable to do much. He got jobs in several lines of work but kept getting fired for different reasons. In a restaurant kitchen, Tom cut his hand while chopping radishes and bled on the food. At a grocery store, he lost control of a floor polisher. He was turned down at a bakery during a tryout because he wasn't able to work the cake-icing applicator. In time, the family had to realize that Tom would never be his old self.

Tom is not retarded. He is brain-injured, and the capabilities of such people run the gamut. There are patients who recover, others who realize moderate improvement, and still others who get progressively worse. Although in recent years there have been significant advances in medicine and science, relatively little is known about the human brain. It is an enormously complicated mechanism. It contains some 100 billion cells, including neurons that are specialized cells of the brain and nervous system. The neurons communicate via a relay system of electrical impulses and neurotransmitters. The brain generates more electrical impulses in a single day than the combined total of all the world's telephones. The brain, a three-pound jellylike mass of fat and protein, is one of the body's biggest organs. It has been compared to a combination computer-chemical factory, and to function properly, the brain depends on many electrical signals by chemical means. Brain cells produce electrical signals and send them from cell to cell on pathways called circuits. And like a computer, these circuits receive, process, store, and retrieve information. The brain is responsible for coordinating our physical activities, assembling our thoughts, and regulating unconscious body processes, such as digestion and breathing. It also holds cherished memories as well as our dreams and hopes. It determines our character, judgment, and ability to reason. No other living thing in the world can perform even the most simple of human tasks such as counting, writing, and drawing a straight line.

An injury to the brain can lead to an imbalance of its chemicals and interfere with its ability to send electrical signals. For instance, it can create a high amount of dopamine, a neurotransmitter in the brain. An excess of dopamine, or other neurotransmitters such as serotonin and norepinephrine, can cause psychosis in people—they hear voices and have hallucinations and strange beliefs and delusions. Why do certain people have an excess? The short answer is that no one knows exactly why. There is much that remains unknown about treating people with brain injury.

"For the acutely impaired, there are assisted-living residences. But Tom failed to qualify for such a government-funded facility. Eventually, in 1993, he found a job that he could keep; it was cleaning bathrooms at a rest stop on Interstate 75 in northern Kentucky. He was paid minimum wages that in time topped out at $7 an hour. His day began at 5 A.M. because he needed a two-hour bus ride (with transfers) to get there, and another two hours to come home. By the time he finished supper, he was exhausted and usually fell asleep on the sofa watching television. Nonetheless, it was a job that he kept for nearly ten years. But it did little for his self-esteem. Whenever asked what he did for a living, he'd answer, 'I clean toilets for a living. I pick up their shit.' This annoyed Rob, who would say, 'Why can't you just say that you work at interstate rest stops?'"[186]

ROB ENTERS THE WORKFORCE

When Rob graduated college in 1987, he was unable to find a job he liked in the Cincinnati area. Following a long talk with his mother, he decided to move to Orlando, Florida. After many interviews with different companies, he took a job driving a hazardous-waste truck as a route service representative for Safety-Kleen, an environmental service company. "Are you sure you want to do this?" the interviewer questioned. "With a college degree, you're overqualified for this job."

"Yes," Rob answered. "I'll take it and show you what I can do. Then you can give me a job with more responsibility."[187]

As a Safety-Kleen route service rep, Rob's job was to make calls on auto repair shops and auto dealers as well as small manufacturers. Prior to their refurbishing a greasy, oily part, it would have to be cleaned in a parts washer, which usually was a sink on a drum filled with solvents. Rob's role was to pick up the hazardous waste materials that accumulated, which were in turn recycled and disposed of by Safety-Kleen. It was a messy job, but Rob wasn't one to worry about getting his hands dirty. He had always loved cars and enjoyed talking about automobiles with his customers. "I'd call on them every two weeks or so," he tells, "and I built up rapport. I'd also sell them other company products such as hand-cleaning and floor-cleaning products or perhaps another solvent tank."[188]

The Safety-Kleen branch manager took a personal interest in Rob and served as his mentor. He even invited Rob over for Thanksgiving dinner and other holidays. Life was going well for Rob. Then a disaster happened.

"Rob's first cousin, John Mader, had also moved to Florida. The two young men went waterskiing on a nearby lake with a friend. When it was Rob's turn to ski, he tried to cross a wave, hit it at an angle, and flew into the air. The ski hit his head, and Rob took a hard spill that knocked him out. He nearly drowned before his two buddies were able to haul him into the boat. By this time, his face had turned blue, and they had to resuscitate him. His skull was shattered, and blood flowed from his head. He was rushed to the hospital, where the doctor was concerned Rob had suffered severe brain damage. Rob, however, was alert enough to plead with the doctor not to call his mother. He explained what had happened to Tom, and didn't want to upset her. 'My poor mom has gone through enough with my brother,' he pleaded. 'It's better that she doesn't know about this.'"[189]

The doctor did call LaVern but downplayed the seriousness of Rob's condition. However, it was serious. For eight months he was unable to work.

Rob explains:

"I couldn't drive. In fact, I couldn't do anything. I received disability benefits, and during this period, I did a lot of reading to learn more about the environmental business. I spent a lot of time in the office, and it was to my good fortune that Safety-Kleen was starting a new division that would service drums used by large industrial companies. I figured that if I could become knowledgeable in this area, when I returned to work, the company would consider me for its new business."[190]

Rob figured right. Upon his return, Safety-Kleen promoted him to branch industrial manager. In this capacity, he called on manufacturing companies; he wore a coat and tie and supervised two reps who did the service work. A soft-spoken, conscientious man, he became a top sales producer. Recognizing his potential, the company enrolled him in several leadership programs. In 1990, he was promoted to sales manager. Rob liked his job and enjoyed his life in Florida. But deep down, he felt guilty about not being at home to help his mother care for Tom. LaVern still worked long hours in real estate, and when she wasn't selling homes, caring for her son consumed almost all of her time. Rob called home regularly, and when he came for a visit, he always left with an empty feeling. A friend who was a physical therapist sensed his guilt. "If you feel you're letting down your family," she told him, "you should move back home."[191]

CARETAKING

Rob recognized that this was good advice. In 1991, he requested that Safety-Kleen transfer him. Not only did the company move him, but it turned out Rob was given an even bigger managerial job in Ohio. "I knew by then that by being around Tom, I could make a difference in his life," he says. "I made this responsibility a top priority. It was something I needed to do."[192]

Although LaVern made few demands on her children to help with Tom, she was thrilled to have Rob back in town to pitch in. "Naturally, I wanted Rob to have a life of his own," she points out, "but at the same time, Tom couldn't drive, and I had to take him everywhere. With Rob here, I'd have some free time."[193]

Once he was back home, Rob saw Tom several times a week. He soon met a young schoolteacher, Brenda Hatton, who is now his wife and mother of their three daughters. During their courtship, Tom regularly joined them on dinner dates, and the three of them regularly attended Cincinnati Bengals and Cincinnati Reds games. Another favorite activity was taking in Highland High School's Friday night football games. The family would also go to little league games to watch their sister's son play. LaVern says, "We'd read the football program and recognize many of the names of players who were children of Tom's and Rob's high-school friends. One time, Tom quietly said to me, 'You know, Mom, I could have a kid that would be out there playing.' My eyes watered, and I just said, 'That's right.' I'm sure when he sees his old high-school buddies who now have families, he wonders what his life could have been had he not been injured."[194]

"I was determined to get Tom back into the world," Rob tells.

"It killed me to see him staying home when other young people our age were out with their friends having fun. He'd just stay home every night and watch TV. He was so lethargic, and on most nights, he'd doze off with the TV still running. He was oblivious to what was going in the world. Plus there was my mom, who was working so hard with a son still at home who doesn't move for hours at a time. On weekends, Tom had nothing to do, so I'd say, 'Why don't you go with me?' and he would. Brenda knew how deeply I felt about my brother, and she was very supportive. I know she realized that my love for him was unconditional, and as long as he needed me, I'd always be there for him. She knew that this was my lifetime commitment, and she still was willing to marry me."[195]

Going places with Rob and Brenda was good therapy for Tom; however, it required a lot of patience and understanding from his brother. For example, at Cincinnati Bengals football games, Tom would excuse himself and be gone for forty minutes or so. Rob recalls:

"He'd go to the men's room, light up a cigarette, and who knows who he'd be talking to. He's just naturally friendly. He didn't always apply good judgment, and I'd be worried about some unsavory character who would take advantage of him. He walked and talked differently from most people, and he had an expression on his face that made him look as if he might be on drugs. So I'd be on pins and needles whenever he'd take too long to return. At the same time, I didn't want to baby him. Whenever we had plans to go somewhere, say to an event a few weeks away, he would look forward to it so much that the least I could do was invite him to join us.

"Another thing: Tom is prone to using poor judgment in routine incidents that can be dangerous. For instance, we'd be in my car at an intersection and a car is coming down a side street. 'Go, Rob, you can make it,' he'd say, when I actually could not have made it. I'd worry about small things, but that's just my nature. I didn't want to take any chances that could possibly harm Tom."[196]

Sometimes on his two-hour bus ride home from work, Tom would fall asleep and miss his stop. He'd wake up, get off at the wrong stop or miss bus transfers, and be walking the streets in Cincinnati's inner city. Rob explains:

"I'd get calls in the middle of the night and have to go looking for him. Sometimes I had to drive around for several hours before I'd find him, and in tough areas, and it frightened me even to ask anyone if they saw anyone like Tom who seemed lost. One time my mom got a call from a man who angrily shouted in her ear that Tom had been wandering in his backyard. Luckily, Tom gave the man his mom's number, and he called her. He could have called the police. Another time, Tom got some marijuana, and he was smoking it on a street corner in broad daylight. He didn't think he had done anything wrong, but a cop came along with a different opinion. After I'd explain things to Tom, he'd look at me apologetically and say, 'I screwed up. Rob, I'm sorry.' It would tear me to pieces when he said that. That's what he'd often say about his car accident and how he screwed up his life. 'We all screw up,' I'd say. 'Just don't dwell on it. Get on with your life.'"[197]

Individuals with a brain injury often acquire self-destructive habits. Tom became a smoker, and he developed a habit of shoplifting cigarette lighters. Rob says, "When I'd explain to him that it's wrong to steal, Tom would reply, 'Why? The store has plenty of lighters.'

"I remember when we were little and we'd be at the bar where my father worked. There was a regular customer who had a brain injury. This guy didn't drink much, but because of the way he behaved, people always thought he was drunk, and they made fun of him. Well, I didn't want people laughing at my brother."[198]

Rob attended a Safety-Kleen awards banquet held at the Omni Hotel in downtown Cincinnati to honor its top producers for their 1993 performances. During the presentation, a company vice president at the head table talked about the honoree who would be the recipient of a plaque. Sitting in the audience with Brenda, Rob whispered in her ear, "Honey, I think he's talking about me and I'm getting the award."[199]

He was right. Rob was invited to the podium to accept and to say a few words. He spoke with emotion, and upon coming back to the table, his eyes were filled with tears. It had reminded him about the All-State football banquet when Tom was honored.

"This one is for Tom," he said softly to Brenda. "I see how hard he works to achieve all he has with his handicap, and that has inspired me."[200]

As kids, Tom was the star and Rob the underachiever. Tom always took care of his little brother. As grown men, their roles have reversed. Today, nobody thinks of Rob as an underachiever. In addition to becoming a sales manager, on his mother's advice, Rob invested in real estate. One property was a small apartment building he purchased at a low price that needed significant repairs. He moved into one of the building's units, and while living in it, fixed it up. Then he rented it, moved into another unit, fixed it up, rented it out, and so on until the entire building was renovated and occupied with tenants. After he and Brenda were married, they lived in one of their apartments. Their plan was to sell the building and with the money buy a house. Meanwhile, they both worked—she teaching school and he in sales.

In 1999, the family-owned Safety-Kleen was sold. Rob explains:

"They treated me well, and I made a good living with them. I never thought about leaving, but with the new owners, it wasn't the same. For example, there was a time when one of my salesmen came to me and said, 'I'm thinking about buying a house for X amount of money. What do you think, Rob?' Under the previous ownership, I would have felt comfortable telling him to go for it. But I no longer felt that way, and that made it difficult for me to manage for a company that I no longer believed in. So I decided it was time to move on and start my own environmental recycling company."[201]

THE START-UP COMPANY: RESOURCE ONE

In 1999, Rob started gearing up for the day when he would open his own shop, which he would call Resource One. He explains:

"To avoid financial pressures in the beginning, Brenda and I downsized our lifestyle. Without my Safety-Kleen steady income, we cut back and mainly lived off her teaching salary. I rented all the units in the apartment building and took out a mortgage to purchase, because I knew that without a job, we soon wouldn't be able to get any credit. I sold my car, my boat, and anything of value that would generate the cash I needed to start my environmental recycling company. The first thing I purchased was a beat-up truck for $800. I had $60,000 in cash to put into my new venture. I worked out of our garage and went out calling on manufacturing companies with which I had contacts. My first sale was to one of those contacts. This guy liked me because he knew that I always did what I'd say I'd do. He gave me a chance. Back then, a lot of companies didn't know anything about recycling but felt they should be doing it. My sales pitch was: 'Don't throw this thing away. I'll pick it up, and I'll recycle it, as opposed to having it go into a landfill.'

"I'd pick up lightbulbs and rags from industrial companies. I'd spend my days making sales calls and many of my evenings researching, packaging, and shipping hazardous materials. There'd be times when I'd put in twenty-four-hour days. Our service was to help companies become zero landfill. Everything can be recycled or reused. Everything. It's kind of neat to be able to say, 'Nothing gets thrown away here.' After I sensed a customer was satisfied with my services, I'd point out, 'You have those chemicals over there. I can manage those for you at a fair price.'"[202]

Rob's first major account was LensCrafters, headquartered in Mason, Ohio, just outside Cincinnati. In its second year, Resource One hired its first employee. Rob's goal was eventually to have ten customers. Today, he has more than 200 customers, including Whirlpool, Sherwin-Williams, and DuPont. Annual revenues are around $10 million. The company does business mainly in Ohio and the surrounding states but also as far away as the Carolinas and Florida. Its largest account is Honda, located in Marysville, Ohio. The initial order with Honda was $500 a month, and it has since become a $1.2 million annual account. There were times when Honda considered not using Resource One because it was too small. But Rob was persistent, and he not only held on to the account, he expanded it. The secret of Rob's success is the diligence that he applies in doing anything and everything necessary to take good care of customers. "It's all about service," he insists.[203]

In 2004, Rob sold his real estate holdings to buy a 20,000-square-foot warehouse/office building in Blue Ash, Ohio, a community just inside the Greater Cincinnati inner belt. Resource One also occupies a facility in Bellefontaine, Ohio, about twenty minutes northwest of Honda's huge plant.

Resource One has prospered. Today, Rob and Brenda live with their three daughters in a colonial-style home in Loveland, Ohio. Their house sits on a wooded lot on top of a hill overlooking a creek. The company has succeeded beyond Rob's expectations, and with his growing family, he is an American success story. As a young man, not yet forty, he could have been content with all he'd accomplished. He was not. Rob still could have no peace of mind knowing that his brother was cleaning men's restrooms. He says, "How could I be happy when Tom had such a poor quality of life? I kept on thinking that there has to be something better for him. Some line of work where he could be trained and gain self-esteem and be able to go home at the end of the day feeling good about what he had achieved. It should be some place safe and one that presents a challenge so he wouldn't feel bored and frustrated.[204]

"One day Tom lost his job. It had nothing to do with his performance. He was reliable and hardworking and rarely tardy or absent.

The company that employed him lost its contract with the state of Kentucky. Although Rob hated that his brother had to clean men's restrooms, it was even more disturbing to see him at home with nothing to do but watch television. It caused Rob sleepless nights. One night he exclaimed to Brenda, "I can't sit around and wait for something to open up for Tom. I have to do it myself."[205]

So Rob decided to start an organization that would employ Tom and others like him. In these jobs, they could work in an environment where they were treated with dignity, and at the end of the day, they'd go home feeling good about themselves.

Rob says, "I probably could have created a job for him at Resource One, but that's not reality. That's a gift. I wanted a place where he could have an opportunity to be productive—and grow. And then if I could do this for Tom, why not for other people like him as well? Just imagine how much it would mean to brain-injured individuals and to their families. I did a lot of homework and concluded that there was nothing out there that provided such a workplace. So it would be up to me to start one."[206]

Rob envisioned having it staffed with skilled personnel who could provide rehabilitation services. Recognizing that he lacked such know-how, he and Kathy O'Brien, his business manager and accountant, made trips to rehab centers in Arkansas, Tennessee, and Illinois. Rob explains:

"We wanted to visit different facilities that we researched on the internet to see what was out there and perhaps find someone who was already doing something similar to what we had in mind. But we had to conclude that there wasn't anyone. Our objective was to set up a workplace for individuals who have sustained a traumatic brain injury, and we would operate it like a real business. Tom and others like him would have specific responsibilities just like any worker on a company payroll. We recognized that it would take a lot of patience because it would require more time for such handicapped persons to master their assignments. But once they did, they could be productive workers who would receive a biweekly paycheck."[207]

A NEW VENTURE: THIS ONE IS FOR TOM

It was clearly a lofty and maybe impossible goal. For starters, Rob had to commit a significant portion of his time to the new venture, and concurrently, Resource One would have to fund it. In 2004, he formed InRETURN, a nonprofit organization housed in a warehouse-and-office facility adjacent to Resource One. The new enterprise was incorporated under the Internal Revenue Code tax exemption Section 501(c)(3). Advantages in addition to its tax-exempt status included being eligible to receive public and private grants, lower postal rates, discounted advertising rates in publications, and free radio and public service announcements provided by local media.

Now, an estimated 50 percent of InRETURN's revenues is generated by its production associates (the title given its workers) assembling absorbent products made from unusable baby diapers. Rob explains:

"We grind up off-spec diapers that a diaper manufacturer, such as Proctor & Gamble, couldn't use for its product line, and our production associates stuff them by hand into what we call 'socks,' because they are shaped like a tube or a snake, that are typically forty-two inches in length. A one-pound sock absorbs up to twenty pounds of liquids—oil and coolants—from spills and leaks that accumulate in manufacturing facilities. The socks are placed on floors underneath equipment. The main benefit of the socks is safety related. A slippery floor is a work hazard, [potentially] causing injury to a worker. Another benefit is that the customer is being environmentally correct. Rather than dumping this waste material in a landfill, we pick it up, and then it's recycled. Isn't that cool? We take someone else's defect material, and instead of throwing it away, we make a useful product from it."[208]

InRETURN invested in a baler machine that bales recyclable materials that have been separated. Paper, cardboard, and plastic containers are sorted for recycling by a team of production associates, keeping the materials out of landfills. The baler is safe and uncomplicated to handle, so it's ideal for production associates to operate. "Cardboard can't live with plastic, and there are several different types of plastics," Rob says.

"We can bale 700 pounds of plastic into a square cube that is converted into a more manageable form for recycling. A lot of companies don't have the manpower to do this, so they pay us to pick it up. Then another team of production associates bale it, and in its new form, we can resell it. So ideally, we generate revenue twice for our services."[209]

Engineer Coordinator Shaun Shipp at Honda Manufacturing Company says that, having been a Resource One customer, he was open to working with InRETURN when Rob told him about another service that the new nonprofit company could do for the Marysville plant. Shipp says, "At the time, I was in the facilities department, which handles utility supplies for the plant. Rob told me about absorbent socks that InRETURN made and how they could prevent our people from slipping on the oil that leaked from our air compressors. We had been keeping oil pads around the base of the compressors to soak up the oil, and we were sending them out to be laundered. By switching to InRETURN for this work, we now ship the socks off as nonhazardous waste to a company that burns it as a fuel. This way, it is recycled, because it has some BTU value and is reused as a form of energy. It also saves money for Honda."[210]

Shipp has visited the InRETURN plant in Blue Ash, and he has seen firsthand how production associates who have suffered brain injury are now gainfully employed. Shipp says, "Yes, Rob's providing us with a good service at competitive price, and as a bonus, it's great to know that we're doing business with an individual who has such compassion and truly cares about other people. With all things considered, I'd much prefer doing business with a person like Rob versus the guy that is only there because he's making a buck and doesn't care who he steps on to get what he wants. Seeing what Rob is doing is a real confidence builder—it tells me that I'm dealing with a man who has a heart, and this is the kind of company I want to do business with."[211]

Neil Schaller is the environmental engineer at Whirlpool Corporation's Findlay Division in Findlay, Ohio. Mary Jakeway at the

All in the family—Rob Groeschen, founder of Resource One/InRETURN, and his brother Tom pose in front of the InRETURN company logo (top); Tom Groeschen stands with his mother, LaVern (bottom).

Hard at work—Tom drains socks (top) and InRETURN associates do book cutting for NewPage Corporation (bottom).

Whirlpool plant in Marion, Ohio, who is a Resource One customer, recommended Rob to Schaller. Schaller explains:

"Whirlpool is the world's largest manufacturer of dish washers, and we paint cabinets at this plant. We use solvents to thin paints and clean paint guns. During this process, the solvents are contaminated and must be disposed [of]. Prior to Resource One, the solvents were drummed and taken to a company in the environmental waste business in Youngstown, Ohio, to be destroyed. The company over there burned them in an incinerator at temperatures of 1800 Fahrenheit. This meant that after we were through using the solvents in our plant, they had no other use. Well, actually they had a small use for the company that we shipped them to. The solvents helped to burn other hazardous wastes.

"So what could Resource One do for us that would be an added value? Rob told us that his company would ship the contaminated solvents to a cement manufacturer in Indiana. They would then reuse the solvents to clean out residues in their railcars, and afterward, the solvents would be used again as a fuel in their 2400-to-2800-Fahrenheit furnaces that would provide complete destruction of the materials. So here was a scenario where the solvents that we discarded could have two additional applications before being destroyed. The added value we get has to do with the U.S. EPA and Ohio EPA regulations that govern us. I won't get into details, but by having these solvents reused as a solvent *and* as a fuel, we are put into a lower category by the government that does not subject us to as much regulation. Considering the amount of time and effort that is now saved, we are significantly ahead by going with Resource One."[212]

Schaller points out that to make sure its vendors are in compliance with government procedures and regulations, Whirlpool audits facilities that handle its waste materials. Both Jakeway and Schaller made a trip to audit Resource One and another recycling company in Cincinnati. Schaller recalls:

"While there, we took a tour of InRETURN, and we watched their production associates make absorbent socks. Seeing these individuals struck a cord with me because my companion has suffered a stroke that has affected her speech. I was touched by what Rob is doing. It is a very noble cause.

"Since that tour, we've been using absorbent socks made by InRETURN. Observing all the good that Rob is doing certainly makes me want to give him my support."[213]

META Manufacturing Corporation is just up the street from InRETURN in Blue Ash. CEO David McSwain explains his business and its relationship with InRETURN:

"We're a contract machine shop, which means we don't make any products of our own. We use computer-controlled metal-cutting tools with lathes and machining centers to manufacture machines for my customers' blueprint designs. For the most part, these are made out of metals—steel, aluminum iron, stainless steel. We have a diverse customer base ranging from automotive to military. We make parts that go on oil rigs, air compressors, and aerospace-related parts.

"We use an industry coolant that's mainly water but is mixed with a small percent of soluble oil to lubricate and cool machines because, as you know, they heat. It also helps to prevent parts and machines from rusting. The machines also use lubricating oils and hydraulic oils, and over time, even a brand-new machine tends to leak. Rather than have oily stuff on the floor and have to mop it, we use the InRETURN absorbents to soak it up.

"We've used other absorbent products, but remember, we're a small company with a workforce between sixty and seventy, so when I do business with anyone, I feel more comfortable when I know who I'm doing business with. I like to have a relationship with people versus buying something over the internet. I like to spend my money with somebody I know. Now this doesn't mean I'll overpay for a company's products. I believe InRETURN is giving us a good value at a fair price. And I've visited their facilities and have seen firsthand how much good they do for the production associates, so that's all the more reason to do business with them versus another company.

"Like other companies, I get solicited for donations, and we are happy to make contributions to worthy causes. I'm not a Proctor & Gamble, so I can't give as much as I'd like to everyone, so I have to pick and choose which ones to support. We help sponsor an annual golf outing that InRETURN has, and there's also another way that we contribute. They need special machines to perform some of the things they do. For instance, they recycle shock absorbers that require removing oil from them. One day, Rob came here and said, 'Dave, I don't know anything about this. How do I get started?' We found him a fairly low-cost machine that they could use. We tooled it and equipped it to do the job they needed done. My toolmaker makes rigs and fixtures for us, and I had him custom make it for InRETURN's process. I wanted to make sure it was safe for the production associates to use, so we went even beyond what standard OSHA regulations require.

"I've been over to their place, and I see how their employees are made to feel productive and how they go home at the end of the day feeling good about themselves. When I see that, I want to do all I can to support Rob and what he's doing. I know him well, and I see how people from all over are coming to InRETURN because they have someone who's brain injured or autistic that they'd like placed there. Doctors, rehab centers, and families are constantly calling him. I know it breaks Rob's heart to turn anyone down, but InRETURN can only hire so many of them. He'd love to grow to the point where he can take them. This makes me want to do business with him so he can get InRETURN to where he wants it to be. He's not there yet, but he'll get there someday."[214]

The new enterprise has a built-in market—Resource One customers. Rob emphasizes that InRETURN receives no assistance from the federal or state governments. "This gives us the flexibility to do our own thing," he states, "and most importantly, function like a real company."[215]

InRETURN's general manager is Charlie Parris, who previously was an executive performance coach and had served as a volunteer for the Mary Rose Mission, a nonprofit organization that cares for the terminally ill. Rob and Charlie met through Sister Bertha, Rob's aunt. Charlie agreed to volunteer two days of his time at InRETURN as a consultant, but upon learning what Rob wanted to do, he came onboard full time. In this position, Charlie manages the InRETURN workforce and plant operations, while Rob spends a major portion of his time in the field with Resource One customers and also drums up business and programs for InRETURN.

Tom was the first InRETURN production associate. There are now sixteen, all of whom have special needs caused by traumatic brain injury, stroke, or autism. Every day they start with a morning ritual: reciting a written statement posted on the wall. One of them acts as the group's lead reader of "My Declaration of Self-Esteem," written by author Virginia Satir. They read in unison: "In all the world, there is no one else exactly like me. Everything that comes out of me is authentically me because I alone chose it—I own everything about me. . . ." It concludes with: "I own me, and therefore I can engineer me—I am me and I AM OKAY."

Charlie explains:

"We create a normal work environment for them. They work fifty minutes and have a ten-minute break, plus a forty-five-minute lunch period. There are five work periods each day. Production associates work in teams usually consisting of three or four coworkers. Each team is assigned a separate task. During the break, they can use the restroom, have a soft drink, or watch TV. We even have a pool table and card table for them. These recreational activities help them develop social skills. It's not unusual for some of them to come to work early and stay late to 'hang out' with their coworkers. We encourage this time together because it's good for their personal growth.

"Having said this, starting with the time they are interviewed, we make it very clear that this is a business and they are here to make a contribution to the company. Everyone is required to sign in each day, and on their breaks, they fill out a time sheet about what [they] did during the last work period. Nobody takes a restroom break during a work period. We feel it's important to treat them like anyone else who works for any other company. It's good for their self-esteem to know that they must earn their keep and not think of [themselves] as a charity case. While they receive minimum wages, they are thrilled to take home a paycheck that is paid in addition to what they may receive from social security disability benefits."[216]

Charlie explains that they punch in at 8:30 and work until 2:00. He continues:

"From 2 to 3 P.M., they participate in a life-skills class. There is always something going on here. For instance, on Mondays, there is a character-development class that includes a handwriting session, and a fitness program on Tuesday. On Wednesday, it's book club day, where they listen to a talking book on tape or watch a movie and then discuss it, giving feedback on how they interpret it. Thursday is cooking class day. Occupational therapists come in regularly, as do volunteers who teach classes on subjects such as art, cooking, and nutrition. Something is planned every day—this is a very busy place."[217]

InRETURN provides transportation to and from work every day. Tom Schwartz, a local BMW dealership owner, furnishes a van and two drivers. Like Tom Groeschen, Schwartz's brother-in-law, Daniel, suffered a traumatic brain injury in an auto accident. He worked as a production associate for about one year. "Mr. Schwartz saw the good things we do here and has become an ardent supporter," Charlie says.[218]

One of the regular van passengers is David Werner, who has been a production associate since October 2007. Dave was only twenty years old on August 22, 2006, when he was brutally assaulted outside a bar in the University of Cincinnati area. It was dark, and nobody knows exactly what happened. He was found unconscious and has no memory of that evening. No witness has ever stepped forward, and the assailants have never been identified. Dave was so badly injured that during his first eight hours in the hospital, his entire body went into septic shock and twice into cardiac arrest. He was not expected to survive the night and remained in a coma for six weeks. Upon being released from the hospital on December 10, his left side was completely paralyzed. "He had to learn everything," his mother, Sharon Werner, tells. "How to walk, talk, feed himself. Everything."[219]

With Sharon and her husband, Rich, both working full time, and with David requiring around-the-clock care, the Werners had to make major changes. After working for years in retail store management, Sharon became a job coach at the Warren County Community Services Board's Office of Mental Retardation and Developmental

Disabilities. Rich, who worked in technology for Avon Products, was permitted to work at home, and he continued doing computer programming for his employer. Working their jobs around Dave's needs, which included daily trips for physical therapy, the Werners did whatever it took to accommodate their son. Slowly, Dave, a left-hander, learned to use his right hand, and although he walks with a limp, he is now mobile.

Sharon says, "Dave got a job at Warren County Production Services, an adult services organization that provides work for people with disabilities. Most of the people there were more disabled than he, so he didn't fit in. The workers were paid piecemeal, and at the end of the day, Dave took home $6. He was working real hard and felt the pay was demeaning. 'I'm better than this, Mom,' he'd tell me. A friend of mine got Dave an interview with Rob at InRETURN. Shortly afterward, in October 2007, Dave began there full time. Then amazing things happened. Within a month, we noticed huge differences in Dave's personality. Every morning he wanted to get up, and ever since, he's been excited to go to work. That's because he has a purpose. He thrives on the classroom atmosphere. He is so grateful to Sister Bertha, who taught him how to write with his right hand. He totally enjoys the exercise classes. InRETURN has been his savior."[220]

One weekend a month, Dave and his parents go to family game night, where they gather with other production associates and their families. "We look forward to these get-togethers," Sharon says.

"We all support each other, and everyone has a good time. At an InRETURN open house, Rob invited Dr. Lori Shutter, Dave's physician, as well as all of the hospital staff that knew him during his long stay. His physical therapists from the rehab center were also invited. Just about all of them came, and they were amazed to see how well Dave had progressed. Only a handful of them had even known about InRETURN. They couldn't get over that such a place existed."[221]

Prior to his accident, Dave worked for a screen printing company that made T-shirts. In high school, he studied photography and was a photographer for the school paper. He has now again taken up photography, and he particularly enjoys photographing flowers and nature scenes. Recently, he donated two of his pictures to InRETURN's annual fund-raising golf tournament. In an auction, they went for $250. In a silent auction at another InRETURN fund-raising event, Dave's photographs brought in $500. "He felt so proud about being able to raise this money for InRETURN," Sharon tells.[222] Dave's dream is to someday be a photographer for *National Geographic*.

The production associates love Charlie, and for good reason. First, he's caring, and second, he treats them with respect. Charlie is constantly seeking ideas from them. He says that it makes them feel good when their suggestions are implemented. He makes sure to let them know why certain of their suggestions are not used. He gives them encouragement, but at the same time, he's strict with them. If somebody steps out of line, much like any other employer, he lets them know it. "Their biggest limitation," he says, "is that they lack multitasking skills. So we try to set up everything that is single tasking. They mainly do assembly-line work. Our manufacturing is user friendly—our first priority is safety and keeping them out of harm's way."

In late 2008, at age sixty-two, Charlie had a bout with throat cancer and was unable to work for eight weeks. Rob recalls:

"When your main guy who runs the shop is down, you're in a bind. It wasn't possible for me to do his job and mine, too, so it looked like we were in deep trouble. To keep the shop running, I'd meet with our production associates a couple of times a week and tell them how proud I was of the job they were doing. I could see how proud they were in themselves. They recognized the spot we were in, and everybody pitched in to make sure the place would operate without Charlie. With a minimum of supervision, our production numbers didn't falter. One production associate, Duane Lehner, stepped up to the plate and assumed much of Charlie's role. When he returned, Duane was named his assistant manager."[223]

Charlie received many get-well cards and letters from the production associates, which he says did wonders for his spirits. "I missed these guys," he says, "and couldn't wait to get back to work. I was touched by the warm reception I received on my return."[224]

One production associate, Chip Norris, is prone to a seizure now and then, which is not uncommon for brain-injured persons. One of the other associates knows exactly how to treat Chip and is able to bring him back to normal within a short time. Tom, who used to have seizures, seldom if ever does today. When he first saw Chip having one, he said to Rob, "So that's what I looked like when I had one." Rob thinks that it's a positive thing for brain-injured people to witness others like themselves. "They know that they are not alone in this world," Rob says. He shrugs his shoulders and adds, "Things happen."[225]

GOOD RETURNS FOR INRETURN

It doesn't take long after employment at InRETURN before one noticeable change occurs: all production associates attain significant improvement in their social interactions. "You clearly see this with every one of them," Charlie points out.

"But then if these individuals didn't have InRETURN, they'd most likely be alone at home every day. When that's so, I coined a phrase for what happens to them—they become "domestically institutionalized" in their own home. It becomes their prison, because they are cut off from the outside world. For example, take Tom. Thanks to InRETURN, he's a different person today. His entire personality has changed. And the change in him is so apparent. He no longer slurs his words. Before, his eyes were downcast. Now he makes good eye contact with people. Tom is enthused about what he does here, and he looks forward to being here every day. He's doing so well that he now helps train new workers, and we've put him in charge of a product line that recycles defective shock absorbers."[226]

Tom's happiness with his work has carried over to his personal life. After being on a long waiting list, he recently moved into his own apartment at a HUD-supported assistant-living facility. To make sure he could adjust to his new quarters, the first two nights, Rob stayed overnight. After dinner, they watched television and played cards. On the third night, the two brothers were having dinner, and Tom said to Rob, "What are you doing here, Rob? I want you to know I'm good. I am sure your little girls miss you. You need to go home."

"You're kicking me out?" Rob chuckled. "Okay, I'm out of here."[227]

Rob explains:

"Tom's unit has a kitchen, so he has the option to prepare his own meals or eat in the main dining room. He looks after everything from doing his laundry to housecleaning. He also routinely works out and has gotten himself into good physical shape. He's truly happy, and I can't begin to say how happy that makes me.

"In the first years after his injury, Tom would never get excited watching a football game on TV. It used to be that I'd see him in front of the set and I'd ask, 'Who's playing?' or, 'Who's winning?' and he wouldn't know. He was just taking up space. Today, he's a happy camper. His retention has vastly improved, and he really gets into things."[228]

LaVern, now in her late seventies, finds peace of mind in knowing that Tom is capable of living on his own. She says, "When he lived at home with me, I would worry about what would happen when I am no longer around. After all, I didn't want him to become a burden to any of my other children. I can't begin to say how happy I am to know that Tom has become independent. And as long as Rob is there, I know that nobody will ever harm Tom. And Tom will not interfere with Rob's life because he has his own life.

"Tom is a happy guy. He loves shaking hands and giving hugs. On those rare occasions when he's down, I remind him about how InRETURN would not have happened if not for him, and because of him, others are benefiting. He feels good about this, and he is so proud of Rob."[229]

Rob recalls an incident that reassured him that his work at InRETURN was getting positive results. It wasn't something that happened in the plant. "The other day," he says, "I was in a pizza place with my family. We were having dinner when I got a tap on my shoulder from behind. It was one of our production associates. He was having dinner with two of the other guys from InRETURN. It seemed so normal—three buddies who work together out getting pizza. I loved it."[230]

Positive changes have been observed in all of the production associates. "One associate is autistic[231]," explains Charlie Parris.

"His family owns a national grocery chain. Last year, the young man's doctor called to talk to me. I reluctantly picked up the receiver and was thinking, 'What could this be all about?' Then the doctor said, 'I don't know what you guys are doing, but keep on doing it. I've never seen Ben better.' We get many calls from parents who say that their loved one is more content, interacting better, and sleeping soundly. That's what this is all about."[232]

In the beginning, InRETURN was fully dependent on Resource One for funding, and Rob contributed hundreds of thousands of dollars to support it. The time and money he'd put into InRETURN as well as the stress he'd endured prompted Monte Hazelbaker, Rob's financial adviser, to say, "Why don't you just give the money to charity and you can rent out the building. You can give Tom a job at Resource One, and financially you'd be way ahead."[233]

Rob says, "Monte was basically telling me that I had another option that could also do some good and with a lot less wear and tear on me. I responded to him that if there was someone out there who was doing what I wanted to do, I would jump right on their ship and help them. But there was no person, and somebody had to start it. 'I have to be that person,' I told him."[234]

The goal today is to make sure InRETURN prospers and becomes self-sustaining without having to depend on Resource One for financial support. "This organization would have never made it without Rob's commitment," Charlie says. "Few people would have had his perseverance and positive attitude. His cup is always half full, never half empty. It's working because Rob has committed to his brother's well-being. He is willing to do whatever it takes for this to succeed."[235]

Today, there have been several production associates who have made such good progress that they have left InRETURN for employment in the "real" workplace. This is exactly what Rob wants to happen. There is a long waiting list of individuals wanting to work at InRETURN, so the plan is to graduate production associates and bring in others to take their places. Rob would also like to see the InRETURN model implemented in cities across the nation. As the word spreads, people from other cities are in contact with him to try and replicate what he has accomplished in Blue Ash, Ohio. Rob is eager to share his ideas, knowing that others like Tom will benefit.

Three Musketeers—Company leaders Kent Thiry, Douglas Vlchek, and Joe Mello convey that fun is part of the company's values, as is the musketeer's spirit of togetherness.

One for All and All for One

DaVita Inc., operates 1,544 outpatient dialysis facilities in 43 states and the District of Columbia, serving an estimated 119,000 patients. It is the leading independent provider of dialysis services in the United States. DaVita® was founded in 1979 as Medical Ambulatory Care, Inc., a subsidiary of National Medical Enterprises, Inc., based in Santa Monica. The company was formed to own and operate its parent company's hospital-based dialysis services business as freestanding facilities. Management envisioned growing the business by developing additional dialysis facilities and by acquiring other companies.

Historically, outpatient dialysis facilities were viewed as a fragmented industry, mainly owned and operated by individual nephrologists and groups of physicians who had partnered to expand their practices. Hospitals also operated dialysis facilities. In the 1980s, there was a race by a handful of key players to become the dominant industry leader in the United States. Some of the bigger companies were even thinking globally. The big companies purchased small and medium-sized private facilities with multiple locations. But the quickest way to gain market share was to do a merger or acquisition. Meanwhile, because of cumbersome government regulations and administrate costs, hospitals began to outsource their dialysis facilities to larger companies.

In 1994, Medical Ambulatory Care was spun off by its parent company and became Total Renal Care Holdings, Inc. Total Renal Care, Inc., was the new name of its dialysis unit. The company had an initial public offering *in 1995 when it became listed on the New York Stock Exchange. Victor M. G. Chaltiel, a Harvard Business School graduate who had held several top executive positions in the health-care industry, became the newly formed company's CEO. With ambitious plans for expansion, Chaltiel went on a shopping spree to acquire dialysis facilities across the country. In a $1.3 billion all-stock transaction, the company acquired its closest competitor, Renal Treatment Centers, in 1997. The acquisition gave Chaltiel's company a 15 percent market share, putting it only slightly behind Gambro Healthcare, a subsidiary of a Swedish renal care company, Gambro AB. The market leader was Fresenius Medical Care AG, a German company that controlled 25 percent of the U.S. market.*

In a November 1997 article in Modern Healthcare, *Chaltiel stated: "We now have the critical mass necessary to ensure our position as the leading independent provider of dialysis services in the U.S. and the resources to rapidly expand." He would soon eat his words. Although the acquisition uplifted Total Renal Care's status as an industry leader, it nearly wrecked the company and led to Chaltiel's ultimate downfall. The company had simply grown too fast and didn't have the infrastructure to support the much larger organization that its CEO had assembled. What had happened to the company was best summed up in a quote from an October 23, 2000,* Los Angeles Business Journal *article that read: "All they did was buy things instead of focus on running the company."*

In the summer of 1999, Chaltiel, at age fifty-eight, stepped down as the company's chairman and CEO. After an extensive search for a replacement, in October 1999, Kent Thiry, also a Harvard Business School alumnus, was named Chaltiel's successor. Thiry, a blond-haired, energetic man, oozed with charisma. A former Bain consultant, the forty-three-year-old Thiry had spent the past decade with Vivra, Inc., a health-care company that operated dialysis centers across the United States. Thiry's assignment was clear. He was brought in to save a ship that had sprung many leaks and was quickly sinking.

&

A BRIEF HISTORY OF DIALYSIS

Kidneys are twin organs located under the rib cage in the lower back and are each about the size of a fist. Healthy kidneys process 100 percent of the body's blood supply about every five minutes. As blood flows through the body, wastes resulting from metabolism of foodstuff in the body cells are deposited into the bloodstream; this waste must be disposed of in some way. A major part of this cleaning of the blood takes place in the kidneys and, in particular, in the nephrons, where the blood is filtered to produce urine. In short, the function of the kidneys is to filter out extra water, minerals, and toxins from the blood as well as to produce hormones that prevent anemia and bone disease. Healthy kidneys work in the same way that a water filter does as it takes the impurities from our drinking water. The cleaned blood remains in the body, and the waste products exit the body in urine.

Kidney failure is caused by disease, genetics, accidents, drug abuse, and certain medications. The most common causes in the United States are high blood pressure and diabetes. Chronic kidney disease affects about 26 million adult Americans, and it is estimated that 90 percent are unaware that they are at risk. The most severe chronic kidney failure is end-stage renal disease (ESRD). At this end stage, the kidneys can no longer sustain life. For people who have lost nearly 90 percent of their kidney function, the only treatment options to avoid death are dialysis or a kidney transplant. Dialysis does not cure kidney failure, but with proper treatment, a patient can sustain his life. However, the patient will still likely have a dramatically shorter life span and impaired quality of life. More than one in five of America's dialysis patients die each year. The number of dialysis patients is dramatically increasing in the United States. In 1982, there were 66,000 ESRD patients in the United States. By 1995, the ESRD population was 200,000. By 2000, it had climbed to 382,000. Today, an estimated 450,000 Americans are on dialysis (119,000, or roughly 25 percent, are DaVita patients). According to the United States Renal Data System, by 2015, there will be as many as 842,000 ESRD patients in the United States. The rise in the number of patients corresponds in part with the escalation of diabetics. It could be said that dialysis treatment is a growth business.

Dialysis comes from Greek word *dialusis*, which means "to pass through." Prior to the development of dialysis treatments, the only option for treating ESRD was a kidney transplant. The procedure was first successfully performed on identical twins because the organs were compatible with both the donor's and recipient's immune systems. By the early 1960s, immunosuppressives that helped decrease the risk of kidney rejection became available, and this made it possible for people who weren't twins to receive kidney transplants. Even so, although rejection has become less common, and a dramatic shortage of kidney donors limits the number of transplants. In the beginning, it was estimated that only about 5 percent of ESRD patients were viable candidates for a transplant, but it is clear that presently that number is much larger. Although the chances of receiving a kidney transplant have increased, there are not enough spare kidneys to go around, which means those in need must wait their turn to receive a kidney from a living or deceased donor.

Dr. Willem Kolff is referred to as the father of dialysis. As a young physician, he built the first dialyzer in 1943 while working at the University of Groningen Hospital in the Netherlands. His research was put on hold during World War II, when the Nazis invaded his homeland and sent Kolff to work in a remote Dutch hospital. Putting his life in jeopardy, the young doctor continued his work during the German occupation and invented the forerunner to the dialysis machine. By 1945, he had treated sixteen patients with acute kidney disease with little success. An exception was a sixty-seven-year-old woman, who came out of a uremic coma following eleven hours of treatment on Kolff's dialyzer. The woman lived for seven years before dying from an unrelated condition. Kolff's machine is hailed as the first modern drum dialyzer. When the war ended, the Dutch doctor donated five of his machines to hospitals in foreign countries; one of them was received by Mount Sinai Hospital in New York City, where Kolff did research after migrating to the United States in the late 1940s. His work was initially scorned by the medical profession, and even the Mount Sinai administrators opposed this type of therapy. Many doctors rejected his work on the grounds that they thought it was impossible for patients to receive indefinite dialysis. First, they refuted the idea that a man-made device could replace the function of kidneys for a sustained period. Second, they believed that the damage done to a patient's arteries and veins from continuous treatment would mean that doctors would be unable to access their vessels to their blood.

Later, in 1960, Dr. Belding Scribner, a young professor of medicine at the University of Washington, invented a shunt, a breakthrough device that used a new material—Teflon—to eliminate the need to make new incisions each time a patient underwent dialysis. Prior to the Scribner shunt, dialysis could only be used for a few cycles, and it was a painful procedure. Glass tubes were inserted into a patient's blood vessels, permanently destroying them for future access. The shunt worked by using plastic tubes, one inserted into an artery and one into the vein. Scribner shaped a loop between the artery and vein, allowing the device, rather than the patient's vessels, to be opened and closed. After the treatment, the circulatory access was kept open by connecting the two tubes outside the body using a small U-shaped device, which would shunt the blood from the tube in the artery back to the tube in the vein. Although no longer used today, Scribner's shunt led the way to improved techniques to access the circulatory system. In 1960, Clyde Shields became the first American with chronic renal failure to be put on long-term dialysis. Shields lived for eleven years before suffering an unrelated fatal heart attack. In 1962, Scribner opened the Seattle Artificial Kidney Center, the world's first outpatient dialysis facility. The center was later renamed Northwest Kidney Centers, and it became the standard out-of-hospital model for dialysis treatment used throughout the world to this day.

The demand for dialysis far exceeded the capacity of the center's six machines. This created a dilemma about who would receive treatment. Scribner didn't want to determine on his own who would live and who would die. Instead, the choice would be made by an anonymous committee consisting of local citizens from various walks of life, plus two physicians not involved in the kidney field. It was the first-ever bioethics committee. It was controversial and referred to by the media as a "death committee."

To create an awareness of ESRD, Shep Glazer, vice president of the National Association of Patient on Hemodialysis (renamed the American Association of Kidney Patients in 1986), put a face on kidney disease in front of a national audience. In 1971, Glazer dialyzed during his testimony to the members of the House Ways and Means Committee. It captured everyone's attention. In October 1972, Congress enacted historic legislation when it approved provisions to extend Medicare coverage for those with chronic kidney failure. The coverage includes even those U.S. citizens under age sixty-five or not disabled. To qualify, a dialysis patient must have paid into social security.

Bob Badal, vice president of payor contracting at DaVita explains: "Approximately 90 percent of our patients are covered by the government. However, the reimbursement from government payors, particularly Medicare, is insufficient to cover our costs, so the company actually loses money on that business. The economics of dialysis require end stage renal disease providers to rely on reimbursement from the remaining 10 percent or so of private payor business to generate enough returns necessary to achieve DaVita's mission of providing industry leading care for our patients."[236]

Today, there are two primary types of dialysis: hemodialysis and peritoneal dialysis. Hemodialysis treatments are generally administered in a dialysis center three times a week for three to four hours. Trained nurses and technicians care for the patients and perform the prescribed treatment under direction of a physician. Some patients have the option of receiving hemodialysis treatments at home, where they are done more often than in-center treatments. Access to the patient's blood, either by their own blood vessels (a fistula) or an artificial graft in the forearm, is needed so that blood can be pumped into and out of the dialysis filter. A less desirable option is to insert a catheter into the heart, where the blood is pulled out of the body, cleaned, and then delivered back into the body. Today, a fistula is the access of choice, because it causes less risk of infection.

In contrast, peritoneal dialysis is a treatment in which a catheter is inserted through the abdominal wall into the peritoneal cavity, and dialysis fluid is infused and removed in several cycles throughout the night or day. Peritoneal dialysis is more often performed daily at home by the patient, who follows a structured training program. An estimated 90 percent of the patients on dialysis in the United States receive hemodialysis as opposed to peritoneal dialysis.

Many medical and technological advances have been made to improve renal care in recent years. Nonetheless, ESRD has high morbidity and mortality rates as well as enormous financial costs. As of this writing, the annual cost for dialysis is around $85,000, and as technologies advance, the cost continues to increase.

A COMPANY ON THE BRINK

During its five years under Chaltiel, Total Renal Care expanded from 40 to 564 facilities serving more than 44,000 patients. Most impressive, revenues climbed from $75 million to $1.5 billion. Because of Chaltiel's contributions to the company's growth, he was hailed as an extraordinary CEO. However, its existing infrastructure simply could not manage the added workload needed to support the much larger organization that had evolved. As a consequence, the company began to fall apart at the seams. An early sign was how the investment community reacted. On November 2, 1995, when the company had its initial public offering, the stock was priced at $15.50 per share, and it had been as high as $50 during the company's expansion period. However, on February 18, 1999, the company released its 1998 fourth-quarter earnings, which fell far short of expectations, and because of extraordinarily heavy trading, the stock price fell from $21.75 per share to $8.87 per share. By March 1999, it hit a low of $2.06 a share. The company was $1.5 billion in debt and defaulting on its loans to its creditors. Shareholder unrest distracted employees, and employee morale plummeted.

The company's growth strategy had been exceedingly aggressive; the straw that broke the camel's back was its overly ambitious purchase of Renal Treatment Centers. Overnight, the company's patient and staff base had doubled. The 600-person billing and bookkeeping office in Tacoma, Washington, could not handle the vastly larger network of dialysis facilities it had inherited. As a consequence, patients were billed incorrectly or never invoiced, and uncollected accounts skyrocketed. The collections problem was compounded by the fact that there was no standardization of reporting and work methods among the centers. The absence of homogeny made routine management activities, such as reassigning personnel and transferring patients from one center to another center, insurmountable. Another operational failing that caused poor cash flow was the company's struggle at processing insurers' and government forms. Private insurers and Medicare personnel would regularly challenge charges and insist on additional documentation. This led them to unilaterally reimburse lesser amounts or suspend payment altogether until they received an acceptable response.

Guy Seay is vice president of finance at DaVita. A Harvard Business School alumnus, he joined Total Renal Care in 1997 and worked at the company's financial center in Tacoma. He was in the thick of the action during the venture. Seay recalls:

"It was a frightening time. We were desperately trying to figure out ways to orchestrate managing our cash flow, and we were incredibly close to not being able to meet our payroll. We had our normal payroll cycle and then our accounts payable cycles, where bills come in, where we would generate checks and send them out. We didn't have a lot of electronic transfers, and we wrote out a lot of checks. It got to the point when I knew we'd be in a position to meet payroll, but I had to make it clear that all checks had to come to me before they went out. I had to decide on which checks would be put in the mail each day.

"Can you imagine that? We were a billion-dollar company, and I'm putting checks in my desk drawer and asking questions like, 'How much do we have in the bank?' 'How much do we think is going to be in the bank?' 'Okay, let's pay this vendor this week, but we'll put the construction guys on hold.' 'Now let's put the law firms on hold until I give the okay.' We had to prioritize on who got paid, because we were worried there would not be enough money to go around for everyone. Our thinking was that we needed supplies for the centers, so let's give our supply vendors first priority."[237]

Lynn McGowan was a marketing executive at Total Renal Care at the time of its fall. She, too, says that the rapid strain of growth hit her department hard. She explains:

"At my former jobs, I always worked with budgets that were strictly adhered to, but Chaltiel never had budgets when it came to marketing materials in my department, so to me, everything was in disarray. The company had acquired a lot of dialysis facilities that were owned by physicians and small companies. Each had its own system in place, and none were alike. As a consequence, if you visited any of the company's facilities, everyone looked different, and the owner would run it any way he or she wanted to. There was no consistency. Chaltiel also had big global ambitions. Under his guidance, we had dialysis centers in England, Italy, Puerto Rico, and South America—all over. And everything was running differently. The company's focus was just run, run, run and as fast as we could.

"In all due respect to Chaltiel, I remember being at trade shows and everybody wanted to join us. Companies were buying out smaller organizations, and a lot of the doctors that had dialysis centers were either buying out other centers or trying to sell out to one of the big firms.

"Employee morale was at an all-time low. Everyone could see what happened to the price of the stock, and all kinds of rumors were spreading about how the company could go under. We worked from week to week not knowing if the company would be able to meet its payroll. We worried about if we were going to be bought by Gambro. And of course, we heard rumblings about how they were going to take Chaltiel off the board. Everyone felt insecure, not knowing the company's future or, for that matter, their own future."[238]

THE SEARCH FOR A CEO

Following Victor Chaltiel's departure in July 1999, Total Renal Care's board formed a search committee to engage a headhunting firm to recruit a new CEO. After an extensive search, the firm recommended

Kent Thiry to head the company. Thiry came with pedigree credentials. Upon graduating from Stanford and, later, Harvard Business School, from 1983 to 1991 he worked at Bain & Company as vice president of the firm's health-care consulting unit. In 1992, Thiry joined Vivra, a dialysis chain based in Southern California, and went on to become its CEO. Under his leadership, the company prospered.

Thiry's time at Vivra ended when the company was acquired by Gambro at a price the board of directors could not refuse. Along with three private equity partners, Thiry bought Vivra's managed care division, Vivra Specality Partners, from Gambro, but the aggressive new business model was not to be, and the venture failed. "We couldn't even return to our investors all the capital they had invested," Thiry says.[239]

Once the asset sales were well under way, Thiry resigned. As this became known, he was called by search firms regarding other CEO positions, but he had told his family he would take six to nine months off to spend more time with them. After that, he expected to leave corporate America for the not-for-profit world. The Thirys were financially secure, and he wanted to give more back to the community. His wife, Denise O'Leary, is also distinctive and accomplished. She was one of the nation's first female venture capital partners and now restricts her professional activities to board seats. She is one of the few women sitting on the boards of three multibillion-dollar companies (Medtronic, Calpine, and US Airways Group). She was on the Stanford Board of Trustees for fifteen years and for a time served as the chair of the Medical Center Committee. She still sits on not-for-profit boards including that of the Stanford Health system. Thiry had worked hard and was now ready to spend quality time with his wife and two small children, Matthew and Christina.

Thiry says, "In September 1999, my assistant walked into my office and said, 'You have a call from Total Renal Care, a dialysis company.' We had expected the call, because they had imploded, and I had a natural résumé for the job, since I had run a dialysis company that was regarded as being quite successful. I took the call and was set to give the same little speech about how I had decided to take six to nine months off to be with my family, therefore not allowing me to interview. But I couldn't. The memories of my time in dialysis at Vivra came flooding back. They were the most professionally fulfilling years I had ever had. I have no idea what I said in that phone conversation. I only know I did not say what I was supposed to say. Then I headed home and walked into the room where Denise was working and mentioned they had called.

"She glanced over her shoulder and said, 'Well, we expected that, because it's a dialysis company in trouble,' and turned back to her desk. A few seconds later, she sensed that I was still standing there, and she turned around with some of the most intense eyes I had ever seen and said, 'You didn't tell them you would interview, did you?'

"I squirmed a bit and said no. But after a slight pause, I added, 'but I would like to.'

"Denise's reaction was understandably swift and severe. 'What about your decision to spend more time with the family? What about the fact that they're headquartered in Torrance?' At the time, we were living in the San Francisco area. She continued the flurry. 'What about the fact they are a turnaround in dire straits? How much of this is you wanting to prove you can do a turnaround, to prove you can run a bigger company?'

"I replied, 'I am sure part of what is going on in my head does have to do with wanting to take on a big business challenge, and I am sure part of that has to do with my ego. But there is another thing going on in a big way, and that is me wondering if this is the place where I can do the most good for society. If I can help to create a great place to work for thousands of people, a place that provides great care and caring for tens of thousands of patients, then that would have an impact that many not-for-profits could never dream of. It's like fate has been preparing me for this.'

"Denise and I went through just a hellacious few weeks in our marriage trying to sort out how much of it was driven by ego or a desire for a big capitalistic score and how much was, in fact, something my innermost spirit wanted to do. I kept thinking that it might be the opportunity to try to lead a for-profit service organization in a very different way, serving society and shareholders with equal intensity.

Twice that month, I turned the Total Renal Care offer down, but each time, I was intensely sad after doing so. Finally, my wife kicked me out of the house, telling me, 'Stop pouting and go do it. If it does not work out, you will find a successor and the kids will still be at home.'"[240]

Thiry called the search firm, and talks resumed. It was on a Sunday, and the final negotiation took place in one of San Francisco's downtown hotels. "A bunch of their board members were penned up in a suite, and I was in another suite," Thiry says.

"Now if that wasn't a waste of money! The search firm team kept going back and forth between rooms, presenting the terms to both sides. None of them had to do with the amount of salary, bonus, or equity, but there were many sticky terms nonetheless. Finally we reached a deal.

"I remember there was a light rain that night, and as I glanced out my room's window, I had an empty feeling in the pit of my stomach. I kept asking myself, 'What have you done?' I kept thinking, 'This thing could turn out to be a freaking nightmare.'

"The next day, I still had that empty feeling, and by this time, I was getting quite nervous. On Tuesday, I flew to L.A. to visit Total Renal Care's headquarters in Torrance and introduced myself around. I was still feeling nervous and was unsure about my decision. The following day, I canceled everything on my morning agenda. I asked Lois Mills, an absolutely wonderful and dedicated dialysis veteran of over twenty years, to take me to a nearby dialysis center. I went there and talked to the facility director, a few teammates, and some patients. The empty feeling in my stomach went way. I remembered why I was coming, and I knew that this is where I belonged."[241]

FIXING THE COMPANY—THE MBA WAY

Upon Thiry's arrival, Total Renal Care was a broken company. It did, however, have some positives. Although they were never effectively utilized, some excellent business school people had been brought aboard during Chaltiel's reign. Thiry determined that there was already a nucleus of operational talent in place that would allow him to quickly jump-start the company and begin rebuilding. Additionally, he would rely on in-house recruiting and his past contacts within the dialysis industry to make sure the company had to right manpower to go forward. But by far, the company's most valuable asset was its people at the dialysis facilities. These were dedicated and skilled caretakers. In spite of the operational turmoil, Total Renal Care provided above-average dialysis treatment, and from a patient's viewpoint, its services were ample. Certainly, there was room for clinical care improvement, and in time, Thiry would raise the bar in this central area of the business. But first things first.

Anthony Gabriel is the company's current chief information officer. He is a graduate of Ohio State's medical school and did his residency in internal medicine at UCLA. In 1996, he made an abrupt career change and enrolled in the Anderson School of Management at the University of California. Two years later, upon his graduation, he joined Total Renal Care as an operational engineer. A few months prior to Thiry's arrival, Gabriel had transferred to the company's IT department. Gabriel explains:

"Just as everything was falling apart, the head of IT jumped ship, so I was given the interim assignment to run IT while the company searched for a new CIO.

"I give credit to Chaltiel for increasing the number of centers tenfold during a five-year period, and that was quite an accomplishment. But when he bought dialysis centers from doctors, he promised, 'If we buy your business, we are not going to change anything about how your center works.' That was fine with one center, but when you have 500 of them and they all work differently, you can't manage that. When Kent came here, it wasn't just about putting new computers out there or installing new software. It was letting everyone know: 'This is the way we are going to document a treatment. This is the way we are going to submit your results to the billing office at the end of the month.' We emphasized, 'We are all going to do it the same way.'"[242]

Gabriel points out that there was some resistance from a few of the facility administrators. He acknowledges that there are always people who resist change, but it was relatively minor. He explains:

"We took a page from Spencer Johnson's book *Who Moved My Cheese?*, a parable about mice showing how people tend to resist change. We called it 'Operation Cheddar.' We talked about how there was going to be a lot of cheese moving for all of us. We promoted the theme about how everyone must get on board and be comfortable with changes that were necessary to put the company back on track. We let them know it's natural for people to oppose change, but in our case, the only choice was that we all had to accept change. 'And a lot of change is going to happen around here,' we told them, 'but understand that it is for the best of the whole organization.' We softened it by using Spencer's parable, and we passed out those cheese hats they wear in Wisconsin, and we distributed the hats to everyone. That's where Kent is from, so he really liked that."[243]

Guy Seay recalls Thiry's first visit to the company's data center operations in Tacoma.

"Kent spoke at a big group meeting and said that he was here to meet us and to learn. He said that it was relatively clear that what we needed to do in the beginning was to collect cash. Second, we had to build a new leadership team. He was insistent on applying the fundamentals in the execution of the day-to-day operations of the business, and he emphasized it must be driven home to the employees that the basics are the foundation upon which everything else is built. 'We must be tenacious and timely with our bill collecting, and we need to start billing on a more timely an accurate basis,' he stressed. After speaking to the larger group, he met with four or five of the directors in finance and accounting. Following a brief talk, he asked if we had any questions. This was only a month or so after Kent came aboard, and at the time, there had not been a top-down kind of edict on doing budgets. I had attempted to muscle it through, because we needed clarity about our plans for the next year. Previously, when I presented this in the summer of '99, I was told, 'We don't want a budget because we don't want to be held accountable to one.' With this in mind, I asked Kent about his views on the budgeting process, explaining that it had never before been a priority. I directly posed the question to Kent: 'What is your philosophy on budgets, and will we have targets?'

"He made it clear that his expectations were how there definitely would be budgets and we would be held accountable for them. We were told that everyone would have two weeks to go back and refresh their numbers. Then they must sign up for it and would be held accountable to meet those numbers. 'This is the deal,' he emphasized. 'You have to understand the numbers. This is part of what you do as a vice president.'"[244]

Thiry's background as a Bain consultant and a Harvard Business School graduate served him well. He had a clear understanding of the importance of having constant dialog with the bankers, who strongly suggested that the company sell parts of the business to pay off debts. The banks pointed out that the company was in violation of some of its agreements because of write-downs of assets and bad debt required by accounting rules. When Thiry joined the company, it was about six weeks from missing payroll. He explains:

"Had the banks asked for any significant payment, we would have had to shut the doors. The only reason they didn't ask is they could not be sure how much money they would get back in a bankruptcy, especially given the fears that would create out in the centers. However, in return for not forcing us into bankruptcy, the banks wanted the capitalistic equivalent of blood—divestitures, operating constraints, onerous penalty clauses, you name it. They were trying to force us to... sell centers, sell the entire company, conduct big layoffs, or agree to mortgage our future by committing to give them an immense amount of our future cash flows rather than being able to use some to build new centers, buy new technologies, and so on. On any given day, if a single bank from the unruly international syndicate had demanded an actual dollar of payment, we would have experienced the equivalent of a run on the bank—only it would be a run on us, and we would have gone belly-up and lost control of our own destiny. We lived that way for eight months. I don't recommend it from a stress perspective."[245]

Thiry and his management team stood firm, refusing to cave in to bankers' demands. Persistency eventually paid off; the loans were restructured, and the default penalties were eliminated. The overseas dialysis centers were sold, thereby allowing management to concentrate on fixing its problems in the United States.

Before Thiry's arrival, the government had put a halt on payments to the company for laboratory tests because of sloppy record keeping and documentation matters. The decision was made to continue performing tests that were in the best interests of the patient, even though the company was not being reimbursed by the government. Meanwhile, the company made appeals to an administrative law judge to reverse unfavorable decisions and collect denied payments. In a period of four years, the company won six successive judgments and was awarded over $90 million.

With each success, communications were dispatched to centers and home office personnel spreading the word that progress was being made. Each victory was celebrated, and in time, it became evident that the company was on the road to recovery. Morale was definitely on the upswing.

BRINGING IN SOME KEY PEOPLE

Like other newly hired CEOs from the outside often do, Thiry recruited to the company some senior people who he had previously worked with. One of Thiry's first choices was Doug Vlchek, whose experience in dialysis goes back to the 1960s, when he was a biology student at Case Western Reserve University in Cleveland, Ohio. Vlchek talks about his experience:

"To earn some extra money, I worked at a dialysis center, and I loved it. After getting my degree in 1969, I was a technician at the dialysis facility at Case Western Reserve's University Hospital in Cleveland. At the time, Willem Kolff, the man who invented dialysis, was running the department down the street at the Cleveland Clinic, and he strongly influenced everything we did. Back then, dialysis was in its very early stages, and you had to have a degree in a field like chemistry, biology, or physics to work as a technician. They didn't use nurses at the time. Technicians did all of the patient care, including giving medications. We even assisted in the surgeries to put in the vascular access."[246]

A few years later, Vlchek joined Hospal, a French manufacturer of dialysis equipment that had been doing research at University Hospital. He later relocated to the company's headquarters in New Jersey. Vlchek moved up the ranks, and by the early 1980s, he held an executive position. Over the years, he developed a reputation as an industry authority. "People from all over the country called me to ask questions, so in 1986, I decided to start my own consulting firm and charge people for the answers to their questions. There were other consultants in the field, and I specialized in technical and clinical consulting."[247]

Vlchek authored five books on dialysis, including one on quality assurance in dialysis that was published by the FDA. He wrote another book for Amgen on continuous quality improvement. In part as a result of his FDA publication, his consulting firm was soon recognized as one of the most prestigious in the industry. His clients included dialysis centers, manufacturers, pharmaceutical companies, the FDA, and the organization that, at the time, was called Health Care Financing Administration. Its name has since been changed to the Centers for Medicare & Medicaid Services (CMS). One particular company that he consulted was Community Dialysis Centers. Its name was later changed to Vivra. He consulted Vivra on implementing total quality management (TQM) at the company's 150 or so dialysis facilities. It was there at Vivra that Vlchek first met Kent Thiry. Vlchek explains:

"At a meeting with Kent, he said, 'Instead of consulting us, I would like you to come to work for us.'

"I didn't want to because I didn't like his company very much. When he asked why, I said, 'I don't think your company is dedicated enough to quality. I think it's interested in making money, not quality.'

"'Fair enough statement," he said. 'But that's why I was recruited—to try to change that, to change the thoughts. So will you give me a chance? Will you reconsider after you watch us for a while as a consultant?'

"I said I would. Within a year, I accepted the job as the vice president for quality at Vivra. I realized that Kent was a really good guy.

To instill quality, we empowered the caregivers. My approach to continuous improvement was to have the people on the front line get involved. Why? Because they are the ones who really know what they are doing. They know how to fix things. But in most companies, those people don't get empowered. They have to take direction from executives who oftentimes don't really know what's happening on the front line. In a period of two to three years, the company went from probably being the worst company as far as quality in most measures to arguably the best. The company was sold to Gambro. Kent left the company, but I didn't. But I stayed for less than six months, because my philosophies didn't mesh with theirs. I went back to consulting."[248]

While Vlchek was at Vivra, he met Joe Mello, president of Vivra's asthma and allergy division and a man who would later be a key member of Thiry's management team.

In the autumn of 1999, while attending a conference in Orlando, Thiry was having dinner with Mello and Vlchek. During their meal, he said to his friends, "I'm fairly sure I'm going to be offered the job as CEO at Total Renal Care."

"That's terrific," Vlchek said. "I'm sure you'll do a great job."

"I'm not sure if I want the job or not," Thiry said. "But if I take it, I'd like you to come with me."

"I really don't want to," Vlchek replied. "I think I've had enough of dialysis. Gambro left me with a bad taste in my mouth. The amount of work required to create a special culture would be amazing. I just don't think I am up for that."

"If you're not going to do it," Thiry answered, "I'm not going to take the offer. You know this is consistent with your own personal life's mission that you've shared with me so many times. You will not get another chance to positively affect so many of the caregivers and patients you love. You've got to do it."

At his hotel room, Vlchek told his wife about his dinner conversation: "You're going to take the job with Kent, aren't you?" she said. When Vlchek told her that he didn't know, she replied, "Yes you are. I know you're going to do it."

Thiry started with Total Renal Care in November 1999, and Vlchek signed on in January 2000. "I would have come sooner," Vlchek says, "but I had to finish up a specific project at Vivra Asthma and Allergy that I couldn't leave undone."[249] Thiry says he gave Yoda (Doug's nickname) the best title in the company—chief wisdom officer.

That June, Joe Mello submitted his resignation and joined Total Renal Care as the company's chief operating officer. Other good people who had formerly worked with Thiry, Vlchek, and Mello were also recruited.

A TOUGH SELL

In the history of American business and industry, there have been failed companies that have made brilliant recoveries. High-profile turnarounds range from Chrysler's resurgence under Lee Iacocca's guidance in the late 1970s and 1980s to IBM's revival under Louis Gerstner's leadership in the 1990s. The art of crisis management has been around for years in corporate America; the fundamentals are taught in leading business schools. Most of the fixes are obvious, such as instilling budgets and holding managers accountable. Certainly, the most urgent one is making sure that a failing company has an adequate cash flow, lest it will surely bleed to death. Turnaround specialists often do this by "killing the cancer," much like a surgeon cuts and removes diseased tumors. A new management team of a large retail chain, for instance, determines which stores are profitable and which are not, and systematically, the unprofitable ones are sold or liquidated. Overhead is slashed, generally requiring extensive layoffs. And, as in the case of Total Renal Care, mending compliance issues is a top priority. This was a high priority because the company was dependent on the federal government for its main source of revenue. Thiry and his management team did all that good turnaround specialists customarily do, and for these endeavors, they deserve much kudos. But many companies have transitioned from a near breakdown only to revert back to their former dysfunctional ways. This is not a book about turning around broken companies. It is about companies with heart and soul. It is what was done to change the organization's culture and build a robust morale that merits telling. This is what they don't teach in business school.

When Thiry joined the company, he had his family's support, but they chose to remain in the San Francisco area. His children were settled in school, and his wife had her own successful career and served on several local boards. And there were grandparents who lived nearby. When Thiry came aboard, he stayed at a Marriott hotel in Torrance three nights a week and then flew back up to be reunited with his family. Later, the company leased a small house, where he and other visiting managers took up residence during the week. Being away from his family was a personal sacrifice, but it allowed him to work long hours focusing on his job. Thiry explains his decision:

"I could be a better father coming home after working a few eighteen-hour days when I was in L.A. than I could have been if they had moved to a new city with new schools with me working late. In the end, I had faced a basic choice: I could have turned the job down and been home more and talked more about leading a purposeful life. Or I could take the job, be gone more, and actually live one. I think my kids have gotten a lot more out of the choice I made than they would have from the alternative. And the irony is that while the job decision had felt like a tremendous burden when I was making it, it became a blessing once I was working, because it forced a level of philosophical clarity I would never have reached otherwise, and it helped me to persevere on the culture front on the days when I otherwise might have given up.

"In 1999, the company was virtually bankrupt both financially and spiritually. The twelve months of implosion had taken quite a toll. People were angry, cynical, and scared. The only healthy way I could think of to look at that first year was to view it as a long, hard sports season. You were going to have some wins and some losses. You were going to have a lot of away games, and you were going to lose some players you don't want to lose. And no matter how much you loved the sport and your team, there were going to be times when you didn't feel like suiting up so many times in a week, but that is what you are going to do."[250]

Just after Thiry's arrival, he set up a corporate executive retreat. At the time, the company didn't have a conference room that was large enough to accommodate the meeting, so it was held across the street at the Hilton Hotel. Thiry called the meeting so the company's top managers could take a look at their new CEO. He says, "We spent a big bunch of time discussing how we were going to avoid bankruptcy and fix the company, of course. But then we also started talking about the company's mission and the need for clear company values and creating a special place for teammates to work.

"When you do that in a situation like this, about a third of the executives are interested in a positive way, thinking that this kind of talk is refreshing. About a third are neutral, listening but thinking that the rhetoric is directionally nice but certainly overstated, and they will just wait and see what actually happens downstream. The final third has a negative reaction, finding it to be a poor use of time and rather insulting, since they are quite sure it is insincere or naïve.

"Yoda's and my perspective was that if we didn't emphasize our missions and values now, there would always be a reason to postpone prioritizing them. It would have been easy to circumscribe the amount of time, effort, attention, and passion that would be required. I believed that if we accepted an excuse the first month, we'd have another in the second month, third month, and so on. I accepted our crisis as a gift. It's a gift because in a crisis mode, everyone is watching and listening to you. Companies pay millions of dollars for Super Bowl commercials. They do it because that's when everyone is watching TV. Similarly, during a crisis, leaders need to be incredibly purposeful about what they say, because everyone is watching and listening.

"Another reason for clarifying and emphasizing our mission and values was because we needed them to guide our decision making. They couldn't guide us if we didn't have them!"[251]

In addition to the retreat's agenda, Thiry, a gregarious and likeable man, made a concentrated effort to shake as many hands as he could, greeting and chatting with the wary crowd. It is said that he worked the room like a seasoned politician. Under normal circumstances, he would have been well received, but not on this day. It would take more than charm to gain favor with this group.

To his credit, Thiry worked on fixing the short-term troubles while concurrently focusing on long-term gains. Certainly, giving immediate attention to dealing with the financial woes was paramount. Had he done otherwise, the company was likely to have gone belly–up, and there would not have been a future company. It was like being on a sinking ship that had sprung many leaks. A captain doesn't have the luxury of plugging one leak at a time; to do so would surely result in a disaster.

Thiry knew that once the financial problems were in order, to attain sustainable, long-term success, the company's culture would have to be changed. "There are things that are done today that are now strong and vibrant DaVita traditions," he explains.

"For example, we have some cheers that instill a teammate spirit. We started experimenting with them because we realized that it was going to be impossible to reach the 800 company leaders who were spread across the country and the 10,000 other teammates in any consistent, in-person way. Sure, we could communicate our message by sending serious voicemails and emails. We could conduct big teleconferences, and we could give serious sermons about the missions and values we advocated. But that would put people to sleep. Instead, we needed to tell *real* stories about *real* DaVita people, along with situations, victories and defeats, decisions, and issues, and discuss them in context with our mission and values. We needed to come up with language and rituals that reminded people of important themes just like the military, sports teams, and religions do." [252]

At his first nationwide meeting as the new CEO, Thiry did what is known today as the company's "New, Ours, and Special" cheer. It bombed. "You get up there in front of 1,000+ people and you do a cheer and there's no response, and you feel like an idiot," he tells.

"It's a humbling experience, but you just ask yourself, 'What kind of a leader am I? I flopped the first time—am I going to stop?' It was daunting, but I wasn't going to give up on it. Later on, I analyzed what happened. My delivery was low energy and slow. There were too many words. I was uncomfortable, and I was worried that the outcome would be exactly what it ended up being. Many people did not believe in the words. It was awkward for everyone. I had to decide on whether I should take a different approach or work on improving it. Since I could not see the DaVita dream ever becoming true until we could have some fun and display some positive energy, having an important message, and reminding us of our values, I decided to give it another try. This time, I would establish more of a context before I did it. Up front I said, 'I know that many of you probably don't believe this, but just for a moment, I want you to accept a premise of authenticity and make this a statement about what kind of leader you are. So forget about me. This is about you, what kind of leader you aspire to be, what kind of work community you aspire to build.' Then I started with more energy, fewer words, and with the conviction that I was not afraid to be there alone if that was the way it had to be. And it changed. It caught on. Not because of me, but because they decided it was about them."[253]

CHANGING THE COMPANY CULTURE

In late January 2000, Thiry called for a meeting of the "Hilton Group" so he could introduce Vlchek to his senior people. As Lynn McGowan explains,

"The Hilton Group was a name of a previous meeting that had actually met at the Hilton Hotel, so whenever the same people who attended that meeting are assembled, it is called the Hilton Group. We have all kinds of groups, including the Cabin Group, the Palmer Group, et cetera. I know this sounds peculiar to outsiders, but it's something we just do."[254]

In his introduction, he gave many accolades to the company's newly hired executive, "Yoda." Thiry kept saying, "And Yoda did this," and, "Yoda did that," and so on. Vlchek explains:

"Kent has called me Yoda for years, going back to when we first met. This is in reference to Yoda, the character in the *Star Wars* fictional universe who was one of the most renowned and powerful Jedi Masters in galactic history. Yoda was known for his legendary wisdom. Kent has often said that he respects me as a teacher, and he has learned a lot from me. He also says that while my ability to teach is good, I teach deeper things beyond management principles, because I teach principles about life and on how to treat people well. He once told me that I've taught him so much, and he loves me for that. I'm not sure if that's really true, and in fact, he's taught *me* so much. When Kent got up in front of the audience at the Hilton Group, he announced, 'We have a new person who has decided to join us. I am so happy to have him here. This is Yoda.' He didn't even say my name. Just Yoda! I've spent a lot of time with his family, and his wife and kids also call me Yoda. I'm not even sure his children know my real name.

"I remember that part way through the meeting, somebody asked, 'What does Yoda do?'

"'He's Yoda. Yoda, Yoda, Yoda,' Kent enthusiastically repeated. That was the only answer he gave.

"I was a vice president, but my first title with the company was Jedi Master. That's what was written in my employment contract, and it was the title on my business card."[255]

At dinner that night, Vlchek was seated at a table with seven vice presidents, all of whom worked in field operations and headed markets across the United States. Vlchek says, "Being with them during dinner, I could see that they were apprehensive about having a new CEO, and now a new guy called Yoda has been brought in. It was natural that they didn't understand this Yoda stuff. During the meal, they started pumping me for information about Kent. They knew that he was special, but they didn't know what to expect. 'Tell us something about him,' they asked. 'He seems dedicated, but is it an act? He sure gets emotional. Is he for real?'

'He's a great human being,' I said. 'I've known him for a while, and you've got to understand what makes him tick.' I paused and continued. 'I've got an idea. I know Kent has a cabin up in the Sierras. I've been up there at a strategy retreat. I did that a couple of times back in my Vivra Renal Care days. I've been there socially, too. Let's have us, or let me arrange to have Kent have us, spend a weekend up there. What do you think? Just with you guys, just operating people so you can get to know him better.' They went, 'Wow. That would be great if we could spend a few days just with Kent like that.'

"'Why don't I just ask him right now? I'll just go over to his table.'

"'Oh no, don't ask him now.'

"'Why not?'

"'We've got to think this through,' one of them said, somewhat apprehensively.

"'Oh, come on, you guys. You can't run the company that way. If you think something is the right idea, let's just go do that,' I said. And so I did. Kent was talking to somebody, and I asked if I could interrupt for a second, and he said it was okay.

"'The operation guys sitting over there,' I said, pointing to the table, and they were all watching me, 'I told them that we should do a retreat up at the cabin.'

"'Great idea,' he said.

"I went back to the table and said, 'When do you guys want to do it? Like in a couple of weeks?' Their eyes were as big as saucers. Up until then, they had had few private conversations with Kent. A few weeks later, ten of us got together at Kent's cabin. He asked me to come as a facilitator because he, too, wanted to have some tough conversations. The meeting is known today as the 'Cabin Group.'"[256]

As the facilitator, Vlchek led a session of "Start, Stop, and Continue." He says, "It was something they had never done before. The idea of this exercise is to get people to come up with ideas on what a person needs to improve. On the first round of the exercise, everything was directed on Kent as a leader. I stood in front of the group and taped three big flip-chart pages to the wall, boldly writing the titles 'Start,' 'Stop,' and 'Continue.' In a brainstorming session, someone would make suggestions on what they thought Kent should start doing to become a better leader. Other comments were addressed to some things that he should stop doing or continue to do. We didn't do it sequentially, and if by consensus the group thought a subject warranted discussion, we'd continue, and if not, we'd stop. When we dropped a subject, we'd immediately start on another or go back to a previous one.

"I started by having everyone address his remarks to Kent from his point of view on 'What leadership things do I need to do?' In the beginning, nobody said anything. Frankly, they were afraid of Kent. Late in the afternoon, I said, 'Okay, this isn't working. Let's talk about some other subjects.' We took a break around 6:00. 'Let's have a glass of wine or two,' I said, 'and we'll come back to this later on. In the meantime, I'd like for everybody to write down some things you'd like Kent to address.'

"One of the comments that someone wrote down was about how Kent sometimes flies off the handle too quickly. Kent said, 'That's a good one. But as you know, I'm a passionate guy, so I do it naturally. Yes, I know I shouldn't. You know, my parents said when I was eight years old that I was like that, and other people have been saying that about me for a long time. I will keep trying to work on it. I will tell you this, however. I don't know if I'll ever succeed, but I promise you I will try harder.' About an hour into the exercise, one of the guys caught up in the moment shouted out, 'I wrote that question. That one's mine.' Then he spontaneously added, 'Let me tell you where I'm going with this one.' That was the turning point. They could see that Kent was sincere and giving honest answers, and boom, the fear decreased significantly with everyone in the room. From then on, they felt comfortable saying what was on their minds."[257]

Around midnight, Thiry asked if anyone wanted to watch the movie *The Man in the Iron Mask*, the 1998 version starring Leonardo DiCaprio, Jeremy Irons, and John Malkovich. "Only four or five of us stayed up," Vlchek says.

"It's the story about how the four musketeers attempted to displace corrupt King Louis XIV. Kent is emotional, and he cries in movies. In fact, he cries a lot, and he doesn't try to hide it. At the end of the movie, the four musketeers are vastly outnumbered by the king's forces and due to face certain death. At this point in the movie, they draw their swords and vow, 'One for all and all for one.' Kent said, 'This is the philosophy that I think this company needs to be run by. I love this whole idea of one for all and all for one.'

"The next day, we talked about core values. I asked them to identify what they believed the company's core values should be.

Remember now, they were in operations, field people. A few weeks later, we had a similar retreat for the business office executives. This time, we met at a beachfront condo in Carlsbad in Southern California. This meeting has since been referred to as the 'Beach Group.' We went through the same process as we did with the Cabin Group, asking them to identify what they thought the company's core values should be. A month later, we did it with all of the directors. Our facility administrators—the men and women who run our dialysis facilities—report to these middle-level executives, who, in turn, report to a vice president. At the time, there were about one hundred of them. Again, we asked these people to identify our core values. I remember how nervous Kent was about it, thinking that they would not come up with the same things that the executives did. I assured him that they would. 'What makes you so sure?' he asked.

"'These are the people who are true health-care workers,' I said. 'They are not here just because they want to make money. They are here because they want to take care of human beings. A lot of them have been caregivers at one time or another. For instance, there are nurses that had become vice presidents. I've been with the company for a few months, and I know that they get it, and that's why they're here. I wasn't sure about the core values that the executives would come up with because I didn't know them well enough, but I am certain about these people.'

"We did the same process that we did with the vice presidents. We had a paper with about sixty words on it. They were value-type words. 'Go through this,' I instructed them, 'and circle the top ten of these words that you would use if you unilaterally were going to get to decide where the core values of this company were going to be.' Then everyone was paired with another person, and the two of them argued it out until they came up with six to eight words. Then those two paired up with two more, and the four of them had to argue it out, and so on. The Cabin Group picked service excellence, accountability, integrity, team, and continuous improvement. The Beach Group added fulfillment, a word that wasn't on my list. The directors picked the same six words!"[258]

Prior to a Hilton Group meeting attended by company vice presidents, and incidentally held at a nearby Marriott, Thiry met with Lynn McGowan in marketing. She says, "We were planning the meeting, and out of nowhere, Kent said to me, 'I'd like to do a skit at the meeting.' Now I had heard rumors about how he did a lot of crazy things, including doing skits, at his previous company. I asked him what he had in mind, and he suggested how he'd like to do one about the Three Musketeers. 'We need to rent some costumes.'

"The skit was awful, but it delivered an important message. The 'One for all and all for one' motto summed up what Kent envisioned the company would become. He got his point across that it would be a place where people cared for each other. And in spite of its corniness, people saw a very human side of our CEO that they liked. He was willing to dress up in this elaborate costume, not caring how he looked. It wasn't so corporate, which is how everything was before.

"I'm sure Kent was aware that some of his audience didn't think it was becoming of a CEO to present himself in such a manner. Just the same, it didn't faze him. He told me to buy the musketeer outfits, which let us know that this was just the first of many skits that he would do. And he always refers to it as his uniform. If you ever want to upset him, refer to it as a costume."[259]

The Hilton Group meeting was a preview for a nationwide meeting held in Scottsdale, Arizona, in the summer of 2000. Approximately 650 people attended. There were two important items on the agenda that would have a marked influence on the future of the company. First, there would be a vote to determine the company's core values, and then a second vote would determine a new name for the company. Again, Vlchek facilitated the exercise, as he had on a smaller scale at previous meetings. This time, the 650 people were broken down into 32 groups of about 20 individuals who put key words on a flip chart, and in the end, the 12 most common words would be put to a vote. The vote selected service excellence, accountability, integrity, team, continuous improvement, and fulfillment—the same six words that the vice presidents and the directors had chosen! These became the company's core values. The seventh most common word was "fun," which didn't make the final cut, but in a vote in 2001, it was added to the company's core values.

Vlchek says, "Fun was added with the thought in mind that running a dialysis facility may be the most difficult job in the health-care field. It's been said that the job is harder than working in an intensive care unit. Remember now, in dialysis care, about 18 percent of the patients die every year. Imagine working at a place where one out of five of the people that you are working with will die this year. It would be easy to let that get you down. Instead, we like to celebrate that we are keeping people alive and vital enough that they can help take care of their grandchildren. They not only live longer, but have a quality life.

And as Kent says, 'The work they do at the centers is harder than being the CEO of a dialysis company.' Now, part of the philosophy of people like Kent, Joe, and me is that if we aren't having fun at our job, we shouldn't be here. We want our people to have some fun, too. After all, they're spending more of their waking hours at work than they are at home with their families, so they better have some fun at work. As it turned out, the people who didn't want to have fun, for the most part, have left the company. Fun is now our seventh core value."[260]

McGowan explains:

"To let everyone know we knew how to have fun, Kent had a dozen or so of us burst into the room at one point during the first national/nationwide meeting and hand out hats and swords to everyone. He wanted everyone to get into the spirit of the meeting, and he had them all raising their swords and shouting in unison, 'One for all and all for one.' Everyone could see that he was really enjoying himself. It's not often that you see a CEO lead a cheer—something which Kent always does at our conferences."[261]

Thiry says,

"Eighteen months later, when we voted on adding fun as one of our core values, those same people who back then thought it was frivolous no longer thought so. They made a statement: 'Fun is an important part of our life.' By the way, 95 percent of them voted it to be added to our core values."[262]

Today, skits are encouraged at major company meetings. These performances are put on by several top executives, many with the Three Musketeers theme, and when so, they are dressed in full uniform. Each skit drives home the message that having fun is not only acceptable but encouraged by the new regime. In one skit, Thiry made his entrance by rappelling down a stone wall—for the first time in his life. Fortunately, Vlchek, who does rappel, gave him a lesson prior to the skit. Thiry had so much fun that he has dared to do even more perilous stunts in future skits, including riding a horse at a conference held at the Hyatt Hotel in Dallas. In this skit, they used the theme from the 1991 movie *City Slickers*. Thiry starred as Mitch Robbins, the character played by Billy Crystal, and rode into the ballroom for the opening reception on a horse next to Vlchek, who was portraying Curly, the character played by Jack Palance. Joe Mello, who has had a fear of horses all of his life, was also in the skit, but he took one for the team and rode a horse for the first time in his life. At the end of a meeting, it was announced that next year's meeting would be held at Disney World. To put everyone in a Disney mood, Vlchek dressed as Mickey Mouse, and Mello dressed as Minnie Mouse. McGowan laughs as she recalls the image of Mello wearing a Minnie Mouse outfit. "It was so funny," she says, "and it's the kind of thing that people remember, because it's not the way managers behave in corporate America. It's like Doug and Joe did that for us for our enjoyment, no matter that it made them look silly. It shows that they've got to care."[263]

After the core values were decided by a consensus, a vote was taken at the Scottsdale meeting to choose a new name for the company. Thiry explained that the name was being changed because people had been saying that with all the changes taking place since his arrival, Total Renal Care was not the same company it used to be. The message he was hearing was, "We don't want the old name because it's associated with some negative stuff." A list that had many names was narrowed down to three names. The name DaVita, an Italian word that means "giving life," was chosen. This was perhaps the first time that a Fortune 500 company had its teammates vote on naming it.

Thus, in the true spirit of a community, home office managers and operational managers selected the company's core values and its new name using a democratic process. As Thiry said at the time, "This isn't about Kent and his objectives, because I'm not going to even be in the room. It's about whether you want to participate in this process with your coworkers."[264]

Mello explains:

"I think what made our approach so different is what we collectively decided to do while fixing the things that were broken. When you're doing a turnaround, there's not a lot of magical stuff that you have to figure out about what to do. It's not all that complicated. But what was unusual here is that our focus went beyond the usual fixing of a company, because we planned to create a very different culture than what existed—and indeed unlike any other company's."[265]

WALKING THE WALK

Joe Mello talks about earning the trust of their employees.

"When we came here, the wind was to our faces because we had no credibility. We had no trust. That was to be expected. People didn't know us well enough to trust us. Credibility and trust come only with time. However, we did have the wind at our backs in two important areas. First, we had these people who work in health care, and in particular, they work daily with patients with chronic kidney disease. These are folks who want to be part of something that's helpful to others. This meant we had this subset of people that wanted to believe. They really wanted to be part of an organization that was different, one that viewed things differently. Patient care always comes first on their agenda. Service excellence was something very endearing to them. A second clear advantage was that in a short time, we had already instituted some positive changes with cash flow and new procedures that we put in place. That was important because in the beginning, those procedures had some people saying, 'You may be here to serve us, but you are creating more work than you are helping us.' So it wasn't an easy matter to say, 'We know these are the things that are broken, and we are committed to fixing them.' They were right when they thought, 'Talk is cheap.'

"A major thing that we did early on was to make a statement that we were going to invest in the personal and professional development of our line-level managers. We were a company with some strong clinical people. For example, there were nurses and technicians that moved up into managerial roles. But they had never been given any management training. We told them, 'We are going to invest in your personal and professional development.' Their response was, 'Yeah, sure you are. We've heard that one before.'"[266]

Walking the walk, the company started DaVita University, which is run out of the Wisdom Department. When it was initiated, it fell under the jurisdiction of Vlchek, as the company's chief wisdom officer. Mello named the department with the idea in mind that the company was dedicated to increasing the knowledge of its teammates. Offering programs in continuous improvement, DaVita University was a five-day event for newly hired facility administrators, and later on, managers and even vice presidents attended classes on leadership development, team skills, and presentation skills, as well as courses on clinical subjects. Mello explains:

"We were excited about that first class, and we celebrated when we did our fifth class, and then we were up to ten, and soon, DaVita University was off and running. Our senior people conducted classes for our facility administrators. Kent, Doug, and I, as well as other senior executives, taught classes. No other dialysis company ever did anything like this before. None had ever made an investment in large numbers of clinical people by bringing them in to attend courses—all at the company's expense. It sent a message to our operations people: 'We said we were going to invest in you to improve your skills, and not only did we do it, but we brought in our senior-most people to coach you.' We could have talked until the cows came home about how much we cared about them. But as they say, the proof is in the pudding. Then they would go back and tell all the folks that they work with: 'Yes, we actually met with Kent, Yoda and Joe. They were teaching us at the head of the class.' All of a sudden, people were saying, 'Well, maybe this is a different kind of company. This does have a different kind of feel to it.'"[267]

It was always a special treat at DaVita University when Thiry, Mello, or Vlchek conducted a class, and the icing on the cake was when one of them participated in a skit. Thiry often came dressed in his musketeer uniform; this, too, delighted the class. It also relayed a message that fun really was one of the company's core values: "It's something to take back to your clinic. Fun should be part of your job, and when you can, get your patients involved."

Bill Shannon was a DaVita senior vice president from 2005 to 2009 and also held the title of chief wisdom officer. He'd spent seventeen years with the Walt Disney Company, and in 1996, he'd helped open the Disney Institute, which helps companies and organizations adapt Disney best practices in service, leadership, creativity, and people management. Shannon has worked with clients such as ExxonMobil, Coca-Cola, Cingular Wireless, Proctor & Gamble, and Duke University. Early in his career, he'd coached high-school basketball in California. At DaVita, everyone called him "Coach." Shannon points out that in 2009, the company conducted its 100th academy. He explains:

"The main idea behind the two-day event is for people to leave the academy feeling more connected to the organization. This means being connected to our village and our village beliefs. This way, they go home feeling energized and engaged to be a better teammate and, if they choose, to be a leader where they work. We don't think leadership is about title or position, but rather about adaptability and capability."[268]

Today, a video of the conference at which the values were voted on is shown at the academy. In the video, Yoda is on center stage pointing to a flip chart that lists different values, and he's asking the audience, "What do you think about this value?" The video highlights the essence of the conference, an event that has become a milestone in the company's history. Also shown is how the teammates voted on the name DaVita; another video presentation documents the conference when fun was added as a core value. Shown these important episodes of the company's history, new people get a clear understanding about how its culture evolved.

Brett Cohen, a director of special projects, is based in DaVita's regional office in the Philadelphia area. A Wharton business school graduate and a former Bain consultant, Cohen explains:

"Some companies put together a mission statement, stick it up on a few walls and in work stations, and then claim they have a strong company culture, but if you dig deeper, you will see that is not the case. DaVita executives' performance is evaluated on our company's values, so it trickles down from the top. Our people take it into consideration when they are working here every day. For example, someone might say at a meeting, 'In the spirit of continuous improvement, I think we should do this.' We are constantly saying, 'We should do this because of this value.' In my former consulting work, where I had contact with many companies, I rarely saw an explicit linkage between people's thinking and actions with their company values. But shouldn't there be a linkage? Shouldn't values be something that you feel strongly about and it really defines who you are as a company? And if so, shouldn't you want everyone to know this is what you stand for? At DaVita, we are consistent with it. It is not just something on a piece of paper but how we actually work."[269]

Thiry told a group of first-year students in a speech at UCLA's Anderson School of Management delivered in 2009 that to be an effective leader, you should speak your dream.

"If you want to create something special, you have to first talk about it out loud, which tends to be sometimes really embarrassing, because half the audience will think you are crazy. Half the people that are working for you think you're using a shrewd, motivational, manipulative technique to get them to work harder, stay longer, and help fuel your career advances. But really funny things happen when you say stuff out loud. It's kind of like you can say, 'Gee, it's assumed that you love your wife and kids, so you don't have to say it.' I think that's really a poor strategy. I think it's really good to say it. Because when you do, it tends to remind you of the set behaviors, decision rules, and guidelines that go along with the fact that you love them.

"There is a great Buddhist quote: 'It is easy to be mindful. It is hard to remember to be mindful.' This is much of what leadership is about. When you speak out loud, you will want to live up to what you say. If you don't say it, you won't have the same standard of behavior."[270]

To remind him of this, the message hangs prominently on Thiry's office wall.

Accountability is one of the company's core values. In the dialysis industry, measurement is vital in clinical outcomes, and to establish credibility, the company kept score of its performances in all aspects. Starting at the highest level, at every board meeting, Thiry would present a list of issues and questions from the last board meeting, and then he would go through his list, one item at a time, with an explanation on the follow-through and results that had since occurred. It was the same at DaVita University. If the company made a promise to its facility administrators—whether it be to take care of a problem or get back with an answer to a question—there would be a response. Thiry would add at the end, "We said, we did." A guest speaker once addressed a DaVita audience, and several times she said, "No brag, just facts." Thiry liked that line so much that he often repeats it after reciting the progress of the company. It has become part of the DaVita vernacular.

When the Thiry team first came aboard to resolve the company's financial woes, they announced that they would never lose sight that the company was first and foremost a clinical care company. They vowed that they would never compromise on this commitment. Guy Seay stresses, "To drive home this pledge, when we report quarterly to our shareholders, we start off with an update on our clinical results. We intentionally address the clinical metrics in these sessions to let everyone know that this is our number-one priority. We do a more formal update with the capital markets when we give presentations, again beginning with the clinical metrics. This sent a message to the people at the dialysis centers that their work was job number one."[271]

A Reality 101 class was also established. All managers at the director's level and above were required to attend a class in a clinical setting to attain first hand knowledge about what it's like to be a dialysis patient. This is a real eye-opener for many Directors and Vice Presidents because it reinforces to the teams at the clinics, that they too, are dedicated to serving the patients."[272]

Early on, just as Thiry held himself accountable to the board of directors, he, accompanied by Mello and Vlchek, held frequent conference calls with the company's top 800 people to update them on the state of the company. On each call, Thiry would start by asking the question: "What is the incremental evidence that we are serious about our mission and values?"[273] Then he would answer his own question. Thiry admits that knowing he'd have to provide answers put pressure on him. The conference calls became a monthly ritual known officially as the "Voice of the Village" calls. Today, these calls are held quarterly. Each has a set agenda, and 2,000 to 4,000 teammates participate by dialing in on a toll-free conference call number. It has the same format as *Larry King Live*, and callers can drill Thiry with tough questions. Anything is fair game, including asking the CEO how much he gets paid.

Anthony Gabriel explains, "The conference calls have a set agenda, which means it will start off with a set script followed by a Q&A session. It's not just Kent who answers questions. Instead, he will head a panel that I, as chief information officer, might be on, as well as other panel members such as our chief operating officer and our chief medical officer. So if someone asks a question about computers, I might take that one. Keep in mind that they can ask any question. It's no holds barred."[274]

Thiry says, "We wanted to show everyone that tough questions could be asked. Then they could personally assess whether the answers sounded intelligent, honest, and pragmatic. It's particularly important to talk about bad news when you're the one who had something to do with it. I was forthright in reporting on those things that I tried and was unable to succeed. I did this to demonstrate that I was willing to share bad news in an honest way. I also wanted to get across the point that we try to be a very human enterprise. We don't promote an environment where people supposedly behave differently here than they do elsewhere in their lives. On the contrary, we try to make work an integral part of people's lives and consistent with how people want to live their lives."[275]

Of main concern to the teammates was their own future. They wanted to know if DaVita and their jobs would still exist in six months or a year. Thiry was careful not to oversell the long-range plans of the company. Instead, he slowly reassured them that there was real progress in small, incremental victories. He explains:

"First, we needed to define what progress was. It was clear we weren't going to be scoring any big touchdowns immediately. So we had to define what would be considered a first down so that people could feel good, and that while we were in deep trouble during those early first months, we were unambiguously making progress."[276]

Thiry says that a sure way to lose credibility is to gloss over setbacks while only discussing successes.

"You've got to give them the bad news along with the good news. If you fail to be up front with them, you will lose their trust. Every year, when I give my state-of-the-company address, I start by pointing out my failures and areas of underperformance. That is not a fun thing to do, but how can I possibly expect others to have reasonable conversations with me about their mistakes if I don't start with my own?[277]

Knowing that open communication is crucial, Thiry announced that DaVita teammates could contact him directly by email. "He made his email address known when he first came here," tells Blaise Tracy, a company communications manager.

"Knowing that he was accessible scored a lot of points right off the bat, because early on, people were apprehensive about the change in executive management. It was especially effective when teammates received emails back from him. If someone asks a question that can be better answered by somebody else, Kent will write back something like, 'Anthony Gabriel is the person to ask about systems, so he'll get back to you,' and he'll cc Anthony. Be assured, there will be a response to all emails Kent receives. It helped institutionalize accountability and integrity, two of our core values."[278]

Teammates get eyeball-to-eyeball answers by attending DaVita town hall meetings. A town hall is held whenever one of the company's more than eighty vice presidents is at a local center or business office and a group of eight or more teammates is present. These meetings may be as short as just five or ten minutes or may run longer, depending on the questions asked. In an informal setting, teammates can ask the visiting executive any question they want. If the vice president doesn't know the answer, he or she makes a promise to get back to the group in the not-too-distant future with one. Most often, town hall meetings are a friendly way for teammates to meet a visiting executive from the home office. And much like the environment of a town hall meeting in a village, people with a common interest are brought together.

IT TAKES A VILLAGE

During Thiry's tenure at Vivra, many people-, team-, and culture-friendly policies were implemented. "These policies were consistent with my basic values," he asserts, "but at the same time, the positive team building was the means, intended to help achieve the end, which was a successful company."[279] He explains that it was different when he came to Total Renal Care.

"This time, the building of a successful company was the means towards the end of building a healthy community. My thinking was based on the fact that humans spend more waking hours at work than anywhere else. So if you are a leader who purports to care about your team, it makes no sense to create a paradigm which concedes all that time needs to be spent in a relatively vanilla-values or sterile-emotional-commitment environment."[280]

Shortly prior to the time when Thiry signed on with Total Renal Care, he contemplated leaving corporate America to devote his life to not-for-profit causes. He decided to stay in the health-care field because he believed that building a world-class dialysis company would fulfill his need to serve others. It gave him a strong sense of purpose above and beyond being motivated by capitalistic reasons. He says, "I came here with the intention that we would create a special place where thousands of people would be able to say to their neighbors and friends, "This is the best company I have ever worked for. It's far from perfect, but it is more fun or more fulfilling or more team–oriented, or it invests more in my personal and professional growth." Whatever the specifics are for each person, the aggregate reality is most teammates are saying this is the best place they have ever worked, knowing that they in fact have been a key part in making it so. It is theirs. Our goal was to create a special kind of environment.

"This was what we had in mind, but then we had to ask ourselves, 'What are we going to do to make that come true?' We understood that it is not just enough to sit back and say, 'Since we have that intent and we are good people, it will happen naturally.' So we developed a plan in a language, with a set of ideas that was just as rigorous and full-blown as we would do had it been the launching of a new product. Our objective was to build a company that was comparable to a healthy, sustainable community. I was raised in a small town outside Milwaukee. In small towns, there is a shared sense of accountability. You take care of each other, and you are responsible for keeping the village healthy. This was the kind of environment we wanted to create here."[281]

The idea was to recast the company as a village, a concept that would better convey to everyone what kind of working community was the ideal. "A village implies a much deeper social contract between the teammates and the leadership," Thiry explains.

"We just didn't want to provide a place where people had a job. We wanted them to take emotional ownership in the company, and they do that when leadership gives them a sense of belonging, a sense that they should care about their coworkers because their coworkers care about them. We wanted to create a real-world community where our people would take care of each other in a real, physical village."[282]

Thirty emphasizes that this village concept let employees know that the turnaround wouldn't be focused only on operating in the black again. It was a different way to view a business. "It let them know that we're not here only to make profits," he says. "No one, no matter how well you're doing financially, can feel good about cash and low turnover unless it's supported by excellent patient care *and* caring for each other. Otherwise, you'd have a sustainable company, but you wouldn't have a soul."[283]

While turning the company around, Thiry recognized the value in honing in on his teammates' desire to do good work. "In our busi-

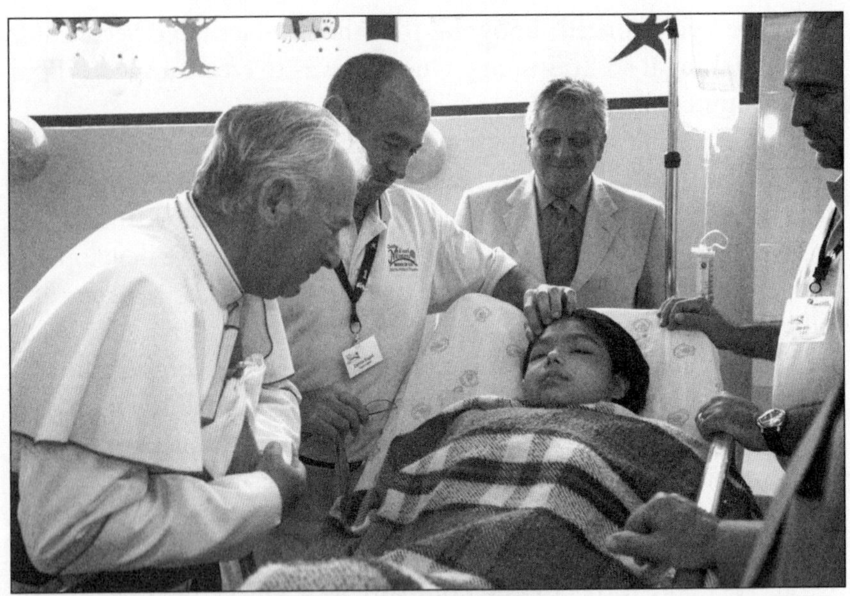

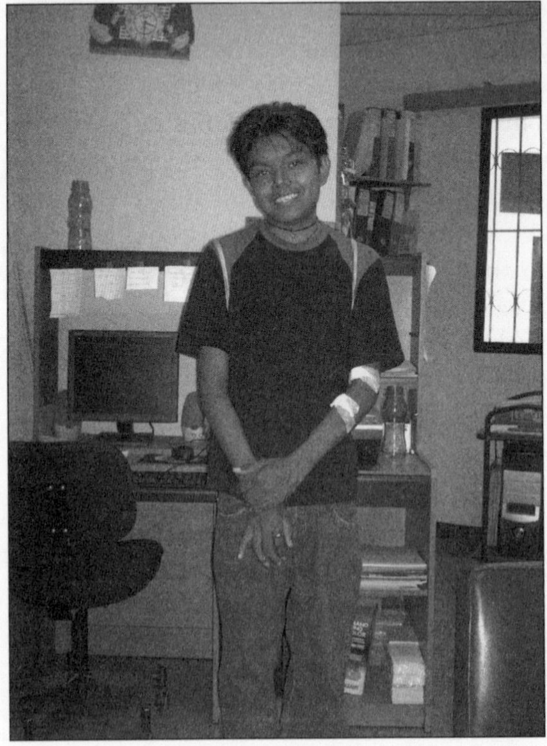

In dire need of dialysis treatments, 16-year-old Juan Carlos is shown here before (above) and after (left) his surgery. He received treatments in a clinic established by Bridge of Life—DaVita Medical Missions.

Tour DaVita 2009—Riders cycle through Michigan for the third annual Tour DaVita in 2009 (top). DaVita event volunteers present at DaVita University Academy, a two-day leadership development and cultural orientation program for new teammates (bottom).

ness, people want to provide good care, and what we had to do was give them the freedom to do it."[284]

Bill Shannon says, "We believe that we are a community first and a company second. We happen to be in the kidney care business. But that's not the end. That's the means to the village versus DaVita, the company. As a community, we are democratic. This is why our teammates, which all people that work here are called, were asked to vote on choosing our core values and our name, DaVita. In a true and healthy community, people care about each other with distinctive consistency and intensity. People care about the community itself and its sustainability. And the community itself provides both opportunities for and safety nets to its citizens, which helps them to realize their full potential while protecting them from unforeseen difficulties.

"We do a lot of things here that are what I call community-like. For example, we have Village Service Days. DaVita launched this program in 2007 to encourage teammates to make a difference, as a team, in their local communities. The teams at the centers choose a specific project that can range from renovating a local community center to reading books to children in need. In other instances, teammates might collectively volunteer their time to refurbish a house in the inner city. Or they might send letters to our troops overseas. Sometimes the combined efforts of several DaVita centers in an area will take on a project. This happened in February 2007 when more than eighty DaVita volunteers did an 'extreme makeover' of the Lions Blind Center in Oakland, California. They did everything from painting and landscaping to larger projects including installing a new water fountain. Another group of about eighty teammates refurbished cottages for Hillview Acres Children's Home, a residential facility for severely abused and neglected children, in Chino, California.

We have another program called DaVita Village Network that focuses on helping teammates in need. It could be a minor thing such as someone's car breaking down, and a teammate would come to her rescue. Or, if needed, a group of teammates might take turns providing rides while her car was in the shop. It could be something more serious, where a teammate's home burns down and his or her coworkers pitch in to rebuild it. It's like they do in an Amish community when a barn burns down and the whole community works together to build a new one."[285]

Joe Mello has a favorite story that he has told many times to DaVita teammates that underscores the spirit of good citizens in a close-knit village.

"Many years ago, a man who had been a village elder now lived at the top of a high hill overlooking the village down in the valley. All the other villagers lived in the bottom of a valley along the river. One day, this man saw that the dam upstream from the village had cracked and was about to break. He knew that he had to do something immediately or else many people would drown. There wasn't enough time to go down the hill and warn them. Then an idea came to him. He set his house on fire. When the people in the village saw the flames, all the men, women, and children came running up the hill to help put out the fire and save the elder's house. When they got there, they heard a loud noise, which was the breaking of the dam. Had they remained in the village, they would have all drowned."[286]

Mello's story is always well received by DaVita audiences. "I first started telling this story at a DaVita University event," he says. "It's a good way to explain our 'one for all, all for one' story."[287]

"He also explains that his story has another message for line-level teammates.

"In a session on leadership, I tell this story to emphasize that all the nurses and technicians that take care patients on a daily basis should think of themselves as leaders. 'I'm just a worker here,' one might say, 'not a leader.' 'Not true,' we tell them. 'There are many selfless acts that you do that have an impact on people, which we view as acts of leadership.'"[288]

Thiry often says in reference to leadership:

"There's an old saying: 'They don't care how much you know until they know how much you care.' This is true leadership. Of course, there are circumstances when this is not applicable. For instance, if you're in a war and you need to take a hill, that's a very finite objective. If you are in a business where everyone is focused on getting a certain product out to take advantage of a spectacular market opportunity, then for a brief period of time, there's not a lot of noise in the system. But in normal life, in normal organizations, over the long course of time, caring does matter. It matters a lot. A leader is accountable, and a leader serves. He serves a cause and serves the people. There is a fundamental difference to whether or not you see yourself as being in charge. But serving versus being in charge and having other people work for you is a fundamentally different texture of leadership."[289]

Bridge of Life—the DaVita Medical Missions™ program—was a non-profit founded by DaVita in July 2006. This program is on the order of the Village Service Days program, but instead of involving teammates doing good deeds in their local community, it extends beyond U.S. borders by providing dialysis to people in areas where treatment is not available. The program is one of Thiry's dreams to create a village without borders. Both home office teammates and field teammates volunteer their own time to build or upgrade dialysis facilities in mainly third-world countries. Although dialysis treatment is available for ESRD patients in the United States, there are many countries in the world that don't have a single dialysis machine. In such places, ESRD is a death sentence.

Ryan Rupp, a facility administrator in Columbus, Ohio, tells about a dialysis nurse who volunteered to participate in the Bridge for Life program in the Philippines.

"Our teammate Lee Lardizabal grew up in the Philippines and hadn't been back since coming to the states. So when he heard that the Bridge for Life program was opening a dialysis center there, he quickly signed up for it. Although the company contributes to the transportation and lodging costs, a teammate is responsible to pay part of his own way. This meant that Lee had to do some fund-raising in order to cover his expenses. The teammates here pitched in to help. The program requires Lee to use some of his vacation time, and he didn't have enough left to be gone for the full two weeks he'd be in the Philippines. Consequently, six teammates at our clinic donated sixty hours of their own vacation time so he could go. It was a team effort, and everyone, including our patients, [was] very proud of Lee's participation in Bridge for Life."[290]

Shortly after Bob Badal joined the company in 2006, he was having a casual conversation with Thiry about charitable organizations. He says, "I mentioned that I would like to get involved in supporting a charitable organization but didn't have anything particular in mind. At the time, Kent didn't make any recommendations. A couple months or so later, Kent talked to Wayne Trebbin, a nephrologist who headed the nephrology department at a hospital in Salem, Massachusetts. The doctor spoke about how he trained international medical school students. 'They constantly talked about how end-stage renal disease was a death sentence in West Africa. If people's kidneys failed, they died,' Dr.Trebbin told Kent. That was in 2006. Trebbin said that he had approached other dialysis companies to help find a way to get dialysis treatment to West Africa and was constantly told, 'Nice idea, but we are not interested.'

Kent told Trebbin, 'I have someone for you to talk to. That's Bob Badal. Call him.' I have no clinical background, and I'm not a physician. I've never set up a facility. So why Kent directed Dr. Trebbin to contact me, I had no idea. Trebbin called me, and we talked for about an hour. While he had limited background in project management, his passion for his mission was convincing, and I bonded with Dr. Trebbin quickly. Normally, my mind-set has always focused on the numbers, and if they don't work, forget it. But I was moved by what he had to say, and I wanted to do something that would make his dream come true. I knew that if I orchestrated it, I could bring in the right people to make it happen—folks that had more expertise than me—and two such people were here at DaVita. One was Doug Luehmann, a vice president of the company's biomedical operations, and the other was Bill Hughson, vice president of DaVita Rx. The three of us sat down and set up a plan and put together a budget. Dr. Trebbin helped us partner with a local hospital in Yaounde, Cameroon. The next step was to select the mission's participants and assemble supplies and equipment. Soon all the pieces fell together, and we were off and running."[291]

A lot of other DaVita people got involved, and in November 2006, the clinic dialyzed the first patient in West Africa. By January 2007, the center had the capacity to serve eight patients, dialyzing three days per week with sufficient supplies on hand. Today, the clinic has eight dialysis machines, and with two to three sessions a day, this translates into a lot of people with end-stage renal disease who are alive today and otherwise would have died.

As vice president of payor contracting, Badal's job is to negotiate with private insurance on fees due DaVita. His face lights up when he adds:

"I like being able to come into work every day and in effect be able to quantify my worth to the company. Either I did a good job by bringing in incremental revenue or I didn't. But when I'm retired and reminiscing about my career at DaVita, I know what I will be most proud of. It will be the role I played, as a part of a broader group, in helping people in West Africa to receive dialysis treatment. I owe this experience to both Kent and Dr. Trebbin."[292]

Bill Shannon points out that the community philosophy carries over to dialysis patients in the centers. "Teammates make a big fuss over celebrating birthdays and anniversaries of patients and teammates," he explains.

"I was at one the other day, and they were having a luau. They even got the ambulance drivers to come in and do a hula with them. They were all wearing grass skirts. We have some facilities that operate bingo games on Fridays. At other places, they play Jeopardy. Both patients and teammates participate. Some centers have gatherings a couple of times a year and invite patients to a local park just to hang out so they can enjoy one another's company away from the machine. We want our teammates and our patients to feel more like family, more like a community. We want fun to be part of the experience. It doesn't mean that we don't take our work very seriously. We don't do this at the expense of clinical care. We know that patients come in and don't feel well. They are full of toxins. They are bloated. They feel weak. They've got a lot of things going on, whether they are young or old, and they come in feeling that way every day. Our teammates literally have people's lives in their hands every single day, hooked up to that machine. It takes a remarkable person who is able to make his or her career in dialysis—a tremendous human being. Clinical care always comes first. Our caregivers know that. And we are proud of those accomplishments. We measure it relentlessly. But when you have a chance to infuse some fun into the atmosphere, we strongly encourage it."[293]

"Every summer, we have a picnic behind our building in our parking lot, where we set up tents and picnic tables," tells Ryan Rupp.

"We have kidney-friendly food that we barbeque. We also have a party at the end of the year at which we celebrate our successes, talk about how many treatments we did and how those treatments extended someone's life. We do 300 treatments a week, which is more than 15,000 a year. That's a lot of dialysis treatments, and we are quite proud of that accomplishment.

"Our sense of community carries goes beyond our teammates. It carries over to our patients and their spouses. For example, there was a group of five women that brought their husbands here three times a week for fours hours of dialysis treatment. Although they came from different backgrounds, they sat in the lobby together and shared a common interest. They bonded. They looked forward to seeing each other as if it was a social hour. They took turns going back and forth to the treatment floor to check on all of the husbands, making sure they were all well, and then came back to be with their friends.

"When one of our patients receives a kidney transplant and goes off dialysis, we are all very excited, and it gives us another reason to celebrate."[294]

During DaVita's nationwide meeting in Dallas, teammates built 350 bikes that went to area Boys & Girls Clubs. This began a chain reaction of building bikes and serving communities all over through Village Service Days. A group of DaVita teammates in Tennessee exemplified this chain reaction when they met in a high-school gym and assembled fifty children's bicycles. They had been told that the objective of the bicycle building was an exercise to develop their teamwork skills. Afterward, fifty children from low-income families were ushered into the gym. The teammates received the joy of seeing the happy face on each child who received a bicycle. Each child was also given a helmet and a backpack. One little girl asked if her new bicycle was her birthday present because it was her birthday. Her father hugged her and said, "It's a present from these good people. You should thank them and be grateful that you don't have to walk fifteen miles a day like I do back and forth to work." When the teammates learned that the man didn't have a car, they gave him an adult-sized bicycle.[295]

"We have several programs to help communities here and abroad," Thirty explains.

"When you create programs that get people to contribute to the community, it has a beautiful humanistic ripple effect on everybody. People want to work at a place where they can do good things to help others. If you believe in community, it would be philosophically inconsistent to say that you only believe in your community. That wouldn't make sense. If you care about one tree, you should care about the forest. Our programs are a way of saying, 'We only live in one tree, but we recognize that we can only prosper if the forest prospers. Therefore we must think about the entire forest.'"[296]

To help create a friendly and warm community environment, a "Wall of Fame" is prominently displayed in the reception area at all 1,500 company centers. Posted here are personal photographs of patients and teammates that depict them in their lives away from the clinic. The walls are also decorated with drawings made by patients, their children, and their grandchildren. "It's a fun way for people to get to know each other," Lynn McGowan says. "And to create some friendly competition, every year the company holds a village-wide contest, awarding those with the most decorative and original displays."[297]

Basak Ertan, once DaVita's Vice President of Marketing, is now VP of Revenue Management. A former Bain consultant, she started with the company in 2001 as manager of guest services. She explains:

"My first job here involved building relationships with our patients. I managed our insurance management team, which helped patients with customer service and insurance-related issues that they had. Our patients are with us three times a week for, on average, seven years. So we see them more often than when they visit a doctor's office once or twice a year. Over this period of time, they have many different questions, and because they can have Medicare coverage as well as commercial coverage through their employer, we want to help them get the best health-care benefits for all their chronic conditions. We have insurance counselors and social workers at the dialysis facility to help them."[298]

The guest services team also provides counseling to those patients who qualify for kidney transplants. Ertan says that there is a lot of information a patient needs to know about how to maintain his or her health prior the transplant as well as after receiving a transplant. It is estimated that about 5 percent of dialysis patients receive a transplant, and about 5 percent of dialysis patients regain use of a kidney.

"We also provide predialysis classes to people with chronic kidney disease who are diagnosed with stage 3 or 4," Ertan explains.

"When they are in stage 5, they go on dialysis. The education program can delay the onset, and when they do start dialysis, they begin as healthier patients. This program educates them on modality options or what therapy would work best for them. It also educates them on the importance of having a fistula placed before they start dialysis. We also invested in building a premier kidney disease website, DaVita.com, which has been recognized as the best disease-state website. Its content includes videos and articles ranging from diet information to describing what it's like to be a dialysis patient. We think this is a positive way to create awareness, not only about DaVita but the disease itself."[299]

DaVita's Community Care programs dedicated to DaVita's vision for social responsibility once fell under Ertan's jurisdiction. One of the Community Care programs is Shining Star Caregivers, a program in which patients give recognition to DaVita caregivers. Another is the Village Greeters program. Here teammates, family members, and patients are in the waiting rooms at clinics to welcome new patients. Ertan explains:

"There's nothing quite like a current patient telling a new patient what it's like to be on dialysis. It's good for a new patient's morale when he or she is greeted by a patient who's living an active life, because it demonstrates that being on dialysis doesn't mean a patient's life has to revolve around his or her kidney failure. Village Greeters provide a wonderful support structure for new dialysis patients, and it is part of the DaVita village concept where neighbors welcome new homeowners into the neighborhood."[300]

DaVita's village concept is present everywhere throughout the organization. You see it at every dialysis center as well as at the company's business office in El Segundo, which incidentally is called Casa DaVita, or Casa for short. Its business office in the Denver area is known as "The Lodge." The aisles in the building have street signs with names like "Be Our Guest" and "Acquisition Ave." Walls have murals depicting village scenes. The office people are casually dressed, and everyone is friendly; when they greet each other, they are just as apt to hug as shake hands. Unlike in typical Fortune 500 company headquarters, which are generally formal and sterile, a walk through the DaVita premises is like a stroll down Main Street at Disney—it's fun and gives you a cheerful feeling. Thiry's office has a sign in front that says "Mayor's House." When asked why "mayor" and not "CEO," he replies, "We like to think of ourselves as a village. And villages don't have CEOs, they have mayors."[301] Naturally, in a place where the top dog is the mayor, nobody is referred to as a "worker" or "employee" but instead as a "teammate" or "citizen." Consider, too, that as a teammate or citizen, a person shares more responsibility and takes more ownership in his community.

There are a lot of odd names for different departments, which is also unusual in a corporate setting. Human resources, for instance, is referred to as "people services." The legal department is known as the "justice league." And of course, how often do you come across a chief wisdom officer in corporate America? Or, for that matter, a senior executive called Yoda?

David Rosenbloom started dialysis treatment at age fifty-seven in 2002 and has since received a kidney transplant. During his treatment, he did limited traveling and dialyzed at different DaVita centers. "I've seen the village concept and how it works all over the country," he tells. "In the beginning, it seemed a little corny to me, but once you get into it, you can see how a lot of people get jazzed by it. I personally liked the way DaVita teammates took a personal interest in me. I knew that they truly cared about me."[302] Rosenbloom, who lives in Glendale, California, makes and designs custom furniture, which he does in his home. Throughout the period he was on dialysis, he remained active in his business, although he does admit there were times when he didn't have the energy to work full time.

"They say being on dialysis is 95 percent attitude, and I believe that if you have the right mental frame of mind, you will get through it. I say this assuming that you don't have a lot of other serious health problems, and of course, age is a factor that you can't get away from. I truly believe that the attitude by the DaVita people directly impacts the patient's attitude."[303]

ACQUIRING GAMBRO

In 1999, just before Thiry came aboard, there were rumors that the company would be purchased by Gambro. At the time, no one could have anticipated that five years later, in December 2004, DaVita would enter into a definitive agreement to purchase the U.S. renal care business of Gambro. After an impressive successful turnaround, the timing was right. DaVita's market capitalization had grown from $200 million to more than $5 billion; the company was positioned to make a $3.4 billion cash offer. Gambro was an early pioneer in the dialysis industry. It began mass production of single-use artificial kidneys and dialysis machines in 1967. Because of customary closing conditions, including Hart-Scott-Rodino antitrust clearance, it took nearly one year to finalize the deal, which closed on October 5, 2005.

The acquisition added 565 dialysis centers to DaVita's operations, giving it more than 1,200 clinics in forty-one states and the District of Columbia. With Gambro's 43,200 patients, DaVita's patient population jumped to 96,000, making it the industry leader. With 84,500 patients in the United States, German-based Fresenius Medical Care dropped to second place. The Gambro unit's revenues of $1.8 billion increased DaVita's $2.2 billion to $4 billion.

Although Gambro was a respected dialysis company, the doomsayers forecast that integrating the company into DaVita's strong, people-oriented culture was a certain recipe for calamity. Their reasoning was that Gambro's management style was bureaucratic and reserved; it was an inflexible European company that could not adapt to DaVita's upbeat, aggressive management style. The contrast between the two company cultures was reminiscent of that between General Motors and EDS when GM acquired EDS in 1984. The highly publicized collusion between EDS's founder, Ross Perot, and GM management epitomized the outcome when different company cultures clash. And like Perot, Thiry was viewed as a maverick. This opinion was held by many former DaVita teammates who had jumped ship upon Thiry's arrival and joined Gambro. These were the skeptics who never got past Thiry's rah-rah-rah antics. So even though on paper the acquisition seemed viable, DaVita could very well find itself in imminent peril of repeating the steps of Total Renal Care's acquisition frenzy, which came dangerously close to destroying the company.

Anthony Gabriel, who was in charge of the integration, explains:

"We have a reputation in our industry for having a strong culture. The Gambro people had the perception that when they came in, they were joining the DaVita cult. We kept hearing remarks from them about how everyone here was drinking the Kool-Aid. Stuff like that. Well, when that's how people think, it's natural they are apprehensive. They heard about the skits, the songs, and Kent in his musketeer uniform. It was so different from where they were coming from. Of course, we anticipated they would be skeptical. How well we remember about how some of us reacted with the same caution when Kent first came here."

"We were prepared for their reaction, and we talked very candidly with them about how we understood what they were experiencing by joining a new company. 'We think we have a very special company,' we told them. 'We think this is a really neat place, and we do a lot of good things, and we will tell you all about it. But for now, we don't expect any of you to just jump on board. It was that way when we were a new company and just starting. It took us a while to adjust. We encourage you to take as much time as you need to make a decision about whether or not this is the right place for you.' We were very open and positive."[304]

Lynn McGowan said that there was apprehension on both sides.

"We all worried, because we had positions, and they had the same positions, so we are thinking, 'Am I going to go, or is she going to go?' I think the merger was more grueling than anything we ever went through, and it was the culture differences that presented the most challenges. I remember the first time I went down to Gambro's former corporate office in Irvine. I wanted to let them know that somebody was reaching out. 'It's not really as crazy as you may have heard,' I said. They asked many questions about such things as about the skits, the cheers, and the village concept. It was all so foreign to them. Some of them were open, but there were others who were so skeptical. Some seemed resistant to any culture change, and it was very obvious that there were going to be radical changes.[305]

From a dialysis patient's point of view, David Rosenbloom says, "I was treated at a Gambro center, and after DaVita bought it, the improvement was like day and night. Gambro was primarily a Swedish manufacturer of dialysis machines and supplies. While my treatment at Gambro was adequate, they didn't do much in the way of patient information and patient spirit. Being in a dialysis clinic is depressing. You never really feel that good doing treatments three times a week. The sessions are long, and you're tired afterward. DaVita's whole team approach to your health with the doctor, technicians, nurses, dietitians, and psychologists all working together and constantly seeing you is great. They all dovetail each other. They are happy to oblige you on anything you want to know about your condition, how the machine works, and so on. The more I knew, the more I felt like I had some control over my kidney disease. I heard a lot of other patients comment on how much better they were treated by DaVita.

"It was an entirely different environment at Gambro. What bothered me was when I was going there three times a week and seeing a lot of the same patients but then someone died. 'Where's so-and-so,' I'd ask. 'Oh, he died over the weekend,' someone would say, and that was it. Nobody would talk about him. I felt, 'This is ridiculous. This person had a life.' Once I asked, 'Can't we somehow celebrate him? Can't we acknowledge him?' I was told, 'Oh, no, we don't do that.' It was entirely different at DaVita. They were open and discussed it with you. 'He was elderly and had a lot of problems,' they'd explain, or, 'He decided that he didn't want dialysis anymore.' The deceased's obituary would be posted on the wall, and perhaps a note from a family member expressing how much he or she appreciated the caring and kindness received at the center by its staff members."[306]

Gabriel explains that the company decided that the best way to make believers out of the nonbelievers was by being very open with them. "During the integration, our communications policy was critically important," he emphasizes.

"We determined that our policy would be no secrets, no surprises, and no hype. By following these tenets, we believed we could eventually establish credability. We were completely open with people about exactly what we were thinking, and they were immediately informed about it. We were so up front that sometimes we'd tell them that we didn't know what is going to happen. For instance, they might ask, 'Which department is going to go?' 'Will the company keep the finance office in Tacoma or Denver?'

"'Well, here's what we are thinking,' we'd say. 'We are looking at it. And we promise you in forty-five days from now, we are going to know the answer. And we promise you that when we do know the answer, this is how it will be: if anyone loses his job over this—if there is a layoff—we will spell out how we are going to take care of those people.' Everything we told them happened. Everything we said we were going to do we did. Over time, it was this credibility that helped to win people over. Again and again, we'd tell them, 'No brag, just facts.' We also made a 'We said, we did' logo that was posted everywhere.

"Yes, there were duplications, and yes, we had to do some layoffs. People understood that this is a big company, and we did a major merger. They understood, for example, that it didn't make any sense to have two accounting departments. We understood that this was an emotional thing. Nobody wants to have his job eliminated. But people can, if you explain it rationally, accept and understand that we don't need two of this function in the company. Each time we did a layoff, we would let everyone know in advance what to expect. We communicated to everyone—the people we had to let go and the people that would stay with us. The important thing was to treat everyone fairly. The people who were staying were watching to see how we treated the ones who were let go."[307]

To combat rumors spreading throughout the company, it published a biweekly newsletter, *The Integration Insider*, to keep everyone in the know. Gabriel explains:

"We decided to do the newsletter when we were doing some normal repair work at our Tacoma office building, and some of the employees saw construction equipment on the site. Thinking the worst, they assumed the building was being torn down. We struggled on how to communicate the right amount of information, and that's how the newsletter on integrating the two companies was started. Someone came up with the idea that it should contain a column, 'Ask Anthony,' which would be modeled like a 'Dear Abby' column. Being Anthony, I thought it was somewhat corny, but I went along with it because I was in charge of the integration process. It was a big hit, and I was bombarded with questions. I was always up front with my answers. If there wasn't a concrete answer, I'd write, 'At this time, we are not sure,' and I'd explain what we were to doing to have an answer. We always gave an honest answer, and the column was very popular. In a photo of me, I was dressed casually, wearing a golf shirt, and looked like a regular guy. My answers were written in a direct, friendly way. For instance, when a writer asked if we were closing Team Music City, the DaVita office in Brentwood, Tennessee, I replied, 'No. They are jackhammering out front of the building so they can fix the water line.' Later on, after the integration was over, we started a similar weekly newsletter that is sent to our teammates in the field. It's called *Questions from the Field*."[308]

Vlchek explains:

"We kept on hearing, 'This isn't going to work. We need to be super-conservative businesspeople.' There were those who scoffed at the village concept, the one-for-all-and-all-for-one philosophy, the skits, and the cheers, and they'd tell us: 'Deep down, you guys don't believe in all this crazy stuff. It's a tactic.'

"'It is not a tactic,' we insisted. 'This is what this company is. You can see what it was like here in 1999 before we changed the culture, and look at the results. We know that it works. As a business principle, we know that it works. It is not a tactic.'"[309]

Gabriel explains that the company had integration meetings for the new Gambro facility administrators and also invited small numbers of its seasoned DaVita teammates to be present.

"Our intent was to have a ratio of one DaVita teammate in attendance for every four former Gambro teammates, so the new people could ask questions to the ones who have been around for five or so years. They'd ask questions like, 'What's the deal with all this talk about a village?' and 'What's with the cheers?' We encouraged the new people from Gambro to talk to their peers. 'Don't listen to us,' we'd say. 'Talk to the people in the field and get honest answers from them.' We never coached anyone on what to say. We had enough faith in our people to let them say what they believed."[310]

Vlchek says,

"Gambro was the company that acquired Vivra Renal Care, where some of our people, including Kent and I, had worked. It is interesting how quickly they dismantled the culture and turned it into this staid Swedish culture. It caused a lot of the Vivra leaders to leave. But what Gambro did get were some very good people who were running their dialysis facilities. This small group at the operating level was receptive to the DaVita acquisition. Their reaction was, 'We are going home.' It was at the executive level where we ran into the most resistance."[311]

Thiry concurs:

"Most of the Gambro executives understandably started out strongly skeptical and/or negative. They were the ones who resisted the most and made comments like, 'They sing dumb songs, they do silly skits, and Thiry puts on costumes.' And some would say I was egomaniacal. But what worked for us in the integration were the nurses and technicians and facility administrators in the 565 former Gambro clinics. We kept putting those people together with our own DaVita veterans at local meetings. As it turned out, it didn't matter that much what I or our other executives would say, but it did matter what the new Gambro people heard from their DaVita peers that worked at our centers. On breaks at meetings, they'd mingle and ask, 'What's the deal here? Is this all a lot of bull, or is it for real? Do you like it here?' When they heard in a straightforward way that they ought to give it a chance because the company culture is a really good thing for them, they were willing to give it a try. Once they were open-minded about our core values and how this was a fulfilling and fun place to work, it made a lot of sense to them. When the former Gambro executives saw how the people in the field were buying in to the DaVita way, they started to think, 'Maybe this will actually work.' And, of course, some former Gambro executives emerged as early leaders even before their teams and helped bring other former Gambro folks along."[312]

"A lot of people say, 'Wow, you guys are lucky,'" Vlchek tells. "Yes we're probably lucky, but everything we've done is intentional. Absolutely intentional. Everything was well thought out with very little being left to chance."[313]

Dr. Allen Nissenson, chief medical officer, says, "Most kidney patients are on a multitude of drugs, and through our subsidiary, DaVita Rx, we have their filled prescriptions sent to the patient's dialysis facility. This way, we are on top of what medicines he's on and can ask questions such as, 'Are you having any problems?' 'Do you have any questions?' We work with our patients' physicians, and our nurses take the information on their chart. By making sure the patient's drugs are adjusted in real time and taken daily provides the quicker drugs benefit and in a more sustained way. We measure the patient's blood on a continuous basis, and we chart his progress from a clinical standpoint. It also reinforces why they should be taking those drugs, and as studies show, DaVita patients' compliance rates are among the highest in the industry. Although we are hailed an industry leader, we are constantly working on ways to improve our clinical numbers. We have numbers to prove that we can make a dialysis patient healthier and have a better quality of life when he or she is with DaVita. I don't think it's a stretch to say that if you are a DaVita patient, you are healthier."[314]

Nor is it a stretch to say that during the six-year period under Thiry's leadership, the company made impressive strides in its quest to be the industry leader in providing outstanding patient care. Documented yearly clinical outcomes on how DaVita stacked up against its competitors substantiated a track record that was "no brag, just facts." To the former Gambro people in the field, this was the most important criterion by which to judge the company's performance under the DaVita way. To these new teammates, patient results were the proof of the pudding that the new culture had merit.

COMPANY CHATTER

Let's go back to that first national conference when Thiry bombed with the "New, Ours, and Special" cheer. It works now because Thiry and other DaVita managers believed in it, and in time, others did, too. The cheer has since become a tradition when teammates assemble. It starts with a leader asking three questions: What is this company? Whose company is it? What could it be? They answer in unison to each question with a near-deafening shout: "New," "Ours," and "Special."

"It started at Kent's first national conference," Vlchek recalls.

"In his talk, he emphasized that the company was definitely new. Actually, we weren't new, because Total Renal Care was still the same company. But it was new in the sense that everything about it had changed. So when he asked them, 'What is this company?' they were prompted to respond, 'New.' We wanted them to know that we were changing everything and would no longer abide by the old Total Renal Care philosophy. Second, at the time, the company was literally owned by a consortium of banks, but we wanted our teammates to take ownership in the organization. With this in mind, we said that the company is under the control of teammates who work for it, and they have the opportunity to make the company what they want it to be. Kent used the analogy that the company was like a village in which its citizens pays taxes to the government, but the village belongs to the people who live there. In this respect, the teammates were the company custodians, or owners.

"Note that when we ask the third question, it is not, 'What *is* this company?' but rather, 'What could this company be?' This is to emphasize that we are always aspiring to be special, and although we may achieve great things, there is still more to strive for, because we are on a never-ending journey."[315]

It took a while, but in time, everyone could see that it truly wasn't the old company. It became evident that positive changes were being made, and the cheerleading began to generate positive responses. It has since become a company tradition, and when these three questions are asked, it is followed by a spontaneous, thunderous roar.

All of the clinical facilities in the United States are broken down into one of five operating teams: Dream Team, Team Galaxy, Team Fusion, Trailblazers, and Avanti. At many national conferences, each team does a five-minute skit. A vote is taken to declare the best skit. No awards are given. The competition promotes teamwork and fosters a sense of pride. A "We Are Here" cheer is a group chant and is yet another way to exhibit group pride. The members of each team sit together at company conferences. When a group leader stands onstage and calls, "Dream Team, are you here?" this induces Dream Team members to rise from their seats and bellow out, "We are here!" The cheer goes around the auditorium, with each team screaming out louder and louder as if they were in a shouting match. The significance of these cheers is not to indicate a physical presence but to voice a shared commitment. As Thiry often says in his speeches, "This is not a dress rehearsal; this is your life." He reminds his audiences that we only live once so we should make the most of it. This message is prominently displayed on his wall as a reminder to him as well.

In the beginning, categorically, there were many doubting Thomases. There were those who went as far as to make accusations that management was using brainwashing techniques. The agnostics scoffed and typically said, "I feel like I have to drink the Kool-Aid." They ridiculed the skits; they balked at the cheerleading. It took awhile, but in time, the nonbelievers started to become believers.

Guy Seay remembers his reaction at the first nationwide meeting.

"I was sitting there watching these senior executives in this skit, and there's the rest of us wearing these musketeer hats and waving these gimmicky swords doing this three musketeers' cheer. 'What's this all about?' I'm thinking. 'Is this just for the day, or was it something that we can expect all the time?'"

A Harvard Business School graduate, Seay was analytical. "I'm asking myself, 'Is there a functional value to it?'" he says.[316]

Bob Badal also recalls when he first joined DaVita. He says, "I had heard about the company culture during my job interviews, but I had no idea! It was only my second day on the job when I went to a DaVita Academy session. There were hundreds of DaVita teammates there; probably 90 percent were nurses, technicians, and clinicians. Most of them had been hired in the last twelve months. I walked in wearing a suit because I didn't know the protocol. Then here comes Kent Thiry, the company CEO, and he's dressed as a musketeer, running up and down the aisles. I literally put my hand over my eyes and shook my head. 'Oh my God, what have I done? I've made the worst career decision of my life!' I muttered, half out loud. I remember thinking, 'This is Disneyland. This isn't appropriate in work. I don't get it!'

"It took me a while to understand the power of DaVita's culture. And though Kent has made it his personal mission to lead by example in constantly feeding our corporate culture, it has a life of its own. It grows everyday, with the contributions of so many teammates.. It's about having a goal of trying to create an environment that makes teammates feel empowered and loved so that they can then take that on when they do their jobs. Kent constantly says, 'They [facility administrators] have the toughest job in the company because they unselfishly take care of others.' So if it takes someone to stand up in a uniform, if it takes someone to sing a song, if it takes someone to do something differently by getting a bit outside his comfort zone, and it makes folks happy and smile, and, in return, this is passed on to other teammates and those we serve, then it's a good thing."

Badal pauses and adds with a chuckle, "I wasn't there in the beginning, but I can only imagine when Kent was sitting there in a room brainstorming with Doug and Joe. Then someone says, 'I got an idea. Let's dress Kent up as one of the Three Musketeers, and we'll do some out of the norm themes at our nationwide meeting.' 'What about spin-offs of *Star Wars* or *Star Trek*?' one of them suggested. Then someone else says, 'How about if we have Kent ride a Brahma bull into a meeting?' Then, they're sitting there, high-fiving and saying, 'Yeah, let's do it.' It took a lot of courage.

It was hard on me at first. I didn't cross that bridge right away."[317]

It is a proverbial bridge to which Badal refers—one that is a DaVita ritual and has become what could be viewed by insiders as a rite of passage. It started when Thiry gave a state-of-the-company speech (now a State of the Village). At the end of his talk, he pointed to a picture of a bridge on a screen. "You have a choice now," he stated. "You can stand on this side of the bridge, and you can say, 'I think I want to wait and see how things are. I'm not ready to embrace this dream on what we can do.' Or you can choose to cross over the bridge."[318]

Thiry philosophizes:

"It is easy in life to fall into a pattern where you are not making clear decisions about how you should be spending your time and energy and what purposes you are serving or pursuing. People tend to fall into the muddle of the middle, and they behave in normal ways with normal intensity—that's a terrible concession to make. Getting back to that Buddhist quote, 'It is easy to be mindful and hard to remember to be mindful,' we try to evoke our teammates to say, 'I want to do something more than just be average. I want to be a part of something that is bigger than the average workplace. I want to be part of building a special place.' So we invite our people privately or publicly to ask themselves: 'Are you just persevering through another average day, or is there an attempt to help us build a special place?' And if they can say to themselves—it doesn't matter what they say to us—that they've crossed that conceptual bridge and their intention is to help build a special place, then that is a beautiful thing in and by itself. At DaVita, we call that crossing over the bridge, and you can always go back if you find out that the other side isn't attractive or other people are not authentic. When you cross that bridge, and you do it with others, it's a significant emotional and practical commitment that you've made to these human beings.

"When a DaVita teammate crosses over the bridge, it signifies that they have become a member of the village. Over the years, thousands and thousands of DaVita teammates have decided to cross the bridge, a beautiful example of striving to live a purposeful life."[319]

When statements are internally made about the company's achievements, a DaVita person will add, "No brag, just fact." It is said in a nonchalant way that it triggers a nod of approval. Or, if someone talking to a large gathering of DaVita teammates adds, after mentioning a significant recent happening, "No brag," the members of the audience will impulsively shout, "Just fact." Today, it has become a routine reaction, and DaVita teammates have fun with it. But at first, Thiry purposely did it when he was making claims about the company's advances in such areas of quality, service, and technology. He did it only after stating quantitative data and specific clinical outcome measures. It was his way of matter-of-factly telling everyone that progress was being made and the new team was living up to its word.

Vlchek says, "At the annual State of the Village, Kent would talk about what our last year's goals were, and then he'd say, 'Anybody can yap about all the great things they want to do. But in the end, unless you actually do it, what good is it if you just yap about it? I want to talk about what it is that we actually accomplished.' Then he'd review such issues as the banking troubles we had and the progress that we made during the past year."[320]

Like clockwork, Thiry and his team did what they said they'd do, and slowly they won the confidence of their teammates. Their actions set the pace and inspired others to follow suit. Those who did not perform were moved out, and new people were hired who could get stuff done, or "GSD." Being praised as a person who excels at GSD is highly esteemed at DaVita.

An axiom that Thiry often repeats is "Begin with the end in mind." He means that we must identify goals and pursue them without procrastination. The CEO says this a lot, and it's not lip service. He had a game plan in mind starting on day one, and others at all levels of the company were encouraged to follow his lead. Thiry is also fond of repeating the Buddhist quote "One cannot pour from an empty cup." He frequently uses this expression, because it reflects one of his basic philosophies about how we all are here for each other. He explains:

"We all must help other people stay in balance, and if you want to differentiate in a human work environment, you can't do it if people are running on empty. I am so intense about making this work for the 34,000 teammates and 119,000 patients and America's health-care system that I can't forget I have to make it work for my direct reports, too. I often underperform in this area, but I am getting better as I get older. The great thing is that because many parts of DaVita actually behave like healthy little villages, our executives can get their cups refilled by the village itself, even when their CEO messes up. When you experience what so many of our teammates do for each other and for their communities, you cannot help but be fulfilled and therefore refilled."[321]

As Thiry also likes to say, "DaVita does dialysis, but it is not about the dialysis. It is about life—for all of us."

One of Thiry's favorite quotes that he repeats often and has framed on his wall was said by Mahatma Gandhi: "Be the change you want to see in the world." These words need no explanation.

Certainly, all companies have buzzwords and acronyms that are unfamiliar to outsiders. And like DaVita, they have axioms and slogans, some that are original and others that are as old as the hills. Originality is not an issue. What does matter is that they are insightful and memorable. On this score, none is more meaningful than DaVita's "One for all and all for one" slogan. No matter that it was initially poorly received, the management team had the insight and gumption to stay with it.

STAYING FOCUSED

"The reason that the musketeer imagery is so powerful," Mello explains,

"is that the motto has become shorthand for so many of our values. It's integrity. It's doing what you say you are going to do. It's accountability. It's teamwork. All these things are embodied in 'One for all and all for one.' The skits are effective because they are not required, but they encourage people to engage in our mission and values. In an unconventional way, via the skits and cheers, we communicated what we stood for, and our teammates became comfortable with it. Later, we presented our mission statement: 'To be the provider, partner, and employer of choice.' Its conciseness is easy to remember. The same is true with the company's ongoing goal to be the greatest kidney care company the world has ever seen."[322]

Many companies are too windy in defining their missions, values, and long-term objectives. Although well-meaning, what they stand for becomes complicated and overstated. It gets watered down. As a consequence, their employees only have a vague familiarity with their company's mission statement, and, for the most part, they are unable to articulate its values. At DaVita, it's easy for teammates to commit the company's mission and values to memory. And to make sure everyone is mindful of them, they are everywhere—in signage at the dialysis centers and throughout the home office, on the company's website, in *DaVita Magazine*, and on walls in senior executives' offices. You'll also hear them repeated again and again at company gatherings.

The constant repetition is a positive reinforcement, because it keeps everyone focused on what the company stands for. Just the same, don't for a moment underestimate DaVita and be lulled into thinking that the company is propagandizing its people with catchy slogans and brainwashing techniques. No longer are the doubting Thomases making accusations about gullible teammates drinking too much of the Kool-Aid. Today, when guests in Thiry's office read the words on his wall, "Speak with your life, not just your words," they know that he speaks with his actions. Thiry has become the change he wants to see in the world. This philosophy permeates throughout the organization and to the patients in the dialysis centers.

The company's relentless pursuit of becoming the world's greatest kidney care company is an ongoing goal, one that has never been compromised, even during the leanest of times. Today, the company prospers, and although there are and always will be challenges, DaVita shows no signs of slacking on its commitment to its lofty mission. Its management continues to look for ways to support what it views as its most valuable asset—its tens of thousands of dedicated teammates who work every day as caregivers at the 1,500+ DaVita dialysis centers throughout the United States. Mello confirms this commitment: "DaVita's top leaders recognize that our teammates on the front line are the ones that provide patient care. With this in mind, our job is to support them in every way possible. Our company culture dictates that we are a community first and a company second. We are a community of caretakers."[323]

Mello explains that senior management puts the needs of the local organization before the needs of its corporate people.

"This is a different culture than what you'll find at other companies. We've created a great place for people to work, and that in turn spawns a great place for patients to receive care. It's interesting, because we keep getting better at what we do. As I have said, 'A culture begets itself.' If you look at our interviewing process, you'll see that it's focused on our mission and values. What's happened here is that our people hire other people who fit the culture."[324]

During the summer of 2007, DaVita scored a major coup when it named Nissenson as its chief medical officer. He finished his medical training in 1976, a time when dialysis was still in its infancy. Thirty-one years later, Nissenson retired from his position at the David Geffen School of Medicine at UCLA, where he was a professor of medicine, associate dean, and director of the dialysis program. One of the foremost nephrologists in the United States, Nissenson is a former president of the Renal Physicians Association and has published over 500 articles on nephrology, dialysis, and health-care delivery and policy. In his current position, Nissenson is responsible for clinical care, which includes monitoring the quality of patient treatment. He also worked closely with Davita Clinical Research®, based in Minneapolis, generating new research knowledge to improve the care of kidney patients. Finally, he served as chief medical officer for VillageHealth℠, an organization within DaVita that specializes in comprehensive care coordination and disease management for the most complex patients. Having a renowned leader in the field of nephrology as a DaVita teammate validates the company's commitment to excellence.

Vlchek, an ordained deacon, retired in 2006 to work in the Catholic Church. In June 2009, he rejoined the company on a part-time basis because, as he says, "I missed it too much." He's a regular speaker at DaVita University, and his message to his audience is part business and part spiritual. He explains:

"I was recently in Baltimore speaking to 600 teammates. I said, 'Do you realize what you do for a living? I want you to shut your eyes and think about it for a few seconds.'

"I let the thought sink in, and I said, 'What you do for a living is *you give life*.'

"Most of them worked in the dialysis centers, but there were others from the home office. 'You may be thinking about how you sit behind a desk in a business office and do billing. Well, you are supporting the people that take care of patients. But what about that person in the cube next to you? If you are not giving life to him, then you don't understand what this company is about. That's because this company is about giving life to one another.'

"I saw smiles appear on their faces, and I continued, 'I want you to turn to the person next to you and say, "Do you know what I do for a living? I give life."'

"'Now what do you do for a living?'

"'I give life!' they yelled out.

"'When you leave and if someone in a black business suit who's sitting next to you on the plane asks you what you do, tell him, "I give life." I promise that you will have a great conversation with that person. Because you are going to tell him about this company and what it really deep down is all about.'

"This is what we all do at DaVita. Our teammates in the clinics know every day that they are helping patients. And those of us far removed from the patient in all areas—in accounting, marketing, warehousing—all of us can also feel good about knowing that by doing our jobs well, the company will grow and help more patients have high-quality care.

"There are certain clinical measurements that keep track of company performances in our industry, and these reveal how DaVita constantly outperforms our competition. In most areas, we score higher than the other big dialysis companies, and most importantly, DaVita patients consistently have a lower mortality rate. We are in a space where a high percent of patients pass away every year, and with a company our size, it can be said that thousands of patients live longer as a result of our work. At the end of the day, our people feel good about working for a company that does this.

"Another thing about this company is that we believe everyone should do—and that is, no matter what your job is—you should give it everything you've got. That's what Kent does, that's what I do, and so do our other senior people. And that's what our teammates in the clinics do."

Vlchek pauses and concludes,

"The spirit of the company was in the dumpster when we first came here. Clinically, it wasn't bad, but it wasn't stellar. It was nothing to be embarrassed about but certainly not an industry leader. Kent and the rest of us said that if we weren't going to be the very best at clinical care, head and shoulders above everybody else, then we had no business being here.

"In the end, we are here to take care of other human beings. That's the central focus. As long as we're doing things the DaVita way, that's always going to be the central focus."[325]

David Steward is the founder and chairman of the board for World Wide Technology.

Doing Business by the Good Book

World Wide Technology, Inc. (WWT) was founded by David Steward in 1990 in St. Louis when he leveraged his life savings of $250,000 to fund it. The company struggled during its early years and has since prospered. Today, with annual revenues around $3 billion, WWT is the nation's largest company with majority African American ownership. WWT specializes in providing advanced technology solutions focused on unified communications security, wireless, and data center technologies. The company offers products from more than 3,000 manufacturers and has strategic partnerships in place with industry leaders including Cisco Systems, Dell, EMC, Hewlett-Packard, J.P. Morgan Chase, Sun Microsystems, and the U.S. Air Force. The company is a systems integrator that provides innovative technology and supply-chain solutions to the commercial, government, and telecom sectors. WWT serves large-enterprise customers with everything from network infrastructure and desktop deployments to the disposition of old products. WWT is one of the largest privately owned companies in the United States. The company operates more than 150,000 square feet of warehousing, distribution, and integration space in twenty facilities around the world. The company's first employee, Jim Kavanaugh, holds an equity position in the company and serves as its CEO.

&

HUMBLE BEGINNINGS

The story behind World Wide Technology's founder, David Steward, is a classic rags-to-riches story that can only happen in America. It begins in Clinton, Missouri, a rural town of about 6,000 people, 230 miles west of St. Louis. Dorothy and Harold Steward raised eight children on Harold's meager income as a mechanic, part-time janitor, night watchman, and trash collector. During the holidays, Harold moonlighted by working as a server for the town's more affluent families. He worked tirelessly to provide for his family, making sure his bills were always paid on time.

"We not only lived on the wrong side of the tracks," David says, "we lived only a stone's throw from the railroad tracks, causing our small-frame home to be in a perpetual state of vibration. My maternal grandparents lived next door to us."[326]

David's strong work ethic comes from his father, and emulating his father, as a boy, he mowed lawns, bucked bales of hay, and sold mail-order Christmas cards. "I saw at an early age what it takes to survive and provide for yourself and your family," he says.

"You take opportunity when opportunity is there. We were poor, but I personally never felt like we were. I do, however, remember a time when my father's shoes were falling apart, and he couldn't afford a new pair, so he wrapped electric tape around his shoes. But we never went to bed hungry, and there was always a roof over our heads. We had a six-acre plot of ground, and we raised a few cattle and hogs. My siblings and I shared the responsibility of taking care of our farm animals. Before leaving for school, my daily chores included milking the cows and making sure the hogs were slopped. I attended Franklin Elementary School on the other side of the tracks. I started first grade in 1957, which was the first year that African American students were permitted to attend the formerly segregated all-white school in Clinton. There were two African American girls in my class, and I was the only African American boy. There were a lot of people that didn't think I belonged there. There was talk about that the Ku Klux Klan was going to stop us. In anticipation, my father and some other black men went on patrol at the edge of town. To this day, I think about the courage those men had."[327]

Growing up in a small rural community in the 1960s, David vividly remembers segregation—separate schools, sitting in the for-colored balcony at the movie theater, separate public bathrooms for whites and blacks, being barred from the public swimming pool, not being allowed to eat at the for-whites-only Wiley's Restaurant, and so on. David's most hurtful experience as a youth was when he finished Cub Scouts, and Clinton's Troop 435, an all-white troop, refused to allow him to join. David recalls how he and his mother both cried that night. Shortly afterward, with some of his friends and their parents, they formed Troop 225, the first integrated troop in Clinton. David's older brothers and sisters attended an all-black school that had only two teachers who taught grades one through twelve. The school was in a dilapidated building, and its worn textbooks were hand-me-downs from the school attended by the white children. David, along with a female student, were the first two African Americans to go through the Clinton school system and graduate.

David says, "When I was a small boy, my mother cautioned me against becoming bitter and resentful. 'David, those feelings are self-destructive and a waste of time,' she said, always citing scripture to support her comment."[328]

Dorothy Steward constantly instructed her children, "You can do anything that you set your heart to. Someday, you will have all those nice things, too."[329]

"My mother always took us to church and made sure we attended Sunday school classes," David tells.

"She spent a lot of her time at that church, teaching classes, serving on committees, singing in the choir, and so on. It was a small, poor church that couldn't afford a minister. Traveling preachers on the circuit would periodically visit to preach the gospel. Church and family were the two focal points of my mother's life, and her values have strongly influenced my life. As a youth, I was blessed to be surrounded by loved ones—nurturing parents and grandparents who enriched my life with wholesome values. These hardworking, churchgoing folks showered me with love and were my introduction to the Word of God. Although they had few material possessions, they diligently taught me what really mattered. They did it by example—by the way they lived. Consequently, I feel as if I inherited considerable wealth from them."[330]

David tried out for his high-school football team as a freshman, but at 5'7" and only 125 pounds, he didn't make the squad. He switched over to basketball but was too skinny and didn't make the team until his junior year. He recalls:

"I was a C student, and I had such a bad speech impediment that I had to take special elocution classes. I was painfully shy and had little self-confidence. The only thing I had going for myself was my perseverance. Once my mind was made up, I had the tenacity of a pit bull.

"During my senior year, my coach told me, 'You're a decent high-school player, but you're too thin. Don't waste your time even thinking about college basketball. Those big college boys will eat you for lunch.' I thanked him for his advice, and in autumn 1969, I enrolled as a freshman at Central Missouri State, a co-ed school with 13,000 students, and I tried out for the basketball team. A Division II school, its schedule included nationally ranked nonconference Division I schools such as Illinois State and Texas Tech, so if I made varsity, I'd be playing big-time basketball. Amazingly, during my college years, my height shot up to 6'5", by far the tallest person in my family's history. My mother likes to say, 'David wanted to play basketball so badly that he *willed* himself to grow tall.' I was as skinny as a rail, but I was tall enough to play. I didn't make the team during my freshman year, but I attended every practice. I must have impressed the coaching staff with my grit and determination, because during my sophomore year, I was given an athletic scholarship. By my senior year, I had put on some weight, and with my stick-to-iveness, I became a fairly decent college player.

"Playing college basketball was a wonderful experience. We flew to some of our away games, and I got to fly on an airplane for the first time in my life. And as a team member, I sat down to my first meal in a restaurant."[331]

Upon his graduation in November 1973 with a B.S. degree in business administration and a minor in industrial organization, David set out to find a job. "With only average grades and being African American, companies didn't come knocking at my door with job offers," he tells.[332]

A few weeks later, David took a substitute teaching job with the St. Louis public schools. As a part-time teacher, he earned little pay, so for a while, he stayed with friends. Five months later, he was hired full time by the Boy Scouts of America. His scouting as a youth helped him secure the position. Although he enjoyed the work, the pay was meager, so he kept mailing résumés to potential employers. In mid-1974, he was hired by Wagner Electric as a supervisor in manufacturing. The job lasted about one year, and he was laid off; again he was back in the job market. David estimates that he sent out more than 400 résumés between the time he graduated and February 1976, when he was hired by the Missouri Pacific Railroad Company as a marketing and sales representative. He says:

"The company was committed to hiring African Americans, and I was one of the first ones hired. I had landed my dream job! The company put me through an extensive fifty-nine-week training program, and then I was set to go. I will always be grateful to the company for giving me an opportunity and investing so much in me.

"I was fortunate to have a wonderful mentor, George Craig, a company marketing vice president who was my biggest supporter. At the time, there were some people who thought that sending an African American sales rep to call on customers was a big mistake. Keep in mind that my territory covered southern Louisiana and southern Texas. Mr. Craig made sure nobody within the company tried to interfere."[333]

While he worked for the railroad, David and his family lived in New Orleans, Milwaukee, Houston, and Los Angeles. He explains, "I decided that moving from city to city was no way to raise a family. We moved back to my wife's hometown, St. Louis, and in 1979, I took a sales position as a senior account executive with Federal Express."[334] David is smart, hardworking, honest, and extremely likeable—he has all the natural attributes to excel as a salesperson, and he did. In 1984, he was named Federal Express's Salesman of the Year. Fred Smith, the company's founder and CEO, presented a trophy to David, announcing his induction into the Federal Express Hall of Fame. "The trophy was an ice bucket with my initials engraved on it," David recalls. "When I looked inside the bucket, I saw nothing. 'Is this what I want in life?' I thought to myself. A pat on the back, and "Atta boy, get back out there and go get 'em.'"[335]

For his outstanding sales performance, David also received a raise in his sales quota from 100 to 150 percent. He says, "I saw the carrot being put a little further out there, and I thought, I don't want to wake up when I'm seventy or eighty and wonder why I didn't do more. At the time, Thelma and I had two small children, a mortgage, and a small bank account. We were living from paycheck to paycheck with all the trappings of success that keep you locked into a job."[336]

Many people who knew how hard David worked at Federal Express, one of America's fastest-growing corporations, were surprised to see him abruptly resign. After all, he was on the fast track to receive a promotion into a senior management position. How could he walk away from that to start his own company?

Perhaps what, above all else, catapulted David to start a business was his burning desire to build a company based on biblical principles. He explains:

"I wanted to operate a company that would have a mission to serve its employees and its customers. I knew that if such a company did this, it would succeed. We are here to serve each other, and as it says in Mark 10:43-45, '. . . whoever wishes to become great among you must be your servant, and whoever wishes to be first among you must be slave of all. For the Son of Man came not to be served but to serve, and to give his life as a ransom for many.' As Jesus gives these instructions to his twelve disciples, my management philosophy is based on these words."[337]

David met with Leo Moore, a man who owned a consulting firm based in St. Joseph, Missouri, that did auditing and reviewing of freight bill charges for various carriers. Because of David's work in the transportation business, they knew of each other mainly by reputation. David says, "Leo was sixty-five and planning to retire, and with my Union Pacific background, I felt comfortable making him an offer for his business. He didn't have any other offers, so he agreed to sell his company to me for $100,000 with nothing down. I levered my assets so that I could pay him over time. This arrangement made it possible for the business to generate some cash flow. The company had a few customers, which were enough to keep it going. I left my $66,000-a-year job that had a car allowance, expense account, and generous fringe benefits. I said good-bye to my security blanket, one that comes with being employed by a Fortune 500 company."[338]

EARLY BUSINESS VENTURES

David had a burning desire to start his own business. "I dreamed about it for years," he tells.

"I didn't want to wake up one day when I was eighty-five or ninety years old and wonder why I didn't have the courage to step into the unknown. I wanted to someday be able to look back and think that what I did was worthwhile for my being here. This is the rent we pay for living on this earth. I also wanted to be the first member of my family to have ever operated a business. If I didn't succeed, I would still have the time to recover. I was determined to start my own company, and no matter how some of my friends and family members tried to talk me out of it, I didn't let their comments discourage me. One of the comments I kept hearing was, '*They* won't let you do that.' I kept thinking [about] who 'they' were. But when I thought about it, I realized this was a reference to slavery—a slave had to get permission from the master. This expression was from the South and passed down from one generation to the next. Even though sharecroppers were free, they also had to get permission from the landowner. This is a mind-set that I refused to accept. And hearing these comments made me all the more determined to start my own business. I wasn't about to allow an invisible person out there stop me from doing what I wanted to do.

"You have to look beyond your circumstances, and to me, this is what faith really is. As the Bible tells us, faith is the substance of things hoped for, the evidence of things not seen. It also says in the Bible, 'My people perish for the lack of vision.' If you can see through God's eyes what He has for you, it is always something wonderful, exceedingly above all that you can think, dream, or pray for. Of course, along with the faith it takes a lot of hard work. Naturally, there will be challenges and many distractions, and when you face them, you can't give in to a naysayer that keeps harping that you can't do it and are bound to fail. These are the times when you must remind yourself that there is a power that works deep inside you and that He is with you through all the challenges that you may be facing. This is when you must look at things differently, through another pair of eyes."[339]

David worked for ten years in corporate America before starting his own company. Making such a transition to the role of sole proprietor is always difficult. As David puts it, "Suddenly I was my own boss and no longer had a supervisor to go to to approve major decisions I made. And if my poor performance resulted in a financial loss, it was my money that was on the line. The umbilical cord was cut. I was on my own to either swim or sink."[340]

Another bold step David took was asking his wife to quit her nursing job so she could be a full-time mother to the couple's two small children. Thelma says, "Dave wanted me to devote my full time to the children so he could give his complete attention to the business. This is when I realized how much faith I had in God as well as in David. I didn't know anything about his new company. All I knew was that he was quitting his job, and we were giving up all of our health insurance coverage because we were on our own. I was 100 percent behind my husband.

"Another thing is that we believed that our business could serve as our ministry and allow us to do God's work. It was an opportunity to serve our employees, and they, in turn, serve our customers. I believed David would be a wonderful model on how one should conduct business, and his example would filter out to others all over the world."[341]

David says, "God blessed me with an exceptional life partner, my wife, Thelma, and her faith in the vision of God is a great source of motivation to me. She demonstrates her faith in God by believing in me. While she doesn't have a role in my business, from the very start, she knew it would succeed. I have an undying need to make a difference in other people's lives, and knowing Thelma recognizes this inspires me to succeed, because I don't want to disappoint her or our children, David and Kim. Nor do I want to disappoint our extended family—the men and women with whom I work."[342]

David changed the name of his newly purchased company, Leo Moore Company, to Transportation Business Specialists, a firm that would specialize in auditing shipping charges for companies to determine if they were overcharged for their shipping services by freight carriers. Most of the company's customers were freight companies that hauled liquid bulk products such as cotton seed oil, orange juice, animal seed, and linseed oil. David figured out a way to make tank truck carriers more efficient. Prior to his service, commercial and private fleets would make freight deliveries to a certain destination and then go back to their home base with an empty tank. As a broker, his company matched his clients with shippers, and as a result, their tanks were filled with bulk products on the return trip. As an incentive to induce the shipping company to use this service, it was charged a discounted rate. His customers enjoyed additional revenues for which David's firm received a fee.

In 1987, David took a different approach when he started a sister company, Transport Administrative Services (TAS), that specialized in auditing undercharges for railroad companies. Although there were companies that did auditing services for overcharges, David did his homework and determined that nobody was auditing what charges were due the railroads that weren't being collected. As he explains, "We were analyzing and reviewing freight bills because the railroads were undercharging themselves."[343]

George Craig, David's mentor from his Missouri Pacific days, was retired in 1987, but it didn't stop him from supporting his former protégé. Craig was well respected in the railroad industry, and he opened a lot of doors by vouching for David's integrity. "All Mr. Craig had to do," David says, "is say, 'David Steward is okay, and he's someone you can trust, and I feel he is an individual you can do business with.' He was so respected in the industry, and by giving me access to people with whom he had long-term relationships, I had instant rapport."[344]

His first customer, Union Pacific Railroad, turned over $15 billion of rate information for David's firm to audit three years' worth of freight bills for undercharges, a sizeable contract from a single client. To handle such a large amount of information, David built a local area network (LAN) system to link all of the railroad's operations. It was one of the largest in the St. Louis area. Considered state-of-the-art technology at the time, the LAN system was a group of personal computers that TAS linked together, as opposed to having a mainframe centrally managed on a huge database. At the time, LAN systems and PC-based systems had just been introduced.

David's company performed a major service for Union Pacific, a huge customer that was by far his biggest account. "We worked day and night to make sure we took very good care of the Union Pacific," David says.[345] The young entrepreneur reaped the rewards of success. Then, one day in 1989, David received a call from his contact at the railroad company.

David remembers:

"It was time to renew our contract, and our work with them had been a big success. Our services had saved the railroad millions of dollars, and their people had always said how much they valued what we did for them. In my mind, it was a routine phone call to discuss the terms of renewing our contract, which I assumed would be automatic.

"Out of the blue, I was told that the Union Pacific made a decision to drop us. 'We were completely satisfied with the work you did for us,' the man explained. 'You saved us a bundle, Dave.'

"I took a gasp to catch my breath and asked, 'Then why?'

"'I'll get right to the point,' he replied. 'We have no complaints, and in fact, you did the work so efficiently that we're now in a position to do it internally, so we're not going to renew your contract.'

"'I was so devastated that the only thing I could manage to say was, 'I'm thankful for the opportunity you gave us to do the work.'

"The Union Pacific account was 80 percent of our total revenues. How we will pay our bills, and how will we be able to keep people on our payroll?

"I needed some cheering up, so I called Thelma to talk, but I didn't have the heart to disappoint her with such horrific news. She could tell from the sound of my voice that something bad happened, so I confided in her. She didn't say anything. That night when I came home, she prepared one of my favorite meals—fried pork chops with mashed potatoes and gravy. Sitting with my family made me feel blessed, and after dinner Thelma said, 'Don't worry, honey, we'll find a way to make it work. I believe in you.' With all that warmth and love in our house, my business problems seemed trivial. I had my loving family, and that's what mattered most.

"Losing Union Pacific was a mammoth setback at the time but was actually a blessing in disguise. I had been setting up technology to support the railroad industry, and had the Union Pacific continued to do business with us, I would probably still be in that business, still auditing undercharges for railroad companies. But having lost my biggest account, I had no choice but to regroup and figure out where to go from there. I remembered what my mama taught me a long time ago: 'Dave, we serve a God that works in division and multiplication, not addition and subtraction. It's an awfully poor rat that only has one hole to go to.'"[346]

A PARTNERSHIP MADE IN HEAVEN

David's first company audited overcharges for railroad customers and later went into the more lucrative field of auditing the undercharges, a service that nobody else offered at the time. David explains the next direction his business took:

"When Union Pacific didn't renew our contract, I concluded that our core business should not be limited to the railroad industry. With my experience in linking Union Pacific's operations through a local network, I recognized the benefits of effectively integrating technology to solve business problems. If it had not been for the experience that I had with setting up technology to support the railroad industry, I would not have seen the opportunity in the IT arena. I was blessed with having a front-row seat in witnessing the coming of the technology revolution, and I wanted to be part of it.

"In July 1990, I invested $250,000, money I accumulated during the past seven years as a business owner, into a new venture, World Wide Technology, Inc. At the time, a quarter of a million dollars was an enormous amount of wealth to me—a sum much more than my family or any of my relatives had ever had. I could have played it safe. I was under forty; plus, with my business experience, I could have landed an executive position and not risk losing my life savings. Starting a business now meant risking everything that I had accumulated over a six-year period. In retrospect, back in 1984, had I failed, my losses would have been minimal. I could have simply closed the business or turned it over to Leo Moore and walked away. In 1990, I had something to lose."[347]

When World Wide Technology was first started, David had a partner who owned a minority interest in the business. David's game plan was that he would continue to run Transportation Business Specialists and Transport Administrative Services, both of which still had a handful of customers. In time, he would shut down both companies and work full time at WWT. Meanwhile, as the owner of the three companies, he would oversee each company. WWT was five miles down the road from his two other businesses.

Just weeks after WWT opened its doors, the first employee, Jim Kavanaugh, was hired. Jim was a sales manager with Future Electronics, a Montreal-based manufacturer and distributor of electronics components. At the time, there was no way for David to know the important role the twenty-eight-year-old Jim would play in the company's future, but as the two men have said many times since, their meeting was the beginning of a wonderful lifelong friendship and business association.

Jim came to WWT with an interesting background. He had attended St. Louis University in the early 1980s, where he was a soccer standout. In 1984, he was a member of the U.S. Olympic Soccer Team, and for eighteen months, he traveled around the world with the team. After returning home, he graduated from St. Louis University in 1986 with a marketing degree. He was the second player picked in the Major Indoor Soccer League's draft and penned a contract with the Los Angeles Lasers. Jim spent the next two years playing soccer with the Lasers and then was traded to the St. Louis Steamers. "The following year, the team went bankrupt," he tells, "and I debated on whether to play professional soccer for the next ten years and be in my thirties without any business experience, or should I leave sports and focus on a business career. I loved the game but didn't think it was going to take me where I needed to go."[348]

Jim was single at the time and was paid $35,000 to $40,000 a year, a pittance compared to players' salaries today. In the off-season, he was interviewed by Future Electronics and took the job, making the decision to pursue a business career. Jim's boss at Future Electronics introduced him to David. At the time, Jim and his boss had been talking about starting a business. David spoke about his two companies that he was in the process of closing down. The conversation also focused on company values. Jim listened intently and liked what David had to say about building a company based on strong principles. "I need someone who shares my values and has strong leadership skills to run WWT," David said.[349]

"I was impressed with Dave's vision of the company he wanted to build," Jim tells. "I liked him from the moment we met. His deep passion was evident, and he came across as knowledgeable in his field. He was also someone whom I felt could be trusted, so when he asked me to join WWT, I accepted his offer."[350]

In the early 1990s, it was unusual for a young white person to join an African American–owned company. When Jim was once asked whether he ever had second thoughts about joining WWT, he answered, "Not at all. I had the good fortune to travel around the world and play soccer with individuals from many different cultures. Consequently, I learned that the color of one's skin has no bearing on an individual's performance—on or off the field."[351]

David says that he was blessed to have people like Jim believe in him, especially when many people were predicting that it was only a matter of time before WWT would go belly-up.

Jim took a substantial pay cut, but he was willing to take a risk, knowing that if the company succeeded, he would fulfill his desire to be an entrepreneur. Because of his excellent track record at Future Electronics and his background as an Olympic athlete, headhunting firms courted him. "What could he possibly be thinking," they questioned, "that he would take a low-paying job with a hole-in-the-wall company?"

He didn't receive equity in the company, but he accepted the position on David's word that he could, based on his performance, receive ownership in the future. "I was more interested in the company's growth potential, so I was willing to earn less in the short term," Jim tells:

"There was nothing in writing, just a handshake. My future would depend on my productivity. This I believed was a fair arrangement. When I started in July 1990, I was the only person working for the company. The other owner didn't start full time for another six weeks. I brought three other individuals from Future Electronics with me, and at the time, Dave was spending the vast majority of his time with his other businesses. It meant that I had to run WWT on a day-to-day basis. It was just what I wanted, and even though it wasn't my own business, I had assurances from Dave that I could acquire ownership in the future. I wanted to be an entrepreneur, and although I technically wasn't an owner, I was taking a risk on a start-up company, and I worked as if it were my own business. Besides, I walked away from an executive position with an established company with $400 million in revenues. Talk about being a risk taker."[352]

When WWT was first started, David had a partner who owned a minority interest in the business. Before the summer ended, the other owner was working full time for WWT. Three months later, on a Friday afternoon, Jim called David and said they had to have a talk and that it was urgent. David came over immediately. When he got there, Jim started the conversation by saying, "Dave, we have a problem, and you have a decision to make. Either you terminate him [your partner], or I leave." Jim explained his reasons, detailing specific improprieties that didn't reflect his values and that he felt were cause to give David an ultimatum. Although neither of them will disclose what the other owner did (or refer to him by name), the following Monday, David met with his partner, confronting him with the wrongdoings that Jim had pointed out. The other owner had no choice but to leave the company.[353] The manner in which he handled the termination confirmed to Jim that Dave Steward was a man who would not compromise on matters of principle.

Jim says of the incident, "Needless to say, terminating an owner who is your boss is a challenging situation, but it had to be done. Dave and I were committed to building a company based on trust, and if a company's principle is not trustworthy, the very foundation of the company will not stand the test of time. Dave and I had a level of trust that only required a handshake. We said, 'Here's how we are going to operate. Here's how we are going to be compensated, and you will be paid the same way that I am paid.' We set up a performance-based model for each of us. We shook hands on it, and to this day we have honored our verbal agreement."[354]

"It was as simple as that," David confirms. "On a handshake we agreed that Jim would someday have ownership in the company. Having explicit trust in each other, Jim knew that I would give him what he was due, and I knew he would do whatever it took to continue earning it."

Jim says, "A company must have a foundation of trust. What I think destroys a company or causes one to deteriorate is when a leader starts to have selective memories and stops living up to the things he originally agreed upon. You see that a lot. Oftentimes success changes people. When some people come into money, they lose their humility. Dave has never deviated from his beliefs. He's the same today as when I first met him—he has not been spoiled by success. With Dave, what you see is what you get."[355]

Jim was named WWT president and ran the day-to-day operations. He brought to the table an expertise in electronics, distribution, software development, and component manufacturing—he had a lot of raw talent for a man who had not yet turned thirty. His strong suit was that he was a team player, a carryover from his soccer experience.

WWT: THE EARLY YEARS

The company first sold computer products, mainly Hewlett-Packard copiers and modems made by Hayes Microcomputer Products. Hayes, a Georgia-based company, was founded in the late 1970s and shut down in the late 1990s. The first WWT customer was AT&T. "A man who helped us set up our Transport Administrative Services network had a contact at AT&T and made the introduction for me," David explains. "AT&T liked what we had done and felt comfortable with my reputation, and consequently, we opened our first account with them."[356]

WWT was incorporated on July 23, 1990, and its revenues through the end of the calendar year were $812,000. David says, "It was enough money to cover our cash flow, but this is a capital-intensive business and requires large investments of money well in advance of any chance for profit. It's the nature of the technology industry that we are in a high-risk business. Then, too, with continual technology changes, equipment and software can quickly become obsolete, and the window of opportunity for a company to get an adequate return on its investment can be limited. I credit my mother for instilling in me the belief that I could succeed if I tried hard enough and refused to give in to failure. 'You have to take that leap of faith, David,' I can still hear her telling me. I've been blessed to have a supportive spouse who has faith that God is working his vision through me. True, there will be setbacks along the way—if not, it wouldn't be called risk taking. Risk takers encounter setbacks along the way but don't allow themselves to be defeated. Instead, they learn from their mistakes and grow stronger, never doubting they will eventually succeed."[357]

Jim calls David the "consummate risk taker." With David's sales and marketing background, his approach to business differs from his partner's. An operations executive, Jim is a disciplined manager with a financial perspective. At 6'5", the athletically built David has a commanding appearance coupled with a dynamic personality. More than a half-foot shorter, Jim is youthful and trim. He is soft-spoken and more reserved. Although different in appearance, both men are full of energy and likeable.

David explains their differences:

"There are areas where he is strong and I am weak, and vice versa. This works in our favor because we complement each other. Do our differences sometimes result in confrontation? Definitely. At the same time, they provide a healthy balance that makes us an effective team. Jim has never been shy about expressing his views, and when he disagrees with me, he is quick to challenge me. I know he does it with the company's best interest in mind, and I welcome it."[358]

Some WWT employees say that David is "Mr. Outside," and Jim is "Mr. Inside." David spends 50 percent of his time on the road, calling on customers, always building relationships. As Jim points out, "It is fortunate that we have different personalities as well as a different set of skills. If we both liked doing the same thing, we would probably be getting in each other's way."[359] When either speaks about the other, it is with admiration and affection.

In 1991, the company's first full year in business, sales increased to $3 million. This is the year the company revised its business plan to focus on doing business with the federal government. "What got our attention was hearing that the federal government was spending $25 billion a year on technology," David says.

"Getting started with the federal government required a lot of time and energy because we had to learn the ropes, build relationships, develop political contacts, learn the government acronyms, its culture, and so on. A lot of companies aren't willing to take the time to do their homework. They don't because they become overwhelmed with all the forms that must be completed, plus the enormous amount of rules and regulations that must be followed. Getting a clear understanding of the government's contracting process is a long, drawn-out event. We had to adjust our *modus operandi* to comply with government procedures. We knew going in that if we wanted this business, this was a requirement. Then, once you get the business, you must anticipate that the government is always making changes, and you must be willing to make changes to accommodate it. To be in compliance, a government contractor must constantly adapt. We figured that the potential for high-volume business makes it worthwhile.

Many companies view all the changing rules and regulations as too restrictive and won't compete on government contracts."[360]

David gives a lot of credit to Maureen Brinkley, who worked out of the Small Business Administration's St. Louis office, for helping WWT receive its initial government contracts. David explains:

"The federal government was seeking out small business contractors, and Maureen approached us to see if we, as a small, minority-owned company, would be interested in applying our technology to the federal government. Maureen and her team were absolutely fabulous to work with. They were not the stereotyped government bureaucrats that you hear about who bog things down. They were real professionals, and although they lived by the letter of the law, they were tremendously helpful in guiding us through what is an arduous process.

"At the time, there were few people in the Midwest that were doing government business on a large scale, and the doomsayers kept warning us to stay out of it. The people in my local community tried to convince me that an African American in the Midwest didn't belong in the technology industry. I listened, but didn't heed their comments. As far as I was concerned, the color of my skin or where I lived hardly qualified as valid reasons to stay out of this industry. I recalled a passage from the Bible where Jesus said, 'No prophet is accepted in the prophet's hometown.' It was as if he had said those words directly to me."[361]

In 1992, sales rose to $8 million; however, David continued to reinvest in technology to operate the business, and the company struggled with cash flow problems. Jim had enough faith in the company to invite his best friend, Joe Koenig, to join WWT. The two had been college roommates at St. Louis University and teammates on the school's soccer team. Each is the godfather to the other's son. They often get together for dinner with each other's family. For six years prior to joining WWT, Joe was with Computer Sciences Corporation and held various positions in sales, marketing, and project management.

Joe explains:

"In late 1992, WWT had landed a big Army contract. Jim and I would get together on weekends, and I always asked about how his new company was doing.

I remember one time he said, 'I would love to bring you over and get you in sales, Joe. I think it would be a good move for you as well as the organization.'

"Jim knew I was on the road Sunday through Friday, and I was planning on getting married. He knew that I wasn't happy about all the traveling my job demanded. However, anytime I'd push him, he'd say, 'I wouldn't ask you to leave yet because it's not the right time.'

"'Okay, Jim, just let me know when you think the time is right.' I'd answer.

"In late 1992, Jim thought the time was right for me to join WWT. I didn't actually start until June 1993. My wife and I had just married and were moving into a new house. We were getting ready to start our family, but because I had so much faith in Jim, I quit my job to work here at a much-reduced paycheck. Sure, I was taking a risk, but I was getting in on the ground floor with a company that I believed had a great future."[362]

At about the same time Joe started, David was winding up his work with Transport Administrative Services and putting in a full day with WWT. In the previous twelve months, sales had risen from $3 million to $8 million, and it appeared as though the company was on the fast track. Then the bottom fell out. A major personal computer deal that the company had won in 1992 was not renewed by the Army Automotive Command. The reason: the company was twelve minutes late in submitting the recompete bid. As Joe explains, "With a government recompete bid, when you're late, you're late. This was Jim's account, and it amounted to nearly 80 percent of the company's revenues. Losing this account meant that the company had to reduce its workforce, and it fell from twenty employees to ten. My timing for joining the company couldn't have been worse. Just the same, I had resigned from Computer Sciences, and I was beyond the point of no return. Although the company struggled, each of us was determined to make a go of it."[363]

Right from the start, WWT focused on big customers—Fortune 500 companies, the government, and large institutions. David's mind-set was to sell a big-ticket item to big customers. He enjoyed the challenges of solving problems for big companies, and he never shied away from thinking big when it came to prospective customers. The obvious upside to this approach is that when a sale is made, it is a big sale. The downside is that it generally takes a lot of time to open accounts with such customers because of the time required to make a major decision. In addition, the bidding process with the competition can be fierce, and it, too, is time consuming. Another disadvantage that makes it a high-risk business is the up-front money, time, and effort generally required to invest in engineering, designing, and other resources. And as a start-up company, WWT invested heavily in recruiting and developing people.

A cure to the company's poor cash flow was to open new accounts. But the situation presented a catch-22 because of the high costs associated with putting new business on the books and the long waiting period before a new account generated a profit. Paraphrasing the Bible, David says, "We knew that we would reap what we would sow. With this in mind, we were willing to make less money in order to have highly qualified people. Plus, we believed that if we put our time, effort, and energy into nurturing and developing our clients, it would pay off in the long run."[364]

It is these early struggles that cause most start-ups to throw in the towel. These are the times that test an entrepreneur's mettle—when the weak fall by the wayside and the strong prevail. During the most difficult periods, WWT had so little cash in the bank that it had difficulty paying employees their salaries. But, David says, "No matter how tough times were, everyone received his or her paycheck, with one exception when Jim received his paycheck a week late.

"However, there were many times when I personally didn't have the money in the checking account to pay myself. Like everybody, Thelma and I had our personal bills to pay, and sometimes there was nothing we could do to stop them from accumulating. Believe me, it's not fun to come home and have to tell your spouse that there wasn't enough money left in the till to cut a check for the family. In

1993, we were $3.5 million in debt, and with a wife and two children to support, I was under constant pressure. It's not a pretty situation when bankers try to shut you down, monitoring your every move with your suppliers. When I think about it, I can still feel a pit in my stomach like I'd get when bill collectors hounded me, making accusations that I was a deadbeat. Overly aggressive creditors made house calls and pounded on our front door. Thelma made sure outside pressures didn't follow me home at the end of the day. She saw my anxiety, frustrations, and sometimes sheer exhaustion. She made sure our home was a sanctuary, a retreat where I could reenergize and find peace with God. When bill collectors made calls to our house, demanding money that both the business and I owed, Thelma screened those calls, making sure I wasn't hassled by their threats and insults. She understood what I was going through at the office and that I didn't need to be coerced at home.

"When friends and acquaintances were aware of our troubles, they'd say to Thelma, 'Well, you guys must like living on the edge.' Another thing she'd hear was, 'Oh, you can do bad by yourself.' This is a rural Midwestern women-to-women [colloquialism] that's said when a husband is going through hard times. It's like saying, 'Why are you wasting your time with that man? He will never amount to anything.' Thelma and I quickly learned to discard conventional wisdom, knowing that what the world thinks is wise God thinks is foolish.

"Despite the name-calling by bill collectors and what people said to her, she never lost faith in me. Thelma has always believed in me and knew that I would always do the right thing. She never doubted my vision for the company would come to fruition. 'I don't know much about your business,' she'd say, 'but I do know you, David, and I know God works within you.' Thelma's faith in God is strong; she knows that He will always provide for her and our children through me."[365]

Those close to David marvel at his glass-is-half-full attitude. He believes that the tough times are one way that God prepares us for the next level. "Think about the process it takes to become a butterfly," he says.

"When it is ready to come out of the cocoon, it has to struggle until it can break out. An observer might want to help free the butterfly, not realizing that what seems like struggle is really nature's way of building up the wing strength the butterfly will need. If you cut the process short, then the butterfly will not be able to fly. No matter what one's calling in life, you cannot have a testimony with a testing."[366]

Employees knew the company was struggling to keep its head above water, and some left to seek employment elsewhere. Jim was privy to the company's dire financial predicament, and like David, he had faith the company would succeed. When a bank employee was dispatched to WWT to help run the business, Jim understood that the bank representative was a turnaround specialist and that the purpose of his being there was to protect the bank's interests by finding ways to extract money from the company and reduce its debt.

David says, "During this trying period, Jim received a job offer that would increase his annual salary by more than 25 percent. Still he stayed. Jim didn't leave because he and I shared a vision of what our company would someday be. When he stood by my side, it reinforced a message to employees and vendors that there was no need to panic—the company would survive."[367]

Jim explains that poor financial discipline and structure attributed to the company's problems in financing products. He demonstrated his commitment to the company when he once took $15,000 from his personal savings to pay for a product so WWT could deliver it to a customer. "I always felt extremely confident in what we were building," he says, "and I didn't want to see the company go down the tube."[368]

The darkest hour occurred in 1993 when David was conducting a meeting and a collection company repossessed his car from the WWT parking lot. A tow truck arrived just before noon and was in full view from the conference room's window. Other employees were leaving the building for their lunch break as the tow chain was being attached to the car. David explains:

"Everyone knew we were going through rough times, but taking my car drew attention to the deep hole we were in. A man's car is his alter ego, and no matter how bad things get, he makes his car payments. In sales, you can't call on customers without your car. Although I was humiliated, knowing that how I reacted would affect employee morale, I didn't dare show my emotions. This was not the time to panic, I thought to myself. So what did I do? I calmly said, 'Oh, they're taking my car, and my briefcase is in it. Please excuse me. I'll be right back.' With that, I calmly walked to the tow truck operator to tell him that I had to retrieve my briefcase in the backseat. Then I returned to the meeting and said with all the confidence I could muster up, 'Okay, now where were we?'

It was embarrassing to have everyone know that my car was being repossessed, and it would have been easy to give up. But I had faith in what we were doing. I'm a believer in the unseen, not the seen. I didn't see this company as what it was. I saw it as what it would be."[369]

Joe had just started to work at WWT and was present at the meeting. "Being the new kid on the block," he recalls, "I should have been wondering, 'What did I get myself into?' But Dave handled it so nonchalantly, I just thought, 'Well, sometimes you get knocked down, so you just get back on the bike and keep riding.'"[370]

Jim says matter-of-factly,

"The way I looked at it, sometimes unfortunate things happen. There are a lot of things that go wrong in business, and having your car repossessed is by no means the worst thing that can happen. The next morning, Dave drove his wife's car to work and used it for the next two years until he felt comfortable being a two-car family. There is no question that we were struggling to keep our heads above water, and I'd say that the odds were better that we'd go belly-up versus staying in business. In retrospect, we learned a good lesson because we became more disciplined in our financial management, an area where we had been lax. We decided to take a more team-oriented approach to developing the company, and subsequently, we opened the company's balance sheet to the key management team to show where we were and where we were going.

"At this early stage of our company, Dave and I started to talk about focusing on our company culture and how it would influence our future success. Dave emphasized how he wanted to build the company on the biblical premise of serving people. He stressed that our job as the company's leaders was to serve our employees, and if we did this, and in turn they served our customers, we'd be successful. Although I am not a student of the Bible anywhere to the extent that Dave is, I shared his philosophy that we should always treat people with respect and be focused on doing what's in their best interest. I believed that if we did what was right for them, they'd do the same for our customers, our vendors, our partners, and everyone that we interacted with. We both agreed that this was the right way to build our business. We concluded that the trick would be to have our people behave this way when nobody is watching them. If they only do it because they are being measured and held accountable, then they were the wrong people. We wanted to build with people who treat others this way because it's who they are and it's the culture of our organization."[371]

In 1993, the company's sales increased from $8 million to $9 million, and in 1994, they jumped to $17 million. Meanwhile, Jim recruited more of his soccer teammates, including Tom Strunk, who signed on as the company's vice president of finance. A certified public accountant, Strunk had formerly worked as a controller for a privately held construction company. Two years later, Bill McKeon, who as a junior was the captain of the soccer team during Jim's freshman year, joined the company. Today, McKeon is vice president of Federal Sales, a division that serves all accounts with the federal government. "I wanted to build a team with people I could trust and who I knew would share our core values," says Jim.

The foundation of the company's core values is trust, and it starts at the top of the organization. David and Jim trust each other explicitly. Jim emphasizes, "What Dave says he will do and what I say I will do is what we will do. It starts with the two of us, and our management team emulates what Dave and I do, and it trickles on down. If this trust isn't there at the top, you won't find it anywhere. Strong management knows that it must walk the talk. People will judge you by your actions."[372]

David stresses, "From the start, I told our people that we would always strive for excellence. This message was routinely repeated, and in time, everyone knew our mission. It is my opinion that employees want to believe in their management. They want to believe that it will stand behind what it says. It goes beyond the spoken word. When we talk about excellence and quality, there will be no compromises. Never. Only one standard is acceptable, and it can never waver. There will always be a temptation to relax one's standard for the sake of convenience. For instance, a time may come when an order must be shipped to satisfy a customer, and someone will say, 'Okay, let's push it out the door this one time. It's no big deal if it's not up to our standard work. It's a rush order, and chances are it wouldn't even be noticed.' The customer might not know the difference, but your people will. Once they realize you have more than one standard, they'll think striving for excellence depends on management's mood at any given time. It may not seem like much, but something has been lost. Your people will think that quality is not as important as they had been led to believe. They get confused, and now your goal about excellence was just plain talk. You've lost their trust.

"Another thing: people want to believe in their management, and they will as long as management never compromises its integrity. A company reflects who you are as a leader. By our words and our actions, it reflects on how we are serving our customers and one another within the organization. My commitment is to serve the people in our organization and to serve them well. To paraphrase the Scriptures, seek first the kingdom of God and His righteousness, and everything else will be added unto you. First, you must do what is right by your people, which includes your time, effort, energy, and resources. And you will begin to see everything else to be added unto you because you are sowing the seed of service, commitment, and investment in them. In time, they will begin to replicate within the ranks of the organization by serving one another better and first. They do this by getting outside themselves. Then they begin to permeate out, and they begin to service their customers and suppliers as well. In this respect, the company is our ministry relative to how we begin to get outside ourselves to serve by serving and supporting one another first. My most important job as CEO is to serve others. If I do this, then, like a pebble cast into a lake, its ripples eventually reach the shore."[373]

A DO-WHATEVER-IT-TAKES MIND-SET

In 1993, WWT had made a big PC sale to the U.S. Army Corps of Engineers based in Omaha. It was a $4 million contract, which represented half of the previous year's sales. Joe explains:

"Back then, we had to find new business from one month to the next to keep our head above water. Jim and I wanted to make sure everything went smoothly with this first big government contract, so we decided that we would personally deliver the merchandise to the Army Corps of Engineers base located in Omaha. We rented a large truck that could do about 50 miles an hour, so the 350-mile trip would take us 7 hours. Jim and I met at the office on a Saturday morning, integrated these PCs, boxed them, loaded them on forklifts, and put them on the truck. On Sunday afternoon, we were on our way to Omaha. We shared a cheap motel room outside of Omaha and took turns sleeping while the other one kept an eye on the truck, making sure all those PCs were safe. The next morning, on our way to the warehouse, we drove past a flashing sign on the road.

"Jim was driving and asked, 'Joe, did you catch what that sign said?'

"'Don't know. I wasn't paying attention.'

"We rounded a curve in the road, and I shouted, 'That sign said low bridge!'

"Jim slammed on the brakes, stopping just a foot from the bridge. We wouldn't have cleared it. We both let out a loud sigh. The PCs weren't insured. 'Close one,' Jim said.

"He backed up the truck, and we took another road to the warehouse. Dressed in sweatshirts and jeans, we pulled up next to the loading dock and started unloading the truck. 'Why are you guys doing this?' one of them asked. We found out that drivers don't normally help them unload. After the PCs were on the dock, Jim and I climbed into the back of the truck and changed into dark business suits. When we got out of the truck, the workers are like, 'Who are you guys?'

"We drove away in our suits, dropped off the truck at an Enterprise Rent-A-Car, and we headed to another location for a meeting with some Army officers. The first thing one of them asked was, 'Are you the two guys who unloaded the PCs and changed into business suits?'

"'Yes, that was us.'

"'Yeah, the guys called and told us what you did.'

"'We wanted to make sure the PCs were there and everything worked out,' Jim answered.

"From that day on, the Army Corps of Engineers has been one of our best advocates, and they still tell that story about the two guys who drove the truck and changed clothes afterward. That's what we did. Whatever it took, we'd do it. Later, when we'd bid on contracts, we used them as a reference, and they gave us raving reviews. They helped us win additional government business. Back then, that $4 million order was huge to us, and it kept us in the game."[374]

Joe smiles, recalling memories of the early days when WWT was fighting an uphill battle to survive. He says,

"Back in those days, we didn't have money to travel by plane. I remember going with Dave on a business trip by car and driving from St. Louis to Kansas City to Omaha to Des Moines and back to St. Louis, putting on over 1,500 miles in a single week. It was just boom, boom, boom, making calls on customers. To keep expenses down, whenever Jim and I traveled, we'd share a room. One time when we drove from Washington to Norfolk, it was near midnight when we arrived at the hotel. We went to the front desk to register.

"The desk clerk said, 'We don't have any rooms left except for a king room.'

"'That's fine,' Jim said.

"'You don't understand. It has just one king bed,' the clerk said.

"'No problem,' I told the clerk. He gave us a strange look when he handed the key to me. Being old college roommates, it was not a big deal. We were beat and just wanted to crash for the night.

"Another time, there was a Marine Corps contract we were trying to win and were scheduled to meet with a major at the Marines Corps base in Quantico, Virginia. The account belonged to our WWT sales rep, and he wanted us to make the call with him. Jim and I got there the night before, and we reviewed the proposal during dinner. It was our first chance to see what our rep and some of our other people had put together. After the waiter took our orders, we started reading it.

"'What do you think?' Jim asked.

"'There's no way we can present this to them.'

"'We've got to come up with something a lot better than this, or we're not going to get the job,' Jim said.

"We quickly ate our dinner, paid the check, and with our laptops, headed to a nearby Kinko's. With our account rep, we spent the rest of the night revising the proposal. We put together a hard copy of the document, and at 6:30 A.M., we went to our hotel, showered, and dressed. Our rep picked us up and drove to the base. The rep acknowledged that the new version of the proposal was a vast improvement.

"We met with the major and some of his people at the base. Jim and I made the presentation. Looking back, we can now laugh, but our sales rep was sitting in the back, and he had actually dozed off. The major was not really happy with him, but he really liked our presentation. 'This is good material,' he kept saying.

"After we finished our pitch, the major said, 'Man, this is good. Did you two guys put this together?'

"'Yes sir,' Jim said. 'Joe and I did it last night.' We explained how we were not satisfied with the original proposal and told him about the all-nighter we pulled to get it right for the meeting.

"'Oh, that's great,' he grinned. 'I appreciate that kind of effort. I am going to make sure you guys get this business. But I don't want to ever see that guy in here again,' he said, pointing to our half-asleep sales rep.

"We ended up with a contract from the Marines."[375]

"At the time, we were treading on thin ice," Jim says, "and we needed that BOA to keep us going. The major was very appreciative that we went that extra mile. He thought what we did was in the true spirit of the Marines."[376]

In the autumn of 1991, David attended a luncheon for Black Republican leaders in Washington, D.C., where Jack Kemp was the feature speaker. While at the nation's capitol, he planned to visit the Small Business Administration. He recalls:

"I checked my coat with two satchels of all my papers that I brought with me. I was seated next to Deborah Diggs, who by coincidence worked at the SBA. When I told her that I was going to visit the SBA, she said, 'Come back after this is over, and I'll introduce you to my boss.' She introduced me to Frank Ramos, who had worked most of most of his career with the government and then at the Department of Defense and the Small Business Administration.

"I told Ramos what we were doing and the rejection we had received with the SBA at the regional level. 'Let me check it out, and I'll see what I can do on it,' he said. Frank was instrumental in helping us get through the process successfully.

Ramos has since retired, but during his time with the government, he saw many companies submit bids for contracts. When asked about his impression of Dave Steward, he says, "I've witnessed a lot of minority-owned companies come to Washington and try to use their minority status to get the business rather than saying, 'Look at my capabilities and see what I can do.' I've dealt with these contractors, and that won't cut it with the government. I'm a minority myself, so I'm not knocking anyone because he or she is an 8A, which is what the SBA certifies as a small, disadvantaged business. But I've seen so many people come in here and say, 'Here I am. What are you going to do for me?' They want a free ride, and then they jump all over you for it. That's not the way it works. This is what sets a person like Dave Steward apart from the others. When he came to the SBA, Steward sought the business based on his capabilities rather than his minority status.

"Over the years, I witnessed so many of them come in, hand in glove, and say, 'I need your help.' And I say, 'What do you do?' They answer, 'I'm a systems engineer.' 'Well, so what? There are thousands of them here,' I'd tell them. I never meant to be condescending to anyone. But I remember how impressed I was when guys like Dave Steward came in and said, 'I'm a systems engineer, and I think I can provide you with a solution.' I recall like it was yesterday seeing how well-prepared Dave was. He knew what he wanted to do. He needed some help. He was ready to provide a service for the client.

"It's a competitive environment, and people measure you on past performance. If you have a good track record, it means a lot when you're seeking a contract with the Department of Defense. Understandably, DOD people are very reluctant to do business with an unknown quality. It is an environment where they are adverse to risk. Risk equates failure. Failure puts the war fighter in jeopardy."[377]

In 1994, WWT's sales were $17 million, nearly double the previous year's $9 million. During the year, the company worked overtime preparing its bid to win a large contract with the Army. David says, "Over a period of six months, we invested thousands of hours in our pursuit to close this deal, including having $150,000 in out-of-pocket expenses. We did everything possible to get this business and, in fact, considered it a make-or-break deal for our company. The contract was so large that it would have tripled our annual revenues. We were still having major cash flow problems, and we badly needed to get this order. In the first rounds of bidding, we beat four companies that were competing for the job, and finally it had been narrowed down to another company and us. We both submitted our final bids. We were confident that we'd get the job, and knowing how hard we worked, we believed we deserved it. The other company, however, ended up winning the job, and all of our hard work, time, and money was for naught. We were down in the dumps, scratching our heads, trying to figure out what to do next."[378]

Joe recalls the disappointment.

"Having put so much into our work to get that Army contract threw us for a loop. We thought we did everything right and were confident we'd get the job. But we didn't. We had built up our hopes, and losing it was devastating. Just afterward, while we were still licking our wounds, I got a call from the major at Quantico. He was a happy camper, and I needed a pep talk from a satisfied customer.

We chatted for a while, and then he got to the point. 'For your information, I am giving your name to someone at General Services Administration. I told them how pleased we were, and he wants to talk to you.'

"'We appreciate it, major,' I said.

"'Well, I don't know what the GSA has in mind, but he's been telling me they've got some new ways to do business, and they have a lot of contracts to put out. I highly recommended your company to him.'

I called the GSA person, and it sounded interesting. I set up a meeting and drove with Dave to Kansas City to meet with the GSA.

"'The major highly recommended you,' the officer said.

"'Yes, he's a good customer of ours,' I said.

We talked for a while longer and were told, 'We're looking for a company with technology expertise to assist us with a new start-up program. Yes, we know your company is small, but we've heard some good things about it. Thank you for coming out to see us. I'll get back to you.'

"When we saw the GSA's interest, we considered our company a viable candidate for its business, and we focused all of our energies on winning the contract. At the time, our cash flow was so tight that our survival depended on getting this order. Miraculously, within sixty days, we had a deal, signed, sealed, and delivered. That was an incredibly short period of time considering that we worked for nearly a year trying to get the Army contract. By July 1995, we were off and running. It was a $75 million contract. I remember one month when we did $25 million with the GSA—that was more business in a single month than we ever previously did in our entire time of existence.

"It was all hands on deck. We had to bring in a lot of people quickly to help service the amount of business we were doing. We wanted people we could trust. We wanted people who believed in our values and would fit in here."[379]

David explains that it generally takes close to a year to close a deal as large as the GSA one. "We were so close to the brink of shutting down that we could not have lasted that long. Instead, the entire process was completed in sixty days," he says.[380]

In 1995, the company's sales skyrocketed to $74 million, up more than 435 percent from the previous year.

On September 11, 2001, at 9:40 A.M., American Airlines Flight 77 departed Washington Dulles Airport bound for Los Angeles. Ninety minutes later, the aircraft, which was hijacked by Al-Qaeda terrorists, slammed into the side of the Pentagon in Arlington, Virginia. At a speed of an estimated 350 miles per hour, the plane penetrated the outer three rings of the building. The Pentagon is the headquarters of the nation's Department of Defense. Later that afternoon, Joe Koenig received a call from EDS, which was the prime contractor of certain computer products for the Navy. He explains:

"I was told that they urgently needed 400 laptops reimaged with a specific image that we did for the Navy. The request included PCs and servers. 'Joe, I need them shipped ASAP.'

"At the time, all air travel was shut down, so there was no air transportation. We needed as many WWT people we could muster up to pitch in at the warehouse to do an all-nighter. It was amazing how everyone was willing to drop everything and volunteer to help. The order was: 'Get these things ready to be shipped immediately.' Our logistics people called the trucking company. They sent two drivers instead of the usual one driver. It was amazing how everyone wanted to do his or her part. Not just our people—the freight company, the Navy, and EDS, which was our supply-chain partner for these products. Everyone worked together that night: we had executives, inside sales reps, and secretaries down in the warehouse, moving crates, unboxing packages, and working their hardest to get this order out the door. I was touched by the way everyone worked together because they wanted to be involved in the fight against terrorism. I was so proud of our people that night. It reminded me about how Americans got behind our troops during World War II. Everyone wanted to do his or her share to win the war. I was so proud of our WWT people that night. I thought to myself, 'This is really what World Wide Technology is all about. We are a team that will go that extra mile. When there is a crisis, we will do what we have to do to get the job done.'"[381]

For its above-and-beyond efforts, the Navy presented WWT with its Small Business Award.

WWT today is a prosperous entity, yet the company has never lost its passion and intensity to serve its customers. There is no evidence whatsoever that indicates the company has abandoned its do-whatever-it-takes mind-set to win customer loyalty and build lifelong relationships. An example of this all-out effort occurred in 2006 when the company bid on and won a large supply-chain contract with AT&T, one of WWT's first customers. Jim explains:

"AT&T was consolidating all of its warehouses throughout the U.S., and it was a complicated operation because the technology at these warehouses was not all the same. As a consequence, AT&T didn't have a handle on how much inventory was out there. It turned out that there was much more than anticipated, and the velocity and quantity of equipment that was flowing into our warehouse to serve AT&T was overwhelming. To make sure everything was done properly, Joe Koenig, Mark Catalano—who was president of Telcobuy, our division that serves the telecommunications industry—and I went down to the warehouse at three in the morning to manage this through. We were dressed in shorts and T-shirts and worked side by side with our warehouse employees. We didn't just do it this one time—this went on for months. From a technology perspective combined with the amount of physical work that was needed, plus from the business solutions perspective, this was one of our most challenging tasks ever.

"There was a continuous line of tractor trailers showing up at our docks, and we were running out of space to put everything in our 150,000-square-foot facility. I remember standing at the dock door, and I started counting tractor trailers filled with equipment. They were backed up one after another. I counted twenty of them. I'm looking at them, and I'm thinking out loud, saying to myself, 'I cannot believe this. Our building is at capacity, and we're expecting more trailer truckloads coming in every day for several months.' The sheer volume was causing technology issues on top of our physical resource issues, and there were lots of logistics issues. This had become a humongous problem, and it wasn't one that could be solved by throwing some people and resources at it to straighten it out.

"Then I got a call from two AT&T executives. I was out in the warehouse, and one of them said, 'Jim, we know you're working overtime on this thing, and you said you were committed to making this happen. Just how are you going to do that?'

"'I'll tell you," I answered. 'I just made the decision to move everything from this 150,000-square-foot building to another building that's about 400,000 square feet.'

"'I don't agree with your decision, Jim,' he said. 'The move will put us at risk from an inventory accuracy perspective.'

"'I understand, sir,' I replied, 'but this is my best judgment, and I will tell you that we will do whatever it takes to make this right.'

"'Are you so sure of your decision?' he said. 'Do you understand what's on the line if you don't get it right?'

"'I understand, and I know there are no guarantees in life. But please trust me to know that we will do whatever it takes.'

"'You're out there right in the middle of this,' he said, 'so you do what you think is best. But remember, you've got to get it right.'

"'Yes sir, I get it.'

"We proceeded to move everything into a new building, and while it didn't happen without challenges, it turned out to be the right decision. We had some bright people within our organization that were quite vocal in expressing their views on why we couldn't do it. 'We are over our heads on this one,' some of them said to me.

"Later, we received some awards from AT&T for this job. We appreciated the honor, but more importantly, we earned their respect and trust. This is something that you can't buy. You earn it by your actions."[382]

It is rare in corporate America for senior managers of a billion-dollar company to dress in shorts and T-shirts and do physical work to inspire their employees to do their best to serve a customer. Jim explains that this is the way that things are done at WWT. "I'm a big believer that you must lead by example. People will respect you for that. Look at how many companies stopped doing what made them successful when they got big. And look at where are they now."[383]

Tim Harden, president of AT&T Supply Chain and Fleet Operations, talks about how his company was making major changes in 2006.

"We were expanding our video product, bringing it online. We were also accelerating our investment, hiring thousands of technicians, and we were building at a rapid pace. We needed a company like WWT that could keep up with our pace, and they stepped up to the plate. Despite a lot of risk, they were determined to get the job done. They moved into the larger facility even though it wasn't known how long we'd require the additional space. It turned out to be a smart move on their part, because the facility has since been expanded. They had the foresight to recognize the upside potential beyond the scope at the time of the initial bid for the job, and it has paid off for them. We consider WWT a trusted partner, and as a consequence, we have expanded the business they do with us into other areas.

"We use them as a model. When I sit down with a large OEM, I talk about how WWT is a shining example on what it means to develop a relationship of trust that can do one thing well and demonstrate that it is capable of swimming upstream with that supplier, doing four or five things in their supply chain as a result of how its business has grown. It's a win-win-win situation. I win because I have a supplier that I know can deliver. The OEM wins because it can shift the margin responsibility to WWT. This is where WWT has done an exceptional job demonstrating it can provide more value-added capability by taking on additional supply-chain services. And WWT wins because its business grows. When a company tells me that they aren't able to bring a diversified supplier on, I say, 'Well, here's a $3 billion diversified company that can do five things for your supply chain—and they can do it tomorrow. Here are the results. Here is what they have done. It is unimaginable to me why you wouldn't sit down with WWT and consider what they have to offer your company.' Then I'll add, 'By the way, I don't even look at WWT as a diverse supplier. This is a company that executes exceptional delivery and support.'

"Dave Steward is a great role model, and from a company-to-company relationship, we feel as though we have a valued strategic relationship. I am sure that if you ask Dave, he would tell you the same thing. It's a relationship that is based on delivery, personal involvement, and just has an overall outstanding track record for running a business."[384]

ONE HUNDRED PERCENT CUSTOMER RETENTION

In business, making a sale is only the starting point. When a customer is revered and pampered, revenues generated from future orders will well exceed the initial order. It's a basic principle in every business—if you take good care of your customers, your customers will take care of you. You are rewarded with repeat orders and referrals. If you fail to serve them well, there is no building process. Neglected customers don't come back, and more money must be spent to attract new customers.

Like all senior people at WWT, Mark Catalano knows the importance of retaining customers. Catalano was a regional vice president at TIE Communications for thirteen years prior to joining WWT in 1997. He served for two years as vice president and general manager of WWT's Telco business unit. Catalano was then named president and chief operating officer of Telcobuy.com, a subsidiary of WWT. He is in charge of the WWT sales organization with the exception of the federal government sales, which is headed by Bill McKeon.

"Our business grows from existing customers," Catalano emphasizes.

"Most of our customers are big, such as our federal and state accounts and international companies such as AT&T, Cisco, and Dell. There are obstacles to entry with organizations of this size. It generally takes us a long time to get traction and engagements with such customers. We put in considerable time, effort, and money to get an initial order, and being in a highly competitive field, we don't bat 100 percent. But what we do strive for is 100 percent customer retention. Once we get in, keeping that customer becomes absolutely critical. We have built a successful company because we've been able to figure out how to keep that customer. We are constantly asking ourselves: 'How do we differentiate WWT from the competition?' 'How do we ensure we are providing service that is over and beyond?' 'And if there is a problem, how do we fix it?' We do whatever it takes to make sure our customers knows we have their best interests at heart. We want them to know we will be there for them whenever they need us.

"We have two approaches to maintaining customers. The first focuses on our technical competencies. We want to assure our customers that they are getting the products they need and what we do adds maximum value to delivering those products. By doing this we are able to differentiate WWT as a service company. This makes it possible for us to expand the relevance we have with our customer. We are constantly discussing our second focus, which is to trade places with the customer by asking, 'What would we want if we were the customer?' We find the answer when we address such questions as: 'How would you like to be dealt with?' 'What would you expect in this circumstance?' 'What do you think is fair?' We take this same mentality and then we ask ourselves, 'What is fair?' 'What is equitable?' 'What would you want that you think will solve your problem, or what would you want to negotiate?' We are constantly looking for ways to serve our customers that result in a win-win for both parties. We never try to negotiate a deal with a customer that is tilted in our favor. We want it to be good for both sides, because we want the customer to come back again."[385]

When Catalano joined WWT in 1997, the company's revenues were $137 million. He says,

"When I first met Dave, I asked him, 'Where do you see this company in ten to fifteen years?'

"'Our revenues will be multibillion dollars,' he said.

"We both laughed, and I said, 'You're crazy.' Dave just smiled.

"We're there now. What made this growth possible are the kinds of organizations that we do business with. For the most part, they are large multibillion-dollar enterprises, and the kind of work we do for them is substantial. Once we get our foot in the door, and a new customer experiences firsthand how committed we are to serve his needs and he sees the results, it leads to more business in different areas of his or her organization."[386]

To people who have never conducted business on a large scale that involves millions and hundreds of millions of dollars, such large numbers can be overwhelming. They think that anything associated with high finance is complex and beyond their grasp. David simplifies it by putting it into proper perspective when he says, "It's all about the Golden Rule, which is perhaps the most quoted scripture in the Bible. Matthew 7:12 says it clearly: 'In everything, do to others as you would have them do to you.' This advice has been around for two millenniums, and nobody has yet come up with a better way to treat people. A Golden Rule attitude is deeply ingrained in our company culture, and it permeates our relationships with customers, employees, vendors, and partners. When it comes to doing business based on the Golden Rule, it is appropriate with small and big companies alike.

"With a constant focus on our customers, every employee is treated as if he or she were a customer. Here's how it works: different people within our organization are customers to other people from other areas of the organization. For instance, marketing people are the accounting people's customers; distribution people are the marketing people's customers. And support teams in various departments have their own customers within their own departments, and so on. In my position as chairman of the board, and Jim as CEO, every company employee is our customer. I strongly believe that good leadership makes a priority of serving the people within an organization. Our focus is always on customers, and every employee has a clear understanding of how his or her job relates to customers. I mean everyone, from the receptionist at the front desk to the dock loader in the shipping area. This applies to an employee who has no direct contact with a customer; what he or she does is still relevant to serving customers. That's because the entire company exists to serve customers.

"We are particularly pleased with partnerships we have with vendors. This is a major part of our business, and we are delighted to engage in joint ventures with them. We're aware that they could have selected one of our competitors, and we feel honored because companies partner with people they care about and trust. I view these partnerships as cherished relationships. When we form an agreement with another company, I pray and ask God to bless the union. I ask Him to bless the coming together of both parties and ask that it be profitable for both sides. A business deal can never be successful if it is one-sided."[387]

Jim agrees:

"Just as we have a customer who is a paying customer, internally, our sales operations may be a customer to our operations people. Our IT logistics is a customer to IT. We have strived to get everybody to understand that there's not just one customer out there. We have customers all over the place. Each of us has these different customers, and each internal customer is treated with the same level of focus and caring that we also have on our external customers. When this is done properly, it has a very positive impact on our bottom line. We are continually working on getting our people to understand that the more we take care of our customers, they will help take care of us."[388]

WWT has built a strong reputation for its integrity and high principles, and its people work hard to keep it intact. As David says, "We're not infallible, and we do make mistakes. But when we do, we'll do whatever it takes to get it right. We'll take whatever resources we have to assure that we make it right for the customer, even if it costs us money to give the value that's expected of us, which is above and beyond. Our attitude is we are only as good as the last deal we did."[389]

Although the company has a 100 percent retention goal, it never compromises its principles to achieve this mark. Joe recalls an incident that happened with a company that partnered with WWT in the early days.

"I was working with partners that both represented million-dollar contracts—each at the time was a significant source of revenue for us. I won't mention either by name, but Partner A was considerably bigger than Partner B. When it passed on a proposal we presented to it, we explained that we were going to offer it to Partner B and were told that wouldn't be a problem.

"After Partner B agreed to partner with us on the business, Partner A came back and said, 'We changed our mind and decided that we want to do it.'

"'We approached you first,' I said, 'and you turned us down, so we took it to this partner. We're sorry, but we're committed to Partner B now."

"Partner A wasn't happy with us, but if somebody is going to take us to the dance, that's who we're going to dance with. Win or lose. It's a matter of honoring what we say we will do.

"The guy at Partner A called me and chewed me out. I said, 'I understand that you are upset, and I am sorry about it. But if you're upset with me because we are living by a commitment that we made to Partner B, then our partnership with you isn't going to work out for us. We made a commitment, and we intend to honor it with Partner B. Would you go back on a commitment that you made with a partner to give a piece of business to us?'

"The guy said, 'Well, that's a totally different story.'

"'No, it's not,' I answered. He was upset with us for about a year, but he finally admitted that he saw our point of view. There were other times when companies wanted to partner with us, and if we suspected they didn't have integrity, we turned down the business. For instance, if a company with a dubious reputation wanted to sub some work to us, and if we thought they weren't on the up-and-up, we'd pass on the business. Even during our early days when we were hungry for business, we never put our reputation in jeopardy by doing business with anyone untrustworthy."[390]

David says that in 1 Thessalonians 5:22, we are taught: "Abstain from all appearance of evil." He explains, "This tells us that in business, we will be judged by the people we associate with. There is truth in the adage, 'Birds of a feather flock together.'"[391]

BUILDING LONG-TERM RELATIONSHIPS

For years, WWT sold Dell laptops and personal computers and had been acknowledged by the company as an outstanding vendor for its services in supply-chain warehousing. WWT's first work with the company was when it sold Dell products to its military customers. Joe says, "We were their customer, so in 2002, we asked our contacts at Dell to introduce us to their associates in areas that we identified as having a need for our services. We told them, 'We'd like to put in a bid to develop a solution for managing suppliers associated with your alpha products.' Alpha products are the small items that are included in the building of a computer. They can be labels, screws, packaging foam, and are generally parts that are tracked as expense items. While each of these subcomponent parts is little in itself, in total, with all the PCs that Dell makes, they exceed more than 200,000 pieces. We placed a bid for this business, and I'm sure that due to our performance in other areas of the company, it helped us get the job.

"We developed a solution for Dell that fundamentally changed how materials are delivered to the company. For instance, multiple supplier deliveries have been replaced by a single-truck delivery containing all replenishment products, arriving in forty-five-minute intervals. Using radio frequency devices, our site coordinators on the factory floor generate demand signals to Dell's co-located distribution center, initiating the pick, pack, and delivery to the factory just prior to consumption. This was an entirely new area for us, so in the beginning, we didn't have a picture-perfect start because we were in uncharted waters. We had to build several interfaces between their systems and our systems to make them compatible. Admittedly, it was tough out the gate. The way this works is we buy units from a component supplier, and just how many we purchase is based on Dell's forecast. We warehouse these parts and supply them to Dell manufacturers. We manage the supply demand, which can include managing the ordering, fulfilling, and warehousing. When Dell tells us how many units they want shipped in a month's time, our job is to analyze what they need.

"It only takes one item, something as seemingly insignificant as a label, packaging piece, or a specific screw—just one slipup of one of these items can shut down Dell's production line. One time, during the first six months, we had to shut down the line. It happened because some software documentation wasn't available. It was the fault of one of our vendors, but since we were the prime contractor on the account, we were held accountable, and we had to take the heat. All I can say is that it wasn't a fun conversation with Dell when the line was shut down. To get everything back on track, we had our people sleeping in warehouses down in Austin to get the line up and running. It's amazing when I think about where we were back in 2002 with Dell and how far we've since come. We recently won their Supplier of the Year award, which we feel is quite an honor. Mark Franke is our vice president who manages this account, and although he's based in St. Louis, he spends a lot of his time in Austin. Mark and his team of more than one hundred WWT employees are constantly coming up with innovations to enhance Dell's supply chain; this is something that this group does very well. Since getting that first job in Austin, we've opened warehouses in Winston-Salem, Nashville, and Reno to support Dell. Today, as they change their model, we make changes to accommodate them. We view what we do with Dell as a trusted partnership."[392]

Ying McGuire oversees global supply diversity at Dell. In this capacity, she is in charge of a program that provides equal access to key opportunities for historically underutilized groups including minorities. "We help these companies grow their business in the U.S. as well as the global marketplace," she explains.

"The size of a company isn't a concern, so WWT is classified as a minority-owned business. Therefore, I still manage the relationship. WWT is not only our supplier but our customer as well. They are extremely customer-focused and very technology-driven. They are exceptionally nimble and fast, which make them a valuable partner. They provide superior customer service support, and they are focused on continuous improvement, always looking for ways to improve their service to customers."[393]

McGuire recalls saying to Steward: "Dave, your company is called World Wide Technology. There is nothing worldwide about it. Let's see if we can make it worldwide." As McGuire tells the story, "He grinned and said, 'Sounds good to me.' We were so pleased with our partnership with WWT that our leadership team sponsored and mentored them and then took the company to Brazil. Today, WWT runs a Dell Brazilian operation. Then, in 2009, some of our senior members made several trips with their people to Asia, where we introduced them to local leaders. We opened doors for them with suppliers. We coached them with the culture in those markets and helped them establish roots in the Asian market. As consequence, WWT opened an office in Singapore that serves as its headquarters for their Asian Pacific operations. Shortly afterward, they established an office in Shanghai."[394]

WWT first sold Cisco products to the GSA in 1994. "Our first five orders with Cisco went through that GSA contract," Joe tells.

"This marked the first time that the company did business with Cisco, and initially, the orders slowly increased. This was the beginning of a long business relationship between the two companies. Jim and I paved the way on this account, and Jim is the executive sponsor, which means he'll work closely with high-level Cisco people. Dave will also meet with their senior people. There's nothing like bringing in the company's founder and chairman of the board to meet with a customer's top brass. He's the consummate goodwill ambassador."[395]

"We started by reselling Cisco products," Jim explains.

"Today, Cisco is both a customer and a partner. It's a relationship based on trust that is deeply appreciated, and we never take their business for granted. We are constantly looking to find ways to better serve them. Cisco is a $40+ billion company, so there are a lot of opportunities for us to serve them at home and abroad, and since its inception, we have found ways to expand our business with them."[396]

With $1 billion in annual sales, today Cisco is WWT's biggest single source of revenue. David explains:

"It took us several months to become integrated with their systems; plus we incurred sizeable up-front costs. We are one of a handful of suppliers and vendors that is fully integrated with Cisco. By developing an expertise in their technology so our systems are compatible with theirs, we are able to do a lot of business with them."[397]

An estimated 100 WWT engineers (of the more than 150 WWT employees who work with Cisco) hold in excess of 500 individual Cisco certifications. These engineers keep abreast of the latest technology developments through continuous training and close working relationships with Cisco personnel. At a 2009 Cisco Partner Summit, WWT received awards as its U.S. and Canada Theater Partner of the Year, U.S. Public Sector DVAR (Direct Video Assisted Redressal) of the Year, and Central Region Security Partner of the Year. It's a two-way street; Cisco also has a deep appreciation for its relationship with WWT.

In the IT industry, it sometimes takes years to open a new account, so a lot of patience is required before the right door opens and an order is placed. "It took us seven years before we did business with the state of Missouri," David says.

"For years the state were doing business with GE Capital, and it didn't matter that they were out of state and we were headquartered here in St. Louis. Being Missouri-based, employing Missourians, and paying state taxes served as no advantage. Nor did it matter that we were supporting the governor and other politicians in Missouri. But when GE was unable to deliver certain solutions to the state, a door opened for us to come in, and we were right there. That's because we were persistent, and even though we weren't doing business with the state, we wanted to keep in their faces. Over the years, I've learned that there are times when you don't think you're making any progress, but when you keep yourself in front of people, and they become aware of your passion and commitment, they start to think, 'They keep coming back, and I keep saying no, but they're adamant about how they can improve the way we are doing things.' Of course, we had to go through a competitive bidding process. The initial orders with the state were a relatively small piece of business where we provided desktop service and product. Today we are the single IT provider for the state of Missouri. In this capacity, WWT processes an average of 1,100 purchase orders a month. We coordinate sales forecasts with key suppliers in order to reserve, build, and stage inventory to be ready for callout and delivery. Suppliers include Dell, IBM, Microsoft, Gateway, and Lexmark, to name a few.

"We've been doing business with the state of Missouri since 2001, and once the state saw how good we were, they gave us more business. The state has since expanded the contract to include the university system, and doors have opened for us to do business with local municipalities, police departments, and fire departments."[398]

Joe emphasizes that going that extra mile for customers is not only an excellent way to win customer loyalty, it is also a great way to attract more business. He says, "The state of Missouri has recommended our services to other states, and today, we have contracts with Alaska, Arizona, California, Connecticut, Idaho, Kansas, Michigan, Missouri, Montana, New Mexico, New York, Oregon, Texas and Washington. Today, when we want to solicit new business and haven't had any contact with a particular customer, we ask one of our partners to make an introduction for us."[399]

While WWT partners with some of the world's biggest companies, it treats all customers equally, regardless of size. David explains:

"Those small customers can say wonderful things about us that could open a door to a big customer. And of course, the small customer can someday turn out to be a big customer. I remember how we were treated by some companies when we were in our infancy. There were people who wouldn't give us the time of day, and then there were others who couldn't have been nicer. Well, when you do become bigger, these are the things you never forget when you're in a position to place an order. You're definitely going to go out of your way to do business with those people. There's a story about how Coca-Cola wouldn't sell to Bill Marriott when he opened his first hotel. They were worried about his credit. But Pepsi was willing to take a chance. As a result, when Marriott became one of the world's largest hotel chains, it remained loyal to Pepsi. The Scriptures tell us to be faithful with a little, and the Lord will bless you with much."[400]

A WWT account manager is assigned to each customer. "This person is like a general manager to the account," Mark Catalano explains.

"Depending on the size of a customer, an account manager might only have one account, such as AT&T, Cisco, or Dell, while other account managers might serve five or six customers, and then others might be calling on as many as a couple of dozen different customers. Of course, it's not just the sales organization that is in contact with our customers. For every one salesperson that's out in front of a customer, there are multiple people behind the scenes to support that customer. It starts with a salesperson, front and center. Then there's an inside sales customer service person who supports the tactical requirements, who does quotations, assures orders are entered, and follows up on delivery and customer satisfaction. We also have presale engineers and postsale engineers that support the salesperson by making sure the product is correctly implemented and being properly used."[401]

Opening new accounts and retaining WWT customers isn't dependent on super salesmanship. It's a long process that involves competitive bidding. A lot of follow-up service by a support team is required to maintain an account. Still, like in every business, strong relationships play an important role in achieving maximum results. This is why Dave Steward spends approximately 50 percent of his time on the road, getting out there in front of customers. "Dave does anything we need him to do," Catalano says. "Whether it's a big customer or a medium-sized customer, he gets very involved in customer engagements. A salesperson just has to ask him, and Dave will do it. Knowing that they can count on Dave to meet with their customers means a lot to our people in the field."[402]

WINNING WITH PEOPLE

"There isn't a business school in the U.S. that offers a management course in love," David contends, "yet Jesus, the greatest leader ever, advocated that we should love each other. He said in John 15:12: 'This is my commandment, that you love each other as I have loved you.' These were not idle words. He commanded it. I am not suggesting that one should embrace employees with hugs and say how much he loves them. That wouldn't have gone over very well when I was in the railroad and freight delivery business. I was dealing with a lot of macho guys who weren't the warm-and-cuddly type. I don't think America is ready for business leaders expressing their love to their subordinates. However, there are other ways that a good leader can express his care for his people. He can do it by inviting them in to share his vision and dreams. He can do it by respecting others when he listens to their ideas and suggestions. Providing them with opportunities and fringe benefits also lets them know that he cares about them. And contributing to their 401(k) plans shows that a company is concerned about their future when they retire."[403]

Tom Strunk was one of Jim's closest friends since their college days when they were soccer teammates at St. Louis University. Strunk had a high-paying job as the controller and CFO at a successful construction company. Jim says, "I had been talking to Tom for months, and in 1993, when we didn't win a big contract that we thought we'd get, I told him that the timing wasn't right for him to come aboard. A few months later, when we won another contract, I felt times were better, so I talked to him again about becoming our CFO. I explained that the company still wasn't on a rock-solid foundation, but we were in a better place than before. I made it clear to Tom that we were by no means out of the woods, and he joined us with eyes wide open. It's an enormous responsibility to hire your friends and in particular those who have families and good jobs. During those years when we were struggling to survive, I had a lot of sleepless nights worrying about whether I made the right decision by recruiting them to join WWT.

"When you hire your close friends, they must be held at a higher level of accountability than other individuals in the company. You have to understand that people are going to look at them and say, 'Well, you're hiring only friends.' This was not the case. I had other close friends—and guys I played soccer with—that I would never hire. The upside of hiring people I knew well was that I knew they had the right work ethic. I also knew they had the intelligence and right values to do what we need to do. My view is that you will limit your organization if you are not willing to tap into people that you know. Certainly, there is the perception that these people are given undeserved jobs and opportunities, and I left myself open for criticism, so this is the downside. However, I wanted to make sure that we built a strong foundation with the right people in the right place—and as a collective team, we then could continue to supplement that team as we moved forward. Definitely, we also brought in some very good people that I didn't know previously, and a lot of them started in low-entry positions and have since risen through the organization."[404]

Joe Koenig agrees that it's okay for good friends to work together in business. He says, "I know some people think it's a bad idea, but when you're surrounded by people you trust and know will be loyal,

No introductions needed—Chairman David Steward presents President George W. Bush to World Wide Technology employees in St. Louis on May 2, 2008 (left). Getting the job done—World Wide Technology employees hard at work (below).

Up close and personal—President George W. Bush engages a World Wide Technology audience in May 2008 (above). All hail the company president and leaders—Joe Koenig, President, World Wide Technology (below left), and WWT Chairman of the Board David Steward and CEO Jim Kavanaugh (below right).

One-on-one supervision—Jim Kavanaugh reviews the work of a WWT associate (above). Putting it together—A World Wide Technology employee fixes a computer modem.

it can be very effective. Frankly, I like some guy watching my back to be a buddy of mine. Jim brought in a lot of his buddies that became a trusted circle of friends that we know are loyal, and through our most difficult times, we all stayed on board. This nucleus of people was the foundation of trust that permeated the organization. To Dave's credit, he recognized and trusted Jim's judgment and supported him when he recruited his friends and old soccer teammates."[405]

Jim points out that when friends are recruited into an organization and their work is not satisfactory, letting them go is an unpleasant task. "At times, you bring people on, and it's not a perfect world," he explains.

"Friends or not, you must do it with a level of integrity, and you have to let them go. When this happens, you have to coach them out of the organization. This is part of leading and managing a business. So if someone doesn't fit or can't perform his job to the level that he needs to, this is something that must be done. This is an organization that has high expectations of what our employees need to do. What people sometimes don't understand is that when you manage somebody out of the organization, there is a proper way to do it with a respect to that individual. You do it by sitting down with this person and having candid conversations about what he needs to do to improve. And you say that you want to help him. It is inhumane when a manager is not willing to have a constructive conversation with an employee and fires him without warning. I think that is grossly unfair.

"However, giving advance warning on what's required of him is a win-win scenario. This way the person knows that there are consequences if he doesn't perform. You made it clear that the company prefers he performs and does a great job. He knows that you want him to continue working for the company. But if he doesn't perform, there is another option that probably neither one of you is going to like, but it's likely to happen. I feel that when you put it like this, it is no longer the responsibility of the leader. It's his responsibility. He's been given every opportunity, and you tried to coach and train him."[406]

Prior to joining WWT as director of human resources in 1997, Ann Marr had worked in human resources for Enterprise Rent-A-Car and Anheuser-Busch Companies. She has since been promoted to vice president of human resources. She recalls:

"I was introduced to Dave through a mutual friend. My friend said, 'When you meet Dave Steward, believe me, you are going to want to work for that company.' I wasn't actively looking for a change in jobs, but Dave had a reputation in St. Louis as an up-and-coming business executive, so I thought he'd be a nice person to know. He's so warm and has such high principles, I immediately liked him. Then I met with Jim Kavanaugh, and the next thing you know, I was leaving the largest car rental company in the U.S. to come to work for a small technology company. People thought I was making a big mistake, but Dave and Jim told me about their future plans, and it sounded so exciting to become part of a company with so much potential. I was impressed with the fact that both Dave and Jim were the kind of executives who will roll up their sleeves and work side by side with their people. They wanted me to build a human resources department from scratch, and I liked the idea of being able to start something from the beginning. It didn't scare me at all because I felt they'd give their support to help me do it."[407]

What Ann liked most about her new employers was that they exhibited a high level of respect toward others in the organization. "This has to come from the top," she explains.

"I learned the importance of respecting others by growing up in a very large family as one of thirteen children. My mother and father taught us to treat each other as we would want to be treated. In a family the size of ours, we had to respect each other! I learned that this is the way you treat everybody. It doesn't matter who they are, or in an organization, what level they're at. If someone is the janitor or a VP, you treat them equally, and when you do, that level of respect is going to come back to you. I grew up with these values, and I wanted to work for a company that embraces those same values. It's a simple concept—the Golden Rule—one that everyone understands. We practice it throughout the organization, and our respect for each other creates a sense of loyalty and camaraderie."[408]

Although Jim recruited several personal friends, Joe is quick to point out that a lot of friends weren't hired. He explains:

"There are some you hire and some you don't. You know which ones are the ones you want and those you don't. You know it from what you observed in the way they played on the soccer field. You know it from how they behaved when you went out with them for a few drinks. So yes, we brought in several friends but not as many as the ones we didn't want because we knew they weren't what we were looking for."[409]

Today, the company has more than 1,200 employees, and it's not possible to recruit friends and former teammates to fill every position necessary to run the company. What worked with personal contacts when the company was small isn't applicable on a large scale. Different criteria are required. Ann explains:

"We have core values that we live by, and when we interview prospective employees, we use these values as a gauge for hiring people. We evaluate an interviewee based on certain qualities to determine whether he or she will be a good fit within the organization. This determines whether this individual qualifies for the next level of the interview process.

"There are certain characteristics we look for. For instance, is a person a risk taker? When I was interviewed here, the fact that I would leave Enterprise for a job with a much smaller company indicated that I was not opposed to risk. On the other hand, if a person has had many job changes, it could be signal he might not be a loyal employee. And certainly, we look for people with passion and a positive attitude, two qualities you can almost see the minute you shake someone's hand. Although not everyone plays team sports, a former athlete can indicate that someone will be a good team player. There are a lot of little things to look for during an interview. For example, when someone keeps on saying 'I' instead of 'we,' that is a clue that he might not be a team player. We also like it when a job applicant's résumé shows that he or she has participated in nonprofit events and community activities. We spend a lot of time interviewing people to assure we get the right ones. By being particular about who we recruit, we have a low turnover of employees. High turnover is expensive and bad for morale."[410]

David stresses that although it is crucial to put the best talent into the right slot within the organization, it is essential that those individuals have good character. He says, "This is why we seek out people with the right attitude and why we emphasize qualities such as integrity, loyalty, and trust. We look for people who are giving and want to make a difference in this world. Jesus tells a parable in Luke 6:43-45 that provides an excellent lesson on hiring the right people. He says that a good tree will not bear bad fruit, nor will a bad tree bear good fruit. Hence a tree is known by its own fruit. Jesus explains that figs are not gathered from thorns, nor are grapes picked from a bramble bush. Likewise, a person with a good heart does good deeds; an evil person will do evil deeds. In this parable, Jesus says that you can separate the two by listening carefully when people speak. To do this, you must listen not only to what is said, but you must hear what comes from within. This is true, because what comes from the heart reveals character and attitude. I believe this scripture is helpful in recruiting the right people."[411]

For the past twelve years, WWT's internship program has hired college students from across the United States to spend a summer working for the company. In 2009, thirty-five interns participated. Interns are engaged in different training programs, and they are given opportunities to learn many areas of the business. At a mini–boot camp, different department heads are invited to speak to the interns, thereby giving them exposure to many areas of the company. Then, at the end of the summer, an internship lunch is held in the home office's main conference room, and top executives including David and Jim are featured speakers. A question-and-answer session is conducted that encourages these young people to ask questions. Questions are asked such as: "What made you successful?" "When you were in my shoes, what gave you the courage to do what you did?" At another luncheon, some former interns who have since moved up the ranks at WWT attend, and again, they also do a Q&A session. The internship program has been highly successful, with 85 percent of the participants becoming full-time employees. Several interns have moved up the ranks, including Mike Moriarty, who today is a regional sales manager; Mike Taylor, who is an IT operations director; and Krista Bush, who has been promoted to a finance controller position.

"We want to retain good people," Ann says, "and to encourage employees to stay with us, we invest a lot in them. In addition to training programs, we are continually educating them to sharpen their technical and managerial skills. Providing them with opportunities and encouraging them to grow, our turnover of employees is low."[412]

The company is particularly generous with providing comprehensive health-care coverage for its employees and their families at low premiums. "This sends a message that we care about you and your family," Ann states.

"With health-care costs skyrocketing, this commitment is a huge financial undertaking. Our coverage is more extensive than most companies, and we study benchmark data and do surveys to make sure we are competitive with other companies. Recently, when I told a newly hired person what the health insurance costs were, he commented, 'That's really a low weekly cost for our family.' When I replied, 'That was the monthly cost,' his jaw dropped."[413]

Joe Koenig reiterates that the company's health-care coverage is exceptional, but he says, "Sometimes it's the little things we give our people that excites them. For example, at the town hall meeting with our employees, Jim announced, 'Next year, our health-care coverage will remain the same, and there will be no increase in what you will pay for it.' This generated a slight response. Then Jim said, 'Based on employee feedback, we went casual last year. This year, again on what you told us, the company will allow appropriate people to wear flip-flops to work.' This evoked a huge ovation. We are committed to taking great care of our people, but we sprinkle it with some nuggets to keep it interesting."[414]

David states that the heart and soul of the company is apparent on a visit to its headquarters.

"It's the spirit of our people. You can see it and feel it when you walk through the corridors here at our world headquarters. It's the commitment they have to give service to others. Our people are excited about being a part of a company that cares about them and their best interests. A visitor picks up on this spirit when he receives a warm greeting by our receptionist. Callers hear it in the friendliness in the voice of the person who takes the call. It comes through everywhere from the front desk to the warehouse."[415]

The warmth that David describes is not an exaggeration. But what he doesn't say is that it is a reflection of his own conviviality. It is, in fact, a testament to his authenticity. To find this spirit in a company, you must look at its highest echelons. People know he cares when a family member is sick and he promises to say a prayer for a speedy recovery. They know it when he sends a Bible or some healing scripture to an ill person. They see it when he invites them to attend a Sunday school class he and his wife conduct at their church. For years, the Stewards have been heading a class called "Doing Business by the Good Book."

People know Dave Steward is respectful and caring when they see him at a company social gathering and approach him with a question. "What are your thoughts on how today's weak economy will affect the company?" "Do you think the government cutbacks will change the way we do things in our department?" His wife, Thelma, says, "On some topical subjects, Dave can be asked the same question again and again during an evening, and he will answer it with the same intensity as if he's hearing it for the first time. I know there are times when he would rather talk about something else, but respectful to the other person, he always feels obliged to give a complete answer. Dave doesn't want to slight anyone."[416]

Not long ago, a regional sales manager invited a prospective sales representative to visit the St. Louis headquarters. The manager passed by David's office, and looking in, he saw that Dave was alone, so with the job candidate, he walked in. "Hi, Dave. Just want to take a minute of your time to introduce you to his young lady from Florida who might join the company." David stood up from behind his desk and walked over to greet his guests and chatted with them for about twenty minutes. "I want to do everything I possibly can to help you be successful," he said. At the end of the meeting, he autographed a copy of his book, *Doing Business by the Good Book*, for her. "This book will tell you about our company and what I believe."

The woman was so overwhelmed that she started to cry. Afterward, she said to the sales manager, "I can't believe such a company exists. I want this job so badly I'll work here for nothing. I'll work strictly on commissions. You don't even have to put me in the health program because I am covered under my husband's."[417]

David said it with sincerity when he told her he wanted to help her. He regularly makes himself available to accompany sales reps when one requests his presence. This kind of assistance from WWT managers is not restricted to David. Jim, Joe, Ann, and other executives also make it very clear to sales reps that they are available to back them up. This teamwork spirit is practiced throughout the organization. Again, it starts at the top.

"I get so excited," David says, "when I hear about our people buying new houses, new cars, and sending their children to private schools and colleges. These kinds of things reflect that, had we not taken a leap of faith, these opportunities would not have been there."[418]

On May 2, 2008, President George W. Bush visited WWT's headquarters, where he spoke to an enthusiastic audience of company employees. The president said that he had heard a lot of good things about WWT and wanted to personally know more about the company. Bush commented on the economic times and said that WWT was a shining example of entrepreneurship at its best. He said that the company demonstrated how technology in the Midwest is making a difference in people's lives, and it is providing jobs and opportunities while setting an example for the rest of the world. "I accompanied the president on a tour, and he graciously shook hands with our employees," David says. "He kept repeating that we are a wonderful example of the American Dream."[419]

CORE VALUES

Phil Styrlund is the CEO of the Summit Group, a consulting firm headquartered in St. Paul, Minnesota. A premier sales training firm, the Summit Group has a wide range of Fortune 500 clients including

AT&T, Cisco, Pfizer, Ritz-Carlton, American Express, and 3M. The company also consults the federal government. Styrlund has worked with WWT for several years, specifically in the area of developing sales teams. An astute business consultant, he attributes the company's success to its strong core values. He explains:

"They have something special that I refer to as WWT's 'secret sauce.' The source of that secret sauce starts with Dave Steward, but it really comes from God. I think Dave truly exudes the teachings of Jesus. Those teachings have created a cascading value system that flows through the company. With everyone at WWT knowing Dave is a true believer with unshakable core values, he has created what I refer to as an unmarked ministry. So many business leaders claim that their job is to serve their people, but they don't actually mean it. Dave does. And although he models Jesus, he never tries to force religion or his faith down anybody.

"What Dave does I call the business blueprint of Jesus. Dave is the ultimate servant leader. We've all heard, 'What would Jesus do?' To a great extent, I think Dave has created a business blueprint that really reflects how Jesus would operate a business. I say this knowing that Dave hasn't just built a highly successful company and created net worth, he's elevated people's life worth. I believe this is significant, because in today's society, the workplace is the number-one place where you can impact people's lives. It can be the greatest engine to develop people, and conversely, it can be greatest engine to damage people. The difference is in the leadership. What's more, Dave brought in two highly gifted people, Jim Kavanaugh and Joe Koenig. Jim is an outstanding CEO, and Joe is one of the most talented presidents and sales leaders I've come across. They are best friends, and those guys are more than the sum of their parts. Their friendship is so strong that they can disagree and still respect each other. And what that creates is a modeling behavior in the company culture that says, 'We can have healthy disagreement, and we don't have to attack each other personally.'"[420]

Styrlund emphasizes that the three key ingredients of WWT's secret sauce are capability, highly competitive products, and extraordinary solutions. He says, "It goes back to the blueprint of Jesus. It's an excellence that comes from doing things good and right. The entire company oozes authenticity. I hear it from their people, their partners, and their customers. They say that everyone at WWT is real. Everyone there tells the truth. They are honest. And because of this, people say, they are easy to do business with.

"Dave has modeled the teachings of Jesus to apply to his business better than anybody I have ever seen and has personified it in the leadership he brought in. I say this because part of the teachings of Jesus is to understand your giftedness and [use] it to serve others."[421]

Ann Marr says that David's strong religious beliefs are admired by employees and customers alike. "You see people who go to church every Sunday but they don't practice their beliefs in the workforce. I admire Dave because he applies his biblical beliefs to his work. At the same time, Dave is respectful of other people's beliefs, and he never preaches or tries to convert anyone."[422]

"There is a great diversity of ethnicity and religion, and even a lack of religion by some WWT employees," claims Mark Catalano. "So religion is not the element that fuels our culture but rather the way people are treated. Respect, honesty, and integrity—this is what permeates the entire company."[423]

Prior to starting WWT, David had been exposed to many mission statements when he worked in corporate America. As a consequence, he is one of a small percent of entrepreneurs who had a mission statement from day one. His was short and right to the point: "People, quality, and technology." He practiced it to the letter. He brought in good people, provided high-quality products and service, and focused on state-of-the-art technology to build his business. For anyone starting a company today who is not sure how its mission statement should read, he advises, "You can apply the Golden Rule to every business as well as all walks of life. You can also use what Jesus teaches us in Mark 12:31: 'You shall love your neighbor as yourself.' Both of these verses are simple, easy to remember, and can serve as guiding principles on how to conduct business every day for as long as you are in business."[424]

Starting around 1999–2000 during the dot-com bubble crash, Jim studied successful companies as a source for ideas on the right core values that could be incorporated into the daily way of doing business at WWT. He observed how many CEOs shared common values and used the same buzzwords to describe what their organizations stood for: honesty, integrity, transparency, accountability—the list went on and on. He then composed a list of the core values that he thought would best guide WWT. He says, "The easy thing to do would have been to list every strong value that you could ever think of, but then you would end up with fifty different things that seem crucial to the organization. However, it was a matter of less is more. Too long a list would be hard to remember and make it difficult to implement on daily basis.

"By this time, our company culture was in place. We adhered to Dave's religious beliefs and built our company on the principle that if we serve our people and our customers, we will be successful. By 2000, our revenues were in the $800 million range. As a smaller company, you can communicate in person or through some type of correspondence, but as you get larger, you need to build a more systematic way to get that message out. As we became a larger organization, we realized that we should commit our beliefs to writing. But we had to figure out what very simplistically conveyed our basic core values and would stand the test of time. By this I mean core values that will drive the culture and the personality of the company, not just for today, but twenty, forty years out. I wasn't interested in something that was time sensitive that just drove a specific action, an internet craze, or a market meltdown. I wanted it to be structured and be a value system that would stand the test of time. I wanted it to guide the company long after our current management was gone. I started to put everything in writing and spent six months coming up with five core values. During this time, I had some discussions with Dave, but it wasn't necessary to spend a lot of time with him, because I knew what he and I believed, and we were on the same page. What made this exercise difficult was that I didn't want to have twenty-plus core values. That would make it difficult for people to remember. It would also make it hard for them to figure out how to apply them, and as a result, it's all wallpaper! I wanted these core values to provide alignment for employees on how they were expected to act. It had to be brief and easy to refer to—something that could fit on a card and carried in one's wallet."[425]

When Jim was through, he came up with an acronym for WWT's core values: EPATH, which is referred to as the company's EPATH for employee and company success. It stands for embracing change and diversity of people and thought, passion and a strong work ethic, attitude and being positive and open-minded, being a team player, and honesty and integrity. "I put down what I thought was most important," Jim explains.

"You're never going to capture everything, but I think it's critical that you keep it simple enough that people can understand it, and you also keep it consistent. Honesty and integrity is the most important core value. It is the foundation upon which the value of embracing change, passion, work ethic, and attitude are built. If you have honesty and integrity as one of your core values and you respond consistently each and every time someone crosses over the line, the message gets delivered."[426]

Jim emphasizes that the CEO needs to do what is right.

"When the organization and the people see those types of decisions being made with consistency, that begins to resonate and drive the values and the culture of the organization. We expect you to treat people with a level of respect and integrity, and your actions need to demonstrate that. We all know what we need to do. You need to have an organization that is willing and ready to make those decisions. For example, it could be a business deal in which you are asked to break a commitment to generate more money. To some, it would be an easy decision if it were a choice of going with another partner and abandon[ing] your current partner. We absolutely believe it's the wrong thing to do from an integrity perspective. If we are committed to a partner, we are going to stay with that partner. We'd rather jeopardize our profit margin than jeopardize the integrity of our company and our people."[427]

To let it be known throughout the organization how important the core values were, Jim integrated them into the employee assessment process. Employees are measured not only on how they perform their jobs but also by how they measure up to the core values. He explains:

"If you're a sales rep, you have a quota to hit. You could hit 130 percent of your quota, but there is also a list of core values and behaviors that we expect, and if you are not performing on those behaviors, there will be consequences. For example, if you're not a team player, or if your communication is deemed disrespectful, we may ask you to leave, because it has been determined that we are being suboptimized as an organization. We won't ask anyone to leave immediately, because we advise one to change his behavior, and then we will attempt to coach him. We make it clear that just because you are over your quota, there is more that also matters. We are totally committed to our core values to the point where there have been times when we have had to ask some star performers to leave. While they were performing their job requirement, they weren't performing relative to the behavioral aspect and core values aspect. Consequently, we didn't feel it was a good mix for the company."[428]

Mark Catalano states that EPATH summarizes the company's core values, goals, and fundamental management concepts.

"It is absolutely central to the philosophy of our company. It is ingrained in every manager. Everything that EPATH stands for is essential. If there is somebody in the organization that has some of those core values but not others, that won't cut it. Can we overlook a guy that is an A player and producing but isn't a team player? The short answer is no, we cannot. Such an individual won't flourish in this environment without embracing all of those core values. We take this very seriously. EPATH is something you will see on walls in every building of this company, on displays on desks, and on our people's badges that they use to get in the door. You will also hear our core values discussed in all management meetings. And while mandatory evaluations are done at the end of the year, typically there are quarterly informal reviews based on real-time performances. When we sit down to do assessments with employees and talk about expectations, there is a matrix that includes their job performance and tactical expectations around their job as well as how they are embracing the core values."[429]

Jim insists, "When you put an emphasis on your core values, you must communicate them, hold people accountable to them, and you must live and breathe them. When we look at our employee performance matrix, we look at how you recruit, how you retain people, how you motivate people, and how you terminate people. This way there are no surprises to your people. They know what you expect.

"Another thing about core values: you must be very careful about what you put out there. If you can't hold people accountable for them, you are better off not putting them out there, because now your integrity is at stake. You've sang one thing, and you're doing something else."[430]

AT&T's Tim Harden says that WWT has a stellar reputation. He explains:

"They are known for their outstanding work and doing everything they can to meet a customer's requirements. We think they are very business savvy. Having said this, what I admire about them is that if they don't think they can do a particular job, they have enough business acumen to say, 'This is not something that's in our sweet spot. We cannot do that, so you will have to give it to another company.' This is why I say it is a relationship of mutual trust, one that has evolved into a strategic relationship.

"Dave Steward is an exceptional leader. In my role, I've worked with a lot of companies, and in this capacity, you can tell the people who are involved and know their business and yet they have enough trust in the people surrounding them, so they can grow and make crucial decisions. Dave excels in this area. He has a clear understanding of his business at the detail level, so he is able to have necessary dialogs to resolve issues and bring in new business. And, at the same time, he is able to step away and let his team manage day to day and grow the business. I've been very impressed with what I've seen of him."[431]

GIVING BACK TO THE COMMUNITY

A few years ago, David was a board member of fourteen charitable and civic organizations. This included serving as the chairman of the board of the United Way of Greater St. Louis, the national organization's fifth-largest division in the United States. In 2008, under David's leadership, $68.4 million was raised. Los Angeles's $56 million serves as a comparison point. St. Louis ranks number eighteen among the nation's most populated cities; Los Angeles has the second-largest population in the United States. The St. Louis United Way supports more than 200 agencies in the greater metropolitan area and, in turn, touches one out of three people in the community. Other boards that David serves on include those of the Boy Scouts of America, Toys for Tots, Barnes-Jewish Hospital, Ronald McDonald House, Webster University, and Civic Progress. Civic Progress is an organization consisting of members of the area's largest companies; its mission is guiding and supporting many charitable groups in St. Louis. David currently serves as the chairman of the board of the St. Louis Variety Club, an organization that supports many children's organizations.

Since 1999, David and Thelma have taught a Sunday school class called "Doing Business by the Good Book." The idea for the class came from Dr. Lynn Mims, the pastor of Union Memorial United Methodist Church. Mims had visited WWT on many occasions and was familiar with David's commitment to building a business based on biblical teachings. The pastor asked the Stewards to conduct a class that would help others follow David's lead so they, too, could prosper. Today, the weekly class is attended by a diverse group of businesspeople, ranging from heads of small start-up companies to successful business owners. Mims has since retired, and the class is now conducted at the Salem United Methodist Church, a larger church closer to the Stewards' home.

David is heralded today as one of St. Louis's most prominent business leaders. Many WWT employees are inspired by his leadership, and they, too, are actively engaged in the community. For example, Jim is an active board member of the St. Patrick Center, an organization that serves the homeless. He also supports other charitable organizations such as the the National MS Society, Ronald McDonald House, Toys for Tots, and the United Way. Ann Marr is also a community leader and serves on the board of the St. Louis Minority Business

Council, Focus St. Louis, the Urban League of Metropolitan St. Louis, and St. Louis Forum. She also serves as chair of the WWT Charitable Foundation. Again, it starts at the top. Employees are encouraged to support charitable and civic organizations, and the company matches their contributions dollar-for-dollar, 100 percent—there is no limit. The employees appreciate that the company supports what they support.

Ann says, "In addition to matching contributions, the company frequently supports organizations in which our employees are actively involved. In addition to making financial contributions, if a WWT employee is involved in a fund-raising event that has an auction, the company will frequently donate items such as computers, laptops, and iPods. The company owns luxury suites for professional football, baseball, basketball, and hockey events, and sometimes it will donate the use of the suites to be raffled off to raise money for worthy causes. For the most part, the suites are used to entertain customers. When there is a cancelation, we will make some last-minute calls to local groups so that they may bring young boys and girls who otherwise might not have the opportunity to see a professional sports event. When so, we provide catered food and beverages to our special young guests."[432]

A 2009 survey by America's Research Group states that 81 percent of American consumers claimed they are more loyal to a company that is active in the community. The survey also reveals that 95 percent of American employees boast about their bosses' civic activities, and it makes them feel proud to work for the company. Although these reports were not the reasons WWT is actively involved in the community, the survey discloses that companies can benefit from their philanthropic endeavors. As Joe says, "All those things that Dave, Jim, and other executive team members do to support the local charities are visible to our employees, and it's something they can wrap their arms around and get behind it. It's something we all appreciate at WWT."[433]

On April 12, 2008, Thelma and David Steward were named Pillar of Strength awardees by Friends of Epworth. For more than 140 years, Epworth Children & Family Services has helped thousands of children overcome severe emotional and behavioral challenges. The awards event was held at the Ritz-Carlton in St. Louis. Dell Computers' Ying McGuire says, "I was Dave's guest at the ceremony. I flew in from Austin to attend the event. I was one of a handful invited that were non–family members. The Stewards have done so much for the community, and we at Dell are proud to be partners of WWT, a company that is the epitome of outstanding corporate citizenship."[434]

When asked about giving his time and money so generously to the community, David humbly says, "This is a part of my life that I cherish. As it says in Luke 12:48, "To whom much has been given, much will be required."[435]

Afterword

AN ACID TEST that I use with each business book I write is this: As a businessperson, would I benefit from reading it? If the answer is no, then it is presumptuous to think others would. Based on this test and at the risk of sounding arrogant, on a scale of 1 to 10, *Heart & Soul* gets a 10. I say this not because I'm its author but because of all that I learned from the men and women who are quoted throughout this book.

Now that you have read *Heart & Soul*, I hope that you will emulate what these five companies do to win employee and customer loyalty. By doing so, you'll not only be more successful, but at the end of the day, you'll feel good about yourself, knowing that you contributed to the betterment of other people's lives.

One valuable lesson that is emphasized throughout this book is how a company's culture is a strong influence on all aspects of the business. This is evident at Mary Kay, Inc., a company founded by Mary Kay Ash, who, over her lifetime, became one of America's most highly profiled businesswomen. When its dynamic and beloved leader passed away in 2001, the company worked overtime making sure that her legacy would live on and ensuring that her values and principles would remain intact. With the Mary Kay spirit going strong, the company has become a symbol of free enterprise around the world. As of this writing, Mary Kay, Inc., is thriving. Had its founder's philosophy of giving and caring been abandoned, we can suppose that there could have been a different outcome.

Since Bill Austin purchased Starkley Labs in 1970 for $13,000, it has become the largest hearing aid company in the United States. Austin's goal was never to be a big company—his motivation was to serve people with hearing loss. He was driven by an obsession to be the best in his profession. His ambition was never to make a lot of money, but by providing outstanding service to his customers, Austin has become a wealthy man. With his wealth, his foundatsion is able to donate hearing aids to hundreds of thousands of needy people, and today Austin spends six months a year traveling around the world making this happen. Bill Austin has become a bigger-than-life legend in the hearing-aid industry. No wonder Starkey employees and independent hearing aid dispensers are so loyal to his company.

Founded in 1999, Resource One is the "new kid on the block." Illustrating the title of its story, "Brotherly Love," Rob Groeschen went into business so he could have a company that would provide employment for his brother Tom and others like him with brain injuries and related disabilities. The company prospers today because it was built on the premise of caring for others, a quality that permeates out its doors and to its customers. Resource One customers know of Rob's good deeds and they say it's the kind of company they are proud to do business with.

At DaVita, a new management team was put into place in 1999 to revive a company on the brink of bankruptcy. By revamping its culture, DaVita became America's leading dialysis company. What happened at DaVita is truly remarkable, because it is widely believed that changing a corporate culture is more difficult than instilling a new culture at a start-up company. DaVita's constant goal is to serve its patients, physician partners, and teammates—to be the greatest dialysis company that the world has ever seen. With its management's passion for perfection, the company keeps ahead of its competition.

Founder Dave Steward built World Wide Technology based on biblical scripture that edifies we are put on this earth to serve others.

In a time when greed and corruption in corporate America are commonplace, Steward's company epitomizes how integrity and caring win employee and customer loyalty.

Although the company cultures may vary, each plays a significant role in the success of these five enterprises. One common element stands out: each company's culture is built on trust and integrity. David Steward's handshake is his bond. The company prides itself in always honoring its commitments. "Even if it means losing money because we underestimated our costs," David emphasizes, "we will always deliver what we promise."[436] Likewise, Bill Austin built his reputation in the hearing aid industry as a man whose word is his bond. In his early years, he, too, did business on a handshake. In an industry that was once known for its high-pressure selling techniques, Starkey Laboratories has stood above the crowd as a company known for its integrity. And to change the culture at DaVita, its new management team had to win the trust of its workforce. Kent Thiry and other senior leaders achieved this by continually communicating what, how, and when they planned to meet certain objectives—and then they let their actions speak louder than their words. "We said, we did" soon became their ongoing battle cry. In time, DaVita's "One for All and All for One" motto was more than a catchy saying—it had a real meaning.

All five companies described in this book were founded by individuals with high principles, who placed the needs of their people and customers above their own.

If there is a single lesson to take away from this book, it is that great companies are built on trust. As an owner of a start-up or a fledgling company, be known for your trustworthiness. Remember that you must earn people's trust every day. You do it, one employee at a time, one customer at a time. You can never compromise your integrity. It takes a lifetime to build a good reputation, and it can be lost overnight. Always surround yourself with individuals you can trust, and build with these people. To do this, you must lead by example. People are watching you, and they will follow you. And if you don't trust somebody, terminate your relationship with him or her. Find people you do trust, and build lifelong relationships with them.

Unfortunately, we live in a time when we no longer trust our governmental leaders. Too many politicians make campaign promises that they fail to keep. We see our congressmen and senators demand special deals for their votes on national issues that result in millions and millions of dollars being funneled to their districts and states. It's a form of bribery, and they obviously do it to win favor with their constituents. Shamefully, being reelected is a higher priority to these politicians than doing what is in the best interests of the nation. They have the chutzpa to justify this behavior by telling us, "That's what legislation is all about—it's the art of compromise."

Worldwide, America has failed to honor commitments to other nations. As a consequence, our nation is no longer held in esteem or trusted in many places around the globe. Unless this situation is reversed, the consequences will be costly. To reverse this trend, those of us in the business community must lead by example. Each of us can make a difference, and in mass, we can restore our nation's image both here and abroad. It will be a slow process, one business at a time. It begins with you.

We can all start by putting our self-interests aside and doing what is best for others. Serve them well, and they will respond in kind. Subordinates will be more loyal and inspired; in turn, they will be more productive. Customers will be more loyal, and they will place larger orders. They will also recommend your services to others. Practice what you have learned in this book, and let it be the focal point in how you do business. Be guided by your heart and soul.

Endnotes

MAY KAY'S WAY

1. Robert L. Shook, *The Entrepreneurs*, Harper & Collins Publishers Inc., New York, NY 1980, p. 107
2. Mary Kay Ash, *Mary Kay*, Kay, Harper & Row Publishers, Inc., New York, NY 1981, p. 15
3. Robert L. Shook, *The Entrepreneurs*, Harper & Collins Publishers, Inc., New York, NY 1980, p. 108
4. Mary Kay Ash, *Mary Kay on People Management*, Warner Books, New York, NY 1984, p. 5
5. Mary Kay Ash, *The Mary Kay Way*, John Wiley & Sons, Inc., New York, NY 2008, p. xxii
6. Robert L. Shook, *The Entrepreneurs*, Harper & Row Publishers, Inc. New York, NY 1980, pg.108
7. Mary Kay Ash, *The Mary Kay Way*, John Wiley & Sons, Inc., New York, NY 2008, p. xxii
8. Ibid, p. xxiii
9. Robert L. Shook, *The Entrepreneurs*, Harper & Row Publishers, Inc., New York, NY 1980, p. 111
10. C. Britt Beemer and Robert L. Shook, *The Customer Rules*, McGraw-Hill, New York, NY 2009, p. 108
11. Mary Kay Ash, *Mary Kay*, Harper & Row Publishers, Inc., New York, NY 1981, p. 4
12. Robert L. Shook, *The Entrepreneurs*, Harper & Row Publishers, Inc., New York, NY, 1980, p. 105
13. Mary Kay Ash, *Mary Kay*, Harper & Row Publishers, Inc., New York, NY 1981, p. 5
14. Speech by Richard Rogers at Mary Kay Seminar in Dallas, 2002
15. Ibid
16. Mary Kay Ash, *Mary Kay*, Harper & Row Publishers, Inc. New York, NY 1981

17. Mary Kay Ash, *Mary Kay on People Management*, Warner Books, New York, NY 1984, p. 124
18. Mary Kay Ash, *The Mary Kay Way*, John Wiley & Sons, Inc., New York, NY 2008, p. 17
19. Mary Kay Ash, *Mary Kay*, Harper & Row Publishers, Inc., New York, NY 1981, p. 41
20. Ibid, p. 62
21. Mary Kay Ash, *You Can Have it All*, Prima Publishing, Rocklin, CA. 1995, p. 222
22. Mary Kay Ash, *Mary Kay*, Harper & Row Publishers, Inc., New York, NY revised edition 1987, p. 139
23. Mary Kay Ash, *You Can Have it All*, Prima Publishing, Rocklin, CA. 1995, p. 222
24. Mary Kay Ash, *The Mary Kay Way*, John Wiley & Sons, Inc., New York, NY 1995, p. 23
25. Mary Kay Ash, *Mary Kay on People Management*, Warner Books, New York, NY 1984, p. 21
26. Mary Kay Ash, *The Mary Kay Way,* John Wiley & Sons, Inc., New York, NY 2008, p. 169
27. Mary Kay Ash, *Mary Kay on People Management*, Warner Books, New York, NY 1984, p. 21
28. Mary Kay Ash, *Mary Kay You Can Have It All*, Prima Publishing, Rocklin, CA, 1995, p. 204
29. Ibid, p. 202
30. Darrell Overcash, interview with author on May 12, 2009
31. Rhonda Shasteen, interview with author on May 13, 2009
32. David Holl, interview with author on May 13, 2009
33. Richard Rogers, interview with author on June 23, 2009
34. Ibid
35. Richard Rogers, interview with author on May 12, 2009
36. Richard Rogers, interview with author on June 23, 2009
37. David Holl, interview with author on May 13, 2009
38. Ibid
39. Laura Beitler, interview with author on May 13, 2009
40. Ibid
41. Ibid
42. Anne Crews, interview with author on June 5, 2009
43. Michael Lunceford, interview with author on May 13, 2009
44. John Wiseman, interview with author on May 13, 2009
45. Yvonne Pendleton, interview with author on May 12, 2009
46. Ryan Rogers, interview with author on May 12, 2009
47. Richard Rogers, interview with author on June 23, 2009
48. Ibid
49. Rhonda Shasteen, interview with author on May 13, 2009

50. Richard Rogers, interview with author on June 23, 2009
51. Elizabeth Fitzpatrick, interview with author on June 2, 2009
52. Ibid
53. Ibid
54. Ibid
55. Sherry Giancristoforo, interview with author on June 4, 2009
56. Ibid
57. Richard Rogers, interview with author on June 4, 2009
58. Rhonda Shasteen, interview with author on May 13, 2009
59. Darrell Overcash, interview with author on May 12, 2009
60. Ibid
61. Darrell Overcash, interview with author on May 5, 2009
62. Darrell Overcash, interview with author on May 12, 2009
63. Sherry Giancristoforo, interview with author on June 4, 2009
64. Barbara Sunden, interview with author on June 19, 2009
65. Richard Rogers, interview with author on June 23, 2009
66. David Holl, interview with author on May 13, 2009
67. Ibid
68. Richard Rogers, interview with author on June 23, 2009
69. Ryan Rogers, interview with author on May 12, 2009
70. Barbara Sunden, interview with author on June 17, 2009
71. Rhonda Shasteen, interview with author on May 13, 2009
72. Ryan Rogers, interview with author on May 12, 2009

SO THE WORLD MAY HEAR

73. Bill Austin, interviews with author on May 17, 19, and 21, 2009
74. Ibid
75. Ibid
76. Ibid
77. Ibid
78. Ibid
79. Ibid
80. Ibid
81. Ibid
82. Ibid
83. Ibid
84. Ibid
85. Ibid
86. Ibid
87. Ibid
88. Ibid

89. Ibid
90. Ibid
91. Ibid
92. Ibid
93. Ibid
94. Ibid
95. Ibid
96. Iibid
97. Ibid
98. Ibid
99. Ibid
100. Ibid
101. Ibid
102. Randy Schoenborn, interview with author on July 3, 2009
103. Bill Austen, interviews with author on May 17, 19, and 21, 2009
104. Ibid
105. Ibid
106. Ibid
107. Ibid
108. Ibid
109. Ibid
110. Tani Austin, interview with author on July 15, 2009
111. Tani Austin, interview with author on May 17, 2009
112. Ibid
113. Ibid
114. Greg Austin, interview with author on May 21, 2009
115. Ibid
116. Ibid
117. Bill Austin, interviews with author on May 17, 19, and 21, 2009
118. Randy Schoenborn, interview with author on July 3, 2009
119. Ibid
120. Bill Austin, interviews with author on May 17, 19, and 21, 2009
121. Jerry Ruzicka, interview with author on May 21, 2009
122. Ibid
123. Ibid
124. Ibid
125. Brandon Sawalich, interview with author on July 15, 2009
126. Ibid
127. Ibid
128. Ibid
129. Ibid
130. Ibid

131. Ibid
132. World Health Organization 2006 report
133. Bill Austin, interview with author on May 17, 19, and 21, 2009
134. Bill Austin, interview with author on June 5, 2009
135. Bill Austin, interviews with author on May 17, 19, and 21, 2009
136. Ibid
137. Ibid
138. Ibid
139. Ibid
140. Fredreic Rondeau, interview with author on June 4, 2009
141. Ibid
142. Ibid
143. Tani Austin, interview with author on May 17, 2009
144. Bill Austin, interviews with author on May 17, 19, and 21, 2009
145. Antonio Esteban, interview with author on May 18, 2009
146. Bill Austin, interviews with author on May 17, 19, and 21, 2009
147. Tani Austin, interview with author on May 17, 2009
148. Mark McCarthy, interview with author on May 21, 2009
149. Tani Austin, interview with author on May 17, 2009
150. Bill Austin, interviews with author on May 17, 19, and 21, 2009
151. Ibid
152. Ibid
153. Tani Austin, interview with author on May 17, 2009
154. Bill Austin, interviews with author on May 17, 19, and 21, 2009
155. Ibid
156. Bill Austin, interview with author on May 17, 2009
157. Jerry Ruzicka, interview with author on May 21, 2009
158. Ibid
159. Tani Austin, interview with author on May 17, 2009
160. Ibid
161. Ibid
162. Susan Dalebout, *The Praeger Guide to Hearing and Hearing Loss*, Praeger, Westport, Connecticut, 2008
163. Bill Austin, interviews with author on May 17, 19, and 21, 2009
164. Taylor Swift's Sound Matters PSA, http://www.aceshowbiz.com/news/view/0022401html
165. Bill Austin, interviews with author on May 17, 19, and 21, 2009
166. www.sotheworldmayhear.com (Sound Matters, a Starkey Foundation Initiative)
167. Bill Austin, *Redbook* magazine, interviews with author on May 17, 19, and 21
168. LaVern Groeschen, interview with author on November 18, 2008
169. Ibid

BROTHERLY LOVE

170. Rob Groeschen, interviews with author on November 4, 2008 and April 1, 2009
171. LaVern Groeschen, interview with author on November 11, 2008
172. LaVern Groeschen, interviews with author on November 4, 2009
173. Ibid
174. Ibid
175. Ibid
176. LaVern Groeschen, interview with author on November 18, 2009
177. Rob Groeschen, interviews with author on November 4, 2008 and April 1, 2009
178. Ibid
179. Ibid
180. Ibid
181. Ibid
182. Ibid
183. Ibid
184. Ibid
185. Ibid
186. Ibid
187. Ibid
188. Ibid
189. Ibid
190. Ibid
191. Ibid
192. Ibid
193. LaVern Groeschen, interview with author on November 18, 2008
194. Ibid
195. Rob Groeschen, interviews with author on November 4, 2008 and April 1, 2009
196. Ibid
197. Ibid
198. Ibid
199. Ibid
200. Ibid
201. Ibid
202. Ibid
203. Ibid
204. Ibid
205. Ibid
206. Ibid

207. Ibid
208. Ibid
209. Ibid
210. Shaun Shipp, interview with author on June 10, 2009
211. Ibid
212. Neil Schaller, interview with author on June 11, 2009
213. Ibid
214. David McSwain, interview with author on June 10, 2009
215. Rob Groeschen, interviews with author on November 4, 2008 and April 1, 2009
216. Charlie Parris, interview with author on November 10
217. Ibid
218. Ibid
219. Sharon Werner, interview with author on April 4, 2009
220. Ibid
221. Ibid
222. Ibid
223. Rob Groeschen, interviews with author on November 4, 2008 and April 1, 2009
224. Charlie Parris, interview with author on November 10, 2008
225. Rob Groeschen, interviews with author on November 4, 2008 and April 1, 2009
226. Charlie Parris, interview with author on November 10, 2008
227. Rob Groeschen, interviews with author on November 4, 2008 and April 1, 2009
228. Ibid
229. LaVern Groeschen, interview with author on November 18, 2008
230. Rob Groeschen, interviews with author on November 4, 2008 and April 1, 2009
231. Charlie Parris, interview with author on November 10, 2008
232. Ibid
233. "After a Brain Injury a Business Plan," *The Wall Street Journal*, New York, NY, July 15, 2008, p. A1
234. Rob Groeschen, interviews with author on November 4, 2008 and April 1, 2009
235. Charlie Parris, interview with author on November 10, 2008

ONE FOR ALL AND ALL FOR ONE

236. Bob Badal, interview with author on June 29, 2008
237. Guy Seay, interview with author on June 30, 2009
238. Lynn McGown, interviews with author on June 29–30, 2009

239. Kent Thiry, interview with author on October 20, 2009
240. Ibid
241. Ibid
242. Anthony Gabriel, interview author on June 29, 2009
243. Ibid
244. Guy Seay, interview with author on June 30, 2009
245. Kent Thiry, interview with author on October 20, 2009
246. Doug Vlchek, interview with author on July 16, 2009
247. Ibid
248. Ibid
249. Ibid
250. Kent Thiry, interview with author on October 20, 2009
251. Ibid
252. Ibid
253. Ibid
254. Lynn McGowan, interview with author on June 29–30, 2009
255. Doug Vlchek, interview with author on July 16, 2009
256. Doug Vlchek, interview with author on July 26, 2009
257. Doug Vlchek, interview with author on July 16, 2009
258. Ibid
259. Lynn McGowan, interview with author on July 29-30, 2009
260. Doug Vlchek, interview with author on July 16, 2009
261. Lynn McGowan, interview with author on June 29-30, 2009
262. Kent Thiry, interview with author on October 20, 2009
263. Lynn McGowan, interview with author on June 29-30, 2009
264. Kent Thiry, interview with author on October 20,2009
265. Joe Mello, interview with author on June 29, 2009
266. Ibid
267. Ibid
268. Bill Shannon, interview with author on June 30, 2009
269. Brett Cohen, interview with author on October 2, 2009
270. Speech on leadership delivered by Kent Thiry on September 16, 2009 at UCLA Anderson School of Management
271. Guy Seay, interview on June 30, 2009. The quote ends after the word "metrics."
272. Guy Seay, interview with author on September 30, 2009
273. "Kent Thiry and DaVita: Leadership Challenges in Building and Growing a Great Company," Jeffrey Pfeiffer, *Stanford Graduate School of Business*, February 23, 2006, p. 1
274. Anthony Gabriel, interview with author on June 29, 2009
275. Kent Thiry, interview with author on October 20, 2009
276. Ibid

277. Ibid
278. Blaise Tracy, interview with author on June 30, 2009
279. Kent Thiry, interview with author on October 20, 2009
280. "Kent Thiry and DaVita: Leadership Challenges in Building and Growing a Great Company," Jeffrey Pfeiffer, *Stanford Graduate School of Business*, February 23, 2006, p. 1
281. Kent Thiry, interview with author on October 20, 2009
282. Ibid
283. Ibid
284. "Medicine Man," Erik Cassano, *Smart Business-Los Angeles*, January 2007
285. Bill Shannon, interview with author on June 30, 2009
286. Joe Mello, interview with author on June 29, 2009
287. Ibid
288. Ibid
289. Speech on leadership delivered by Kent Thiry on September 16, 2009 at UCLA Anderson School of Management
290. Ryan Rupp, interview with author on June 25, 2009
291. Bob Badal, interview with author on June 29, 2009
292. Ibid
293. Bill Shannon, interview with author on June 30, 2009
294. Ryan Rupp, interview with author on June 29–30, 2009
295. Lynn McGowan, interviews with author on June 29–30, 2009
296. Speech on leadership delivered by Kent Thiry on September 16, 2009 at UCLA Anderson School of Management
297. Lynn McGowan, interview with author on June 29–30, 2009
298. Basak Ertan, interview with author on June 29, 2009
299. Ibid
300. Ibid
301. Lynn McGowan, interview with author on June 29–30, 2009
302. David Rosenbloom, interview with author on July 31, 2009
303. Ibid
304. Anthony Gabriel, interview with author on June 29, 2009
305. Lynn McGowan, interview with author on June 29–30, 2009
306. David Rosenbloom, interview with author on July 31, 2009
307. Anthony Gabriel, interview with author on June 29, 2008
308. Ibid
309. Doug Vlchek, interview with author on July 16, 2009
310. Anthony Gabriel, interview with author on June 29, 2009
311. Doug Vlchek, interview with author on July 16, 2009
312. Kent Thiry, interview with author on October 20, 2009
313. Doug Vlchek, interview with author on July 16, 2009
314. Allen Nissenson, interview with author on July 16, 2009

315. Doug Vlchek, interview with author on July 16, 2009
316. Guy Seay, interview with author on June 30, 2009
317. Bob Badal, interview with author on June 29, 2009
318. Ibid
319. Kent Thiry, interview with author on October 30, 2009
320. Doug Vlchek, interview with author on July 16, 2009
321. Speech on leadership delivered by Kent Thiry on September 16, 2009 at UCLA Anderson School of Management; Interview with author on October 30, 2009
322. Joe Mello, interview with author on June 29, 2009
323. Ibid
324. Ibid
325. Doug Vlchek, interview with author on July 16, 2009

DOING BUSINESS BY THE GOOD BOOK

326. David Steward, interviews with author on September 2, 2009 and December 9, 2009
327. Ibid
328. Ibid
329. Ibid
330. Ibid
331. David H. Steward, *Doing Business by the Good Book*, Hyperion, New York, NY 2004, p. 95
332. David Steward, interviews with author on September 2, 2009 and December 9, 2009
333. Ibid
334. Ibid
335. David H. Steward, *Doing Business by the Good Book*, Hyperion, New York, NY 2004, p. 29
336. David Steward, interviews with author on September 2, 2009 and December 9, 2009
337. Ibid
338. Ibid
339. Ibid
340. Ibid
341. Thelma Steward, interview with author on December 9, 2009
342. David Steward, interviews with author on September 2, 2009 and December 9, 2009
343. Ibid
344. Ibid
345. Ibid

346. Ibid
347. Ibid
348. Jim Kavanaugh, interview with author on September 3, 2009
349. David Steward, interviews with author on September 2, 2009 and December 9, 2009
350. Jim Kavanaugh, interview with author on September 3, 2009
351. Ibid
352. Ibid
353. Jim Kavanaugh, interview with author on September 3, 2009
354. Ibid
355. Ibid
356. David Steward, interviews with author on September 2, 2009 and December 9, 2009
357. Ibid
358. Ibid
359. Jim Kavanaugh, interview with author on September 3, 2009
360. David Steward, interviews with author on September 2, 2009 and December 9, 2009
361. Ibid
362. Joe Koenig, interview with author on September 3, 2009
363. Ibid
364. David Steward, interviews with author on September 2, 2009 and December 9, 2009
365. Ibid
366. Ibid
367. Ibid
368. Jim Kavanaugh, interview with author on September 3, 2009
369. David Steward, interviews with author on September 2, 2009 and December 9, 2009
370. Joe Koenig, interview with author on September 3, 2009
371. Jim Kavanaugh, interview with author on September 3, 2009
372. Ibid
373. David Steward, interviews with author on September 2, 2009 and December 9, 2009
374. Joe Koenig, interview with author on September 3, 2009
375. Ibid
376. Jim Kavanaugh, interview with author on September 3, 2009
377. Frank Ramos, interview with author on September 9, 2009
378. David Steward, interviews with author on September 2, 2009 and December 9, 2009
379. Joe Koenig, interview with author on September 3, 2009

380. David Steward, interviews with author on September 2, 2009 and December 9, 2009
381. Joe Koenig, interview with author on September 3, 2009
382. Jim Kavanaugh, interview with author on September 3, 2009
383. Ibid
384. Tim Harden, interview with author on November 2, 2009
385. Mark Catalano, interview with author on September 2, 2009
386. Ibid
387. David Steward, interviews with author on September 2, 2009 and December 9, 2009
388. Jim Kavanaugh, interview with author on September 3, 2009
389. David Steward, interviews with author on September 2, 2009 and December 9, 2009
390. Joe Koenig, interview with author on September 3, 2009
391. David Steward, interviews with author on September 2, 2009 and December 9, 2009
392. Joe Koenig, interview with author on September 3, 2009
393. Ying McGuire, interview with author on September 9, 2009
394. Ibid
395. Joe Koenig, interview with author on September 3, 2009
396. Jim Kavanaugh, interview with author on September 3, 2009
397. David Steward, interviews with author on September 2, 2009 and December 9, 2009
398. Ibid
399. Joe Koenig, interview with author on September 3, 2009
400. David Steward, interviews with author on September 2, 2009 and December 9, 2009
401. Mark Catalano, interview with author on September 2, 2009
402. Ibid
403. David Steward, interviews with author on September 2, 2009 and December 9, 2009
404. Jim Kavanaugh, interview with author on September 3, 2009
405. Joe Koenig, interview with author on September 2, 2009
406. Jim Kavanaugh, interview with author on September 3, 2009
407. Ann Marr, interview with author on September 2, 2009
408. Ibid
409. Jim Kavanaugh, interview with author on September 3, 2009
410. Ann Marr, interview with author on September 2, 2009
411. David Steward, interviews with author on September 2, 2009 and December 9, 2009
412. Ann Marr, interview with author on September 2, 2009
413. Ibid

414. Joe Koenig, interview with author on September 3, 2009
415. David Steward, interviews with author on September 2, 2009 and December 9, 2009
416. Thelma Steward, interview with author on December 9, 2009
417. C. Britt Beemer and Robert L. Shook, *The Customer Rules*, McGraw-Hill, New York, NY 2009, p. 57
418. David Steward, interviews with author on September 2, 2009 and December 9, 2009
419. Ibid
420. Phil Styrlund, CEO, the Summit Group, interview with author on September 9, 2009
421. Ibid
422. Ann Marr, interview with author on September 2, 2009
423. Mark Catalano, interview with author on September 2, 2009
424. David Steward, interviews with author on September 2, 2009 and December 9, 2009
425. Jim Kavanaugh, interview with author on September 3, 2009
426. Ibid
427. Ibid
428. Ibid
429. Mark Catalano, interview with author on September 2, 2009
430. Jim Kavanaugh, interview with author on September 3, 2009
431. Tim Harden, interview with author on November 2, 2009
432. Ann Marr, interview with author on September 2, 2009
433. Joe Koenig, interview with author on September 3, 2009
434. Ying McGuire, interview with author on September 9, 2009
435. David Steward, interviews with author on September 2, 2009 and December 9, 2009

AFTERWORD

436. Ibid

Index

L

M

N

T

About the Author

ROBERT L. SHOOK is a bestselling author of many business books, five of which have appeared on *The New York Times* bestseller list, including *Longaberger*, a number-one bestseller. His books are published in more than twenty-five languages. Prior to becoming a full-time author, Shook was the founder and chairman of Shook Associates Corporation and American Executive Life Insurance Company. He and his wife live in Columbus, Ohio. His email address is: shookbooks@aol.com.